IN STATU NASCENDI

JOURNAL OF POLITICAL PHILOSOPHY AND INTERNATIONAL RELATIONS

Vol. 5, No. 1 (2022)

Special Issue:
The Work of Haruki Murakami

About In Statu Nascendi

In Statu Nascendi *(ISN) is a peer-reviewed journal that aspires to be a world-class scholarly platform encompassing original academic research dedicated to the circle of Political Philosophy, Cultural Studies, Theory of International Relations, Foreign Policy, and the political Decision-making process. The journal investigates specific issues through a socio-cultural, philosophical, and anthropological approach to raise a new type of civic awareness about the complexity of contemporary crisis, instability, and warfare situations, where the "stage-of-becoming" plays a vital role.*

Any views expressed in this publication are the views of the authors and are not necessarily shared by the editorial board of this journal. *In Statu Nascendi* is committed to freedom, liberty, and pluralism of opinions and endeavors to contribute to unconstrained public discourse and debate on relevant social, political, and philosophical matters.

ISN welcomes all types of partnership and collaboration for fostering a knowledge-based society, organizing events, and framing new projects. If you are an academic institution, a non-profit organization, research center or research funder, and you are willing to become a long-term partner for *ISN's* activities, please contact us on *irinstatunascendi@yahoo.com*, and we will get back to you as soon as we can.

More information about *ISN*, including information on the editorial board, membership, and all our initiatives can be found on the *ISN* website at

https://irinstatunascendi.wixsite.com/journal

Bibliographic information published by the Deutsche Nationalbibliothek
The Deutsche Nationalbibliothek lists this publication in the Deutsche Nationalbibliografie; detailed bibliographic data are available on the Internet at http://dnb.dnb.de.

Bibliografische Information der Deutschen Nationalbibliothek
Die Deutsche Nationalbibliothek verzeichnet diese Publikation in der Deutschen Nationalbibliografie; detaillierte bibliografische Daten sind im Internet über http://dnb.d-nb.de abrufbar.

In Statu Nascendi—Journal of Political Philosophy and International Relations Vol. 5, No. 1 (2022)

Stuttgart: *ibidem*-Verlag / *ibidem* Press

Erscheinungsweise: halbjährlich / Frequency: biannual

ISSN 2568-7638

ISBN-13: 978-3-8382-1699-7

Ordering Information:
PRINT: Subscription (two copies per year): € 72.00 / year (+ S&H: € 6.00 / year within Germany, € 10.00 / year international). The subscription can be canceled at any time.

Single copy or back issue: € 44.00 / copy (+ S&H: € 3.00 within Germany, € 5.00 international).

E-BOOK: Individual copy or back issue: € 28.99 / copy. Available via amazon.com or google.books.

For further information please visit www.ibidem.eu

In statu nascendi (Latin)

In the process of creation, emerging, becoming

Table of Contents

EDITORIAL

When I decided on the idea of a special issue on the work of Haruki Murakami, I could never have imagined the huge positive response that it has received. It is my privilege to introduce volume 5.1 of *In Statu Nascendi* which has been made possible by the generosity of the contributors whom I truly thank for their time and support. For anyone who has read the secondary literature on Murakami, many of the names on the contents page will be familiar, and once again I thank these authors for choosing to publish their work with us. I believe, however, that all of the papers in this special issue will be of great interest to Murakami scholars around the world; it is perhaps testament to Murakami's immense appeal that so many excellent papers have found their way here. And for those readers unfamiliar with Murakami, I hope that you will be inspired to research further and engage critically with his work. Also, of course, to pick up his books and allow them to take you, at least for a little while, into a *Murakami-world*.

Clearly, research on Murakami continues to grow and spaces to share ideas, such as this project, will continue to emerge. I predict that work with Murakami will continue down different paths; that is, away from traditional literary approaches. In a truly global sense, readers have found a *depth* to Murakami's fiction; a depth which gathers strong curiosity and diverse engagement. Whether it is sociological, psychoanalytical, mythological, political, or so forth, individuals are motivated to extend Murakami's texts: to think and work with them long after their initial reading.

The reason I decided on the work of a Japanese literary writer as the topic of a philosophy journal is because I believe that the depth to Murakami's stories is philosophically important and that this *extension* itself is a philosophic activity. The *philosophic* in Murakami's work is ready to be uncovered, communicated, and developed; it has no original language and is not limited to any one academic field. Therefore, it is hoped that this special issue on Haruki Murakami will explore the *depths* of his works from an interdisciplinary perspective in order to present novel involvement and arguments to the growing research community.

We begin **Part I** of the special issue with **Jonathan Dil's** "Oh My Kamisama! God in the Fiction of Murakami Haruki." Dil masterfully examines the role of divinity in Murakami's work from a Jungian standpoint; the paper examines the existential importance of Murakami protagonists discovering an 'inner God' as against a cold and distant 'outer God'; finally, Dil connects Murakami to 'postsecular fiction.' This is an essential paper on Murakami which *In Statu Nascendi* are proud to publish. Following this, we are honoured to present **Tomoki Wakatsuki** and **Matthew C. Strecher's** "Rebels With a Cause: A Cosmopolitan Examination of Haruki Murakami and Kazuo Ishiguro." Wakatsuki and Strecher explore 'cosmopolitanism' in Murakami's work through a comparison with the Japanese-born, British novelist Kazuo Ishiguro; drawing on the personal experiences of the two authors, Wakatsuki and Strecher maintain that it is their 'memory' that connects them to cosmopolitanism, as well their commitment to issues such as identity and belonging. Rather than postsecular fiction or world literature, Wakatsuki and Strecher relate Murakami to 'global literature.' **Megumi Yama** also puts forward a Jungian perspective in "Haruki Murakami, Novel as a Method: 'Memory' and his Creative Process." Yama's work examines the creative process of Murakami by offering insightful biographical information; additionally, it links with the preceding work through the concept of 'memory'; Yama considers not only Murakami's particular, historical memory, but also introduces the notion of a 'collective memory.' It is argued that Murakami's stories resonate with the psyche or soul of his global readers. **Ype De Boer's** "Ethics of a Split Existence: Murakami's *Hard-Boiled Wonderland and the End of the World* as a Poetico-Philosophical Experiment" embodies the objectives of this special issue as it puts forward a convincing and sustained philosophic approach to the work of Haruki Murakami. De Boer considers the experience of a 'split existence' in Murakami's fiction; further, Murakami's texts are understood as 'poetico-philosophical experiments' in which the mode of existence (the *ethos*) of the writer and reader is called into question; De Boer skilfully articulates the existential responses to such a split in one's identity and world; it is maintained that Murakami protagonists tend to embrace the 'split' in their existence; therefore, De Boer presents a genuinely new and important reading of the novel. Next we have **Amber A. Logan's** "Haruki Murakami's Non-Traditional Portrayals of Shadows and Doppelgangers" which also examines *Hard-Boiled Wonderland and the End of the World* as well as offering a Jungian perspective. Logan explores why Murakami's shadows and doppelgangers are frequently portrayed positively; it is argued that Murakami's 'unconventional' shadows may be due to Japanese cultural differences that are lost in translation or are to be approached as 'idiosyncratic symbols' which are interpreted on an individual basis by readers. **Gemma Scammell's** "The Cityscape and Haruki Murakami's Despondent Characters: the use of magical realism in the creation of heterotopic space" is an excellent interdisciplinary paper which draws on literary studies as well as the work of Foucault. Scammell considers 'space' in Murakami's fiction as centrally related to society and power; it is asserted that Murakami characters seek 'other' spaces in order to escape a despondency caused by their hollow, late-capitalist lifestyles. 'Space' is connected to a recurring theme in Murakami's work: maintaining one's identity. In my own paper (**Joseph Thomas Milburn**), "Haruki Murakami and Carl Gustav Jung: A Post-Jungian Perspective," I examine various Jungian-influenced interpretations of Murakami, such as Strecher's and Yama's previous works; I argue that the 'other' or 'metaphysical' worlds in Murakami's fiction are to be understood as fundamentally related to *this* world and to relations with other ('real') people. I maintain that Jung and Murakami are frequently drawn together because of their metaphorical attitude towards existence. Further, a post-Jungian perspective is offered which considers the terms 'Self,' 'Psyche,' and 'Dasein.' In the final paper of Part I, we have **Chikako Nihei's** "Time for Spaghetti in Haruki Murakami's Fiction: What Cooking Time Means in a Consumerist Society" which is appearing for the first time in the English language. Nihei examines an often-overlooked aspect of Murakami's work: the protagonists' laidback lifestyle and preoccupation with spending time cooking good food. Like Scammell's paper, Nihei applies the interpretation to capitalist society as well as gender roles. Importantly, it is noted that the lifestyle of Murakami protagonists may be difficult for many readers to achieve.

Matthew C. Strecher's "Seeking the Living Among the Dead: The Other World of Haruki Murakami" starts off **Part II** of the special issue. It is particularly valuable as it outlines Strecher's extensive work on the 'Other World'; further, the paper explores the function and development of this central aspect of Murakami's fiction. **Olaf Schiedges** also presents his illuminating work on Murakami in "A spatial approach to the fictional world of Murakami Haruki" which focuses on the significance of space, particularly spatial opposition, and the crossing of boundaries (physical or metaphorical): be it personal (identity), socio-historical, intertextual, or cultural. There are connections to be made with Scammell's paper here, and, arguably, productive comparisons with Strecher's essential findings. **Karen Connie M. Abalos-Orendain's** "Layered Frameworks: Thoughts on Japanese-ness and the Cosmopolitanism of Haruki Murakami" provides more illuminating ideas on the cosmopolitan in Murakami's fiction as well as an examination of its relation to 'pure' Japanese literature; a musical metaphor is put forward, *'basso ostinato,'* to argue that there is something essentially 'Japanese' about Murakami's work. The next part of the special issue includes author introductions to their recent publications on Murakami. **Jonathan Dil** introduces *Haruki Murakami and the*

Search for Self-Therapy: Stories from the Second Basement (2022) and **Masaki Mori** introduces *Haruki Murakami and his Early Work: The Loneliness of the Long-Distance Running Artist* (2021); I am sure readers will appreciate the overviews provided of their key works. Additionally, an interview with **Gitte Marianne Hansen**, co-editor of *Murakami Haruki and Our Years of Pilgrimage* (2022), reveals insight into Hansen's past and present research as well as personal engagement with the work of Murakami. **Midori Tanaka Atkins** provides an in-depth, scholarly review of Murakami's most recent novel, *Killing Commendatore* (2017/2018) in "*Killing Commendatore* Book Review: From *Boku* to *Watashi*, Healing on Canvas and in the Darkness of the Pit" which also considers classical Japanese literature and the importance of first-person pronouns, including, for instance, reference to Murakami's recent short-story collection *First Person Singular* (2020/2021). **Ken Lawrence**, author of *The Murakami Pilgrimage: A Guide to the Real-Life Places of Haruki Murakami's Fiction* (2016), provides a highly readable reflective piece on his personal involvement with Murakami in "Murakami Pilgrimage Reflections: How Murakami's Fiction Makes the Mundane Magical" which I am sure readers will enjoy. Finally, **Eric Siercks** has graciously introduced the newly opened Haruki Murakami library, also called the Waseda International House of Literature, at Waseda University, Tokyo. "Just Like Breathing: Celebrating the Opening of the Haruki Murakami Library" includes further information about the design of the building and recent research activities. I expect many of you will be eager to visit the Haruki Murakami library and, if you do, please look out for a copy of this special issue!

Last, and by no means least, I would like to thank **Piotr Pietrzak**, the Editor-in-Chief of *In Statu Nascendi*, who has tirelessly worked on this project in its final stages and who gave me the opportunity to start it in the first place. Here's to the next one!

We hope that you enjoy this special issue,

Joseph Thomas Milburn
Guest Editor, *In Statu Nascendi*

PART I:
WORKS

Jonathan Dil

Oh My Kamisama!
God in the Fiction of Murakami Haruki

Abstract: *Though Murakami Haruki is an on-the-record atheist, references to God appear in his fiction from time to time. This God, however, is usually cold and distant and seemingly unrelated to the forces of destiny guiding the central protagonist's journey. Prominent examples of this cold, distant God are found in the short story "all god's children can dance" (1999) and in the novel 1Q84 (2009-2010). Yet seen from a Jungian perspective, it can be argued that the forces of destiny guiding each of Murakami's protagonists is simply God by another name, particularly if we accept Jung's claim that "God is an archetype." This essay argues that a Jungian conception of God is a vital framework for understanding the forces of destiny operating in Murakami's fiction, and it uses the short stories "all god's children can dance" and "Cream" (2019) and the novel 1Q84 as prominent examples. In each of these stories, a protagonist's discovery of an "inner God" is an antidote to a cold, distant, or judgmental "outer God" that is tormenting the protagonist in some way. This "inner God" is Murakami's answer to the crisis of meaning and the rise of religious fundamentalism in contemporary society, issues that for him crystalized in the wake of the Aum Shinrikyō sarin gas attack of 1995. Murakami's conception of an inner God as an antidote to an outer God also connects him with trends in what John McClure has labelled postsecular fiction.*

Introduction

Murakami Haruki is an on-the-record atheist, though this is not necessarily something you will pick up from reading his fiction alone, which is full of the strange and the mysterious, and where even God gets a mention from time to time. This is why Murakami is always careful to distinguish between his personal beliefs and the ideas found in his fiction. Talking to Laura Miller and Don George for the website Salon, for example, Murakami explained:

> I write weird stories. I don't know why I like weirdness so much. Myself, I'm a very realistic person. I don't trust anything New Age—or reincarnation, dreams, Tarot, horoscopes. I don't trust anything like that at all. I wake up at 6 in the morning and go to bed at 10, jogging every day and swimming, eating healthy food. I'm very realistic. But when I write, I write weird. That's very strange. When I'm getting more and more serious, I'm getting more and more weird. When I want to write about the reality of society and the world, it gets weird. Many people ask me why, and I can't answer that. (Miller and George 1997)

This contrast between Murakami the health-conscious realist and Murakami the weird-writing fantasist is an important part of his public persona and reassures readers that the man behind the strange stories they love is as grounded in mundane reality as they (perhaps) are. At the same time, these stories are there to offer readers a break from reality—a suspension of disbelief and entry into an imaginative world where anything is possible. And one of the possibilities the atheist Murakami offers his readers in these fictional spaces is God, or more precisely, two Gods—an inner God and an outer one—that tend to appear in his fiction together and play off one another. Murakami's fictional loyalties lie with the inner God—God as something like a Jungian archetype which is always just beyond our conscious awareness, but which is still there shaping and directing our lives in significant ways. What his fiction also suggests is that this inner God can fill the God-shaped hole left by the outer God, not necessarily because this outer God is not there, but because, like an absentee father, He is cold, distant, and disengaged from the meaningful details of our lives. The emergence of these two Gods in Murakami's fiction is one example of his ongoing engagement since 1995 (the year of Aum Shinrikyō's coordinated sarin gas attack on three lines of the Tokyo subway system) with questions of religion, spirituality, and meaning in contemporary Japanese society and the world at large.

This essay begins with a brief survey of statements Murakami has made about his personal beliefs, looking at both his atheism and his openness to what he has described as a parallel reality running alongside the more mundane reality we normally inhabit. It then examines two of Murakami's short stories and one of his novels where examples of this "God without" and "God within" can be found: "all god's children can dance" (1999), *1Q84* (2009–2010), and "Cream" (2018). The essay concludes by considering the applicability of the postsecular label to Murakami's fiction, a term which has gained some attention in approaches to spirituality in contemporary Western literature, but which is still largely absent from similar approaches in Japan.

Murakami's Personal Beliefs

In 2005, I interviewed Murakami in Boston, and as I was questioning him about the influence of Carl Jung on his writing and thinking, the conversation turned to his own beliefs (or lack thereof) regarding religion and the supernatural. The relevant part of this conversation is below:

> **Jonathan Dil:** Are there any things in particular about Jung that you have trouble with, where you see a big difference between his approach and your approach?

Murakami Haruki: One thing is, when I'm writing, I believe in supernatural things, or synchronicity, or those things, but when I'm not writing, I don't believe in anything. I'm a very practical man. But he's not. He's totally attracted. When I'm writing, I go to the other side and come back; but when I'm not writing, I'm just here.

JD: So when you're in this world, you don't believe in anything—God, religion, the supernatural?

MH: No, not at all. My grandfather was a Buddhist priest, and my father was a teacher and priest, but I'm not. I believe in some kind of atmosphere of Buddhism because my father and my grandfather believed in that respected religion, so I grew up in that atmosphere. I'm not a Buddhist in the religious sense, but that atmosphere might be important to me. But I don't think of religion much.

JD: Do you believe in life after death?

MH: No. We are born from nothing and when we die, we return to nothing. That's my belief.

Murakami's grandfather, Murakami Benshiki, was the head priest at Anyōji Temple in Kyoto until the age of seventy, when he was struck by a train during a typhoon and killed. Murakami's father, Murakami Chiaki, was a schoolteacher in Nishinomiya City (near Kobe) but also worked part-time as a Buddhist priest. Murakami has described his father as the possessor of a "sincere faith" and one of his strongest childhood memories is of his father's daily morning ritual of reciting Buddhist sutras in front of a statue of a Boddhisatva kept within a cylindrical glass case in the family home. Once, as a boy, Murakami asked his father why he performed this ritual, and his father explained that he was praying for those who had died in the war, both ally and enemy alike (Murakami 2019). Despite this early home environment, however, Murakami does not believe in nor practice Buddhism himself, nor any other religion. There are times when Murakami will identify as a Buddhist out of convenience. In his travelogue *Uten enten* (Come Rain or Shine), for example, he describes a trip he made to several monasteries in Greece where he ate and stayed overnight. This experience gave him several opportunities to talk to monks and pilgrims, and in these conversations, he would sometimes be asked about his religious beliefs. In these moments, Murakami found it more convenient to describe himself as a Buddhist rather than as an Atheist. At the same time, he emphasizes for his readers that he is embarrassed to say he does not know much about Buddhism, nor about religion in general (Murakami 2016, locs. 230, 502, and 594).

Murakami belongs to the roughly 70–80% of Japanese today who describe themselves as without religion (*mushūkyō*) (Shimada 2009, loc. 133;

Roemer 2009, 307).[1] As Shimada Hiromi points out, this label is more about explicit and exclusive religious belonging and identity than it is about the presence or absence of religious ritual in such people's lives (Ibid., loc. 184). Many Japanese who describe themselves as *mushūkyō* will (like Murakami) also describe themselves as Buddhists or Shintoists on occasion, and many will participate in religious rituals, such as visiting shrines and temples, where they will pray and give offerings. Much of this activity, of course, may be more customary and cultural than it is religious (if this distinction is even meaningful), but the fact remains that these religious practices remain alive and relevant for many Japanese. At the same time, Murakami is clearly not alone in leaving behind the specific religious tradition of his father and grandfather. In terms of formal, institutional religious identity, Japan is one of the most secularized countries in the world.

Shimada suggests that for much of the postwar period, most Japanese who described themselves as *mushūkyō* were apologetically so, seeing religion in general as a positive thing, and he suggests that many, in fact, were slightly embarrassed by their lack of a strong and clear religious identity (Ibid., loc. 98). He also argues that events like the Aum attack and the rise of religious fundamentalism more generally have started to change this attitude to some degree (Ibid., p. 301). Considering that strong religious faith at times leads to acts of violence, why would it not be a good thing to hold one's faith less exclusively and with less certainty? The discussion which follows about Murakami's inner and outer Gods is best seen in this context of shifting Japanese attitudes towards questions of religious faith, practice, and belonging in recent years.

Though Murakami's early fiction makes little mention of God or religion, this began to change after 1995. The general attitude to God (or gods) and religion in this fiction is generally skeptical: religion is, at best, a fiction that allows people to cope with life's uncertainties; at worst, it is a divisive factor that leads to tribalism. In Murakami's 2002 novel, *Kafka on the Shore* (*Umibe no kafuka*), for example, a mysterious character called Colonel Sanders, who explains that he is neither a God nor a Buddha, downplays the concept of God in postwar Japan in this way:

---

1   Shimada references several surveys that show that about 70% or more of Japanese identity with the mushūkyō label, but he also notes that this number went as high as 80% in the aftermath of the Aum attack (13). Roemer presents data from the Japanese General Social Surveys (JGSS) and reports that for those sampled between 2000 and 2003, 66.96% of respondents said they had no religion, 22.8% said they had a household faith that they did not actively practice, and 10.21% said they had a personal belief in a particular religion.

Listen—God only exists in people's minds. Especially in Japan, God's always been kind of a flexible concept. Look at what happened after the war. Douglas MacArthur ordered the divine emperor to quit being God, and he did, making a speech saying he was just an ordinary person. So after 1946 he wasn't God anymore. That's what Japanese gods are like—they can be tweaked and adjusted. Some American chomping on a cheap pipe gives the order and presto change-o—God's no longer God. A very postmodern kind of thing. If you think God's there, He is. If you don't, He isn't. And if that's what God's like, I wouldn't worry about it. (Murakami 2005, p. 265)

In *1Q84*, explored in more detail below, one of the characters, a cram-school teacher called Tengo, ponders the problems of the world and laments the inability of the gods to do anything about it. The narrative offers us this insight into his thoughts:

You could bring all the gods of the world into one place, and still they couldn't abolish nuclear weapons or eradicate terrorism. They couldn't end the drought in Africa or bring John Lennon back to life. Far from it—the gods would just break into factions and start fighting among themselves, and the world would probably become even more chaotic than it is now. (Murakami 2011, p. 380)

In the same novel, a cult leader portrays religion as a compensation for those who are unable to face life's painful realities:

Most people are not looking for provable truths. As you said, truth is often accompanied by intense pain, and almost no one is looking for painful truths. What people need is beautiful, comforting stories that make them feel as if their lives have some meaning. Which is where religion comes from. (Ibid. p. 441)

Such attitudes toward God (or gods) and religion might be described as postmodern tolerance at best, modern skepticism at worst. Yet while religion and God are not normally portrayed in an overly positive light in Murakami's fiction, the inner quests of individuals to find meaning and significance beyond what secularized societies alone can offer is taken seriously. This is the search for the "inner God" which will be discussed in more detail below.

The one "outside-the-box" idea Murakami has professed a belief in is that of a parallel reality running alongside the more mundane reality we normally inhabit. Speaking to Deborah Treisman in *The New Yorker*, for example, Murakami put the idea this way:

My basic view of the world is that right next to the world we live in, the one we're all familiar with, is a world we know nothing about, an unfamiliar world that exists concurrently with our own. The structure of that world, and its meaning, can't be explained in words. But the fact is that it's there, and sometimes we catch a glimpse of it, just by chance—like when a flash of lightning illuminates our surroundings for an instant. (Treisman 2018)

Another place Murakami has talked about this parallel world is in an interview with the German newspaper *Die Zeit*, where he explained:

> I am not religious. I only believe in the power of imagination. And the fact that there isn't only one reality. The real world and another, unreal world exist at the same time; they are strongly connected. Sometimes they overlap, blend. And if I want, if I concentrate a lot, I can cross the border. I can come and go. That is what's happening in my books. That's the point. My stories take place on one side, then the other, and I don't even recognize the difference anymore. (Düker 2014)[2]

In 2019, I again had the opportunity to interview Murakami, and I used the occasion to try and clarify what he meant in the interviews above. At first, Murakami expressed some confusion when I used the phrase "parallel reality" with him (I was speaking to him in English), but he eventually came to suggest that what he was talking about in his interview with Treisman was the idea of synchronicity. He explained:

> I believe in synchronicity. It's a kind of parallel reality. It's similar. Because I have experienced those kinds of things from time to time in my life. So they could happen. But I don't believe in any ghosts or anything … If you don't believe in synchronicity or in a parallel reality you cannot write fiction, I guess. So if you write a novel, there are many synchronicities in that story. You need that. And you have to believe that. So that is my opinion I guess … Anything could happen. That is what I believe. Anything could happen. So you cannot predict anything at all. I have written a story called "Chance Traveler." I wrote something like that in that story.

"Chance Traveler" is the story of a gay piano tuner who eventually reconciles with his sister with the help of some uncanny coincidences. He is not sure how to explain these examples of synchronicity in his life, joking that perhaps a god of jazz or a god of gays is behind it all. In the end, the story suggests, it doesn't matter how one explains these mysterious moments in life—they simply happen, and they have the power to bring about personally meaningful outcomes in our lives. The story also opens with the narrator, "Murakami Haruki," sharing two examples of synchronicity from his own life.

In my 2005 interview with Murakami, he mentioned synchronicity as something he believes in when he is writing but not when he is not writing (and this in the context of his explanation of how he differs from Jung). In my 2019 interview, on the other hand, he was willing to go on the record as a believer in synchronicity, and not just as an idea which supports him when

---

2   I have referenced the original interview in German here. I couldn't find the full English translation of the interview online but the quote I am using here is found several places online without a specific source.

he writes. Instead, he acknowledges that he has experienced synchronicity in his life at times. Murakami is clearly wary of being tainted with either the New Age or Jungian brush, and so in interviews he is careful to distance himself from these topics. While usually leaving Jung out of the conversation, however, Murakami has periodically expressed his belief in a parallel reality running alongside our own that manifests in our lives at times as synchronicity, indicating that his belief comes from first-hand experience rather than from any larger religious or metaphysical commitments.

While believing in synchronicity is not necessarily the same thing as believing in God, it is an indication of an openness to something beyond ourselves (at least our conscious selves) that can touch and guide our lives at times. The Japanese Catholic writer Endō Shūsaku, who did believe in God, but who was also a serious student of Jung in his later years, came to view God less as an object than as a force that works in our lives, most often through other people (he came to call this force the *hataraki*) (Endō 2006, locs. 173–176). For Endō, religion was less an idea you believe in (like Marxism say) than a call from the unconscious (Endō 2009, p. 7). While Murakami brings less religious baggage to his explorations of God than Endō did, there are parallels in their commitment to a God of the unconscious (or what I am calling, following Jung, the God within). For Endō, this call from the unconscious led him deeper into his Catholic faith, but also into the deep river of faith and religion more broadly. Murakami keeps his distance from religion, but not from the call of the unconscious, and it is this "religious-free" approach to questions of God and spirituality that makes him potentially a post-secular writer, a topic I will return to at the end of this essay.

all god's children can dance

The first story in Murakami's oeuvre to offer a clear treatment of an inner and outer God is his 1999 short story "all god's children can dance," which originally appeared in the magazine Shinchō, and later in the short story collection *kami no kodomotachi wa mina odoru* (all god's children can dance, 2000). In English, the same collection of stories was published in 2002 as *after the quake,* this title based on the running Japanese title *jishin no ato de* (After the Quake) which was used to introduce the first five stories in the collection when they first appeared in Shinchō (the sixth and final story in the collection, "honey pie," did not appear in Shinchō, but was added to the first five stories when they were later published as a book). The English title, *After the Quake,* highlights the fact that all the stories in the collection are set after the Kobe earthquake (also known as the Hanshin-Awaji Daishinsai, which occurred on

January 17th, 1995) but before the Aum Shinrikyō sarin gas attack (which occurred on March 20th, 1995). The Japanese title, on the other hand, suggests that "all god's children dance" is a central story in the collection and a useful starting point for understanding its message. It is also a central work for those wishing to understand treatments of religion and spirituality in contemporary Japanese literature. Philip Gabriel writes, "No one story can fully capture present-day Japanese literary attitudes toward the spiritual, but the one that perhaps comes closest is Murakami's 'All God's Children Can Dance'" (Gabriel 2006, p. 175).

Mentions of God are not entirely absent from Murakami's pre-1995 fiction, though these are lighter treatments that have little comparison to the works being discussed here. One early example worth mentioning is "Shika to kamisama to seiseshiria" ("Deer, God, and Saint Cecilia") published in 1981 in *Waseda Bungaku*. Like several of Murakami's early short stories, this is a story about the process of writing a story, and the narrator shares with us the struggle he goes through as he tries to write a short story for the June edition of *Waseda Bungaku*. At the end of this account, the narrator, who sounds like Murakami himself, shares the story of meeting his future wife in classroom 301 of Waseda's Literature Department. He then tells us how when he is depressed (something which happens to him about once every three months or twice every five months) his wife will tell him the story of Saint Cecelia, a nine-year-old girl who God appeared to one morning and declared that she would die that night. The wife asks the narrator what he would do in such a situation, and he offers suggestions such as writing checks that will bounce. The young girl's response, on the other hand, is to only do the things she normally does—attend school and then sing songs with her friends while holding hands. The narrator then imagines God appearing to him and declaring that he too will die that night, but also telling him that what he should do is to bring in the washing, complete his unfinished essays, and destroy his failed stories sitting in his drawer. This story of Saint Cecilia never fails to cheer up the narrator—arguably a message about how the mundane activities which fill our days may in the end be the most important things we ever do, and how we should live each day as if it were our last. The story finishes with this thought: "Why do people write stories? Only God knows" (Murakami 1981, p. 10).

It was the events of 1995, and in particular the Aum attack, however, that really pushed Murakami to wrestle with the idea of God in his fiction in a more substantial way, with "all god's children can dance" the first prominent example. In thinking about this short story, we can start with the way it deals with the God "out there," and particularly in the way it casts this God in the role of the absentee father. Yoshiya, the main protagonist of the story, grows up not knowing his biological father, but instead being told by his mother that (like Jesus before him) he is a product of immaculate conception and a special child of God (the name Yoshiya sounds a lot like Joshua, another name for Jesus). This is cold comfort to Yoshiya, who has little need for a father who sits removed high up in the heavens, but who instead needs someone who can teach him something practical, like how to catch fly balls in baseball. While Yoshiya never rejects the notion of a God out there, he sees little need for a spiritual father who offers him no concrete benefits, and, above all, he is turned off by this God's emotional distance: "the unending coldness of the One who was his father: His dark, heavy, silent heart of stone" (Murakami 2003, p. 59). Japanese religion is often said to be more focused on "this-worldly" benefits than "other-worldly" promises of salvation, and Yoshiya's approach to God seems to align with this general sentiment. What use is a God who will not get involved in the details of his life here and now?

The way Murakami portrays this God "out there" is arguably colored by his relationship with his own father. Scholars in the psychology of religion have explored the ways conceptions of God are shaped by people's attachment styles, which in turn are shaped by their relationship with their parents or primary caregivers (Kirkpatrick 2005; Granqvist 2020). As Murakami has openly acknowledged, he and his father clashed in his teenage and early adult years over his life decisions and they hardly spoke to each other once he became an adult, only briefly reconnecting before his father's death in 2008 (Murakami 2019). Murakami's fiction is filled with avoidant character types, figures who are cut off from their biological families and who struggle to form meaningful relationships with others. It is thus not surprising when these same characters, thinking about God, come to imagine Him as a cold and emotionally distant father.

Yoshiya abandons his mother's faith when he is fourteen years-old; yet this does not solve his existential or practical problems. He is trapped in a potentially incestuous relationship with an unstable mother, which makes his search for a "father" an urgent one. The classical Freudian narrative describes the drama of a boy who unconsciously wants to kill his father and sleep with his mother, but who then overcomes this stalemate by accepting the authority of a new father figure (the superego). In Yoshiya's case, there is no biological father around, and the surrogate spiritual father who is supposed to take his place also appears to be absent. Mr. Tabata, who is the closest thing to an earthly father-figure Yoshiya has, while he later confesses to having lustful thoughts towards Yoshiya's mother, is too timid and bound by his religious convictions to do anything about it. Yoshiya is thus trapped, scared that if he leaves his mother alone, she may hurt herself or worse; petrified that if he stays with her too long, they will transgress the incest taboo. His quest to find his father is about finding a way out of this deadlock.

Once he rejects the supernatural narrative offered by his mother for his birth, Yoshiya reverts to the naturalistic narrative to make sense of his life—the story of how his mother had slept with a doctor who had performed two previous abortions for her, and who had been careful to use condoms when he had begun sleeping with her. This man's rejection of her following her pregnancy with Yoshiya—based on his firm conviction that the child could not be his—had brought her to the point of suicide, and she was only saved at the last minute by her encounter with Mr. Tabata, a member of a religion that worships a figure they call the Okata. This, it should be mentioned, is a rather formal, emotionally distant way to refer to a deity, and this formality and distance arguably contributes to Yoshiya's alienation from this God "out there." As mentioned, he needs a hands-on Dad who can teach something useful like how to catch fly balls in baseball, not an emotionally distant father who refuses to get involved in the details of his life.

Katō Norihiro explains that one of the literary influences on "all god's children can dance" is John Irving's *The World According to Garp* (Katō 2004, p. 123). Garp, like Yoshiya, grows up without a father, the result of "an almost virgin birth" (his mother, a nurse, sleeps with an incapacitated and dying soldier so that she can fulfill her wish of having a child without the entanglements of a father) (Ibid. p. 13). The mothers in Murakami and Irving's stories are significantly different—Yoshiya's mother is a lost soul who finds hope in religion but who is unaware of her own sexuality and the temptation she poses to her son; Garp's mother is someone who is uninterested in sex altogether and is confused by human lust and who, through her unorthodox decisions in life, goes on to become an accidental feminist icon—but what they share are ideas which put them on the outside of mainstream society, and a commitment to raising their sons without a father (or in Yoshiya's case, at least not a father of "this world"). What Garp and Yoshiya share is a need to find their own sense of meaning and purpose in a fatherless world, with Garp often turning to the metaphorical space of a padded wrestling room in search of answers and Yoshiya eventually turning to a baseball diamond (both symbolic wombs).

The one thing Yoshiya knows about the man he assumes is his biological father (besides the fact that he is a doctor) is that he is missing his right earlobe, the result of a dog attack. Garp lost his left earlobe in the same way as a boy, suggesting, in some symbolic, literary sense, that Yoshiya is Garp's "son"—someone who is carrying on Garp's search for meaning in a fatherless world. Consequently, when Yoshiya spots a professional-looking man one day on the subway with a missing right earlobe, he believes that he may have found his father and he begins to tail him, first by train, then by taxi, and finally by foot. Near the end of this chase, the man disappears down a long dark alley that is barely wide enough for two people to walk past each other. Yoshiya follows him into this dark alley but finds himself reaching a dead end—a sheet metal fence. Searching for an exit, he finds a split in the fence, and he squeezes himself through it, emerging on the other side onto a baseball field. At this point, he realizes that the man he was following is gone and that he is alone. The imagery here (the journey down the dark alley and the emergence through the split in the fence into the safety of the baseball diamond), as Katō points out, is suggestive of a birth in reverse, a return to the womb from where Yoshiya can confront the question of his existence (Katō 2004, p. 124). Yoshiya, it would appear, needs to be born again.

As Alex Bates notes, Yoshiya's spiritual crisis began with his unanswered prayers about learning how to catch fly balls in baseball, so the setting of the baseball diamond for his spiritual epiphany is significant (Bates 2017, p. 148). What also comes to play an important part in his rebirth is the symbolism of the circle. The first thing Yoshiya comes to realize on the baseball diamond is how he has been circling the question of his father and his birth for years, but also how he may never reach a satisfactory conclusion to his quest. He describes this discovery as follows: "What I was chasing in circles must have been the tail of the darkness inside me. I just happened to catch sight of it, and followed it, and clung to it, and in the end let it fly into still deeper darkness. I'm sure I'll never see it again" (Murakami 2003, p. 64). Rather than this circling search leading to despair, however, it opens Yoshiya up to a new discovery within himself and a feeling of connection with the universe. Climbing the pitcher's mound, Yoshiya begins to dance, and as he does so, he finds himself swinging his "arms up, over, and down in large circles" (Idem.). Yoshiya's college girlfriend had called him "Super Frog" because of his long limbs and the way he would flay them around when he danced, a pet name he had not been fond of at first, but which he has since come to embrace. Yoshiya gives himself up to this dance, the circular motions of his body somehow expressing something he cannot adequately express in words. His final cry is "Oh God" (Ibid. p. 68).

So what does Yoshiya's final cry on the baseball diamond mean? Who is he calling out to, if not the absent God of his childhood he has clearly left behind? Readers of *after the quake* will notice that Yoshiya's pet name "Super Frog" connects him with another character in the collection, the frog from "super-frog saves Tokyo." In that story, a human-sized frog approaches a man named Katagiri and recruits him for an underground battle with Worm, a figure who causes earthquakes when he gets angry. Katagiri is an every-man—someone who has been selected by Frog for the heroic but unheralded way he deals with his personal challenges in life, and he was a character inspired in part by Murakami's interviewing of ordinary Japanese in the wake of the Aum attack for his non-fiction book *Underground*. Before the Kobe Earthquake and Aum attack, Murakami had been living in The United States, but these two events encouraged him to move back to Japan to look at the country of his birth again with new eyes. While Murakami is someone who never wanted to join what is sometimes disparagingly called Japan Inc.—to get a regular job as a salaryman—what this experience interviewing ordinary Japanese caught up in the Aum attack offered him was a new appreciation for the quiet dignity many ordinary Japanese bring to their lives amidst daily challenges. The battle with Worm, which the story tells us takes place in "the area of imagination," is about the silent battles which go on in every human heart—a battle which when won goes unnoticed, but when lost causes "earthquakes" of various kinds (Ibid. p. 110).

The character "super-frog" may also have been inspired in part by Irving's *The World According to Garp*. In that novel, Garp and his family often talk about the "Under Toad," a family reference born out of a child's imagination and misunderstanding. Garp, a naturally anxious parent, had often warned his sons when they went swimming at the beach near his mother's home to be careful of the undertow, and one of the sons later confesses that he had always thought his father was warning him about the "Under Toad," a creature he imagined that was lying in wait under the water to get him. This childhood vision of the Under Toad later becomes the family's "code phrase for anxiety." The narrator explains, "Garp and [his wife] Helen evoked the beast as a way of referring to their own sense of danger. When the traffic was heavy, when the road was icy—when depression had moved in overnight—they said to each other, 'The Under Toad is strong today'" (Irving 2018, pp. 408–409). *The World According to Garp* is a story in which anxieties abound and where many of the character's worst nightmares come true, but where they are still able to keep moving forward through life's tragedies. The "super-frog" who appears in Murakami's short story, is less a "code phrase for anxiety" (that role is arguably taken on more by Worm), than an expression of that part of our ourselves which heroically continues to fight this battle with fear and anxiety in the human heart. At the same time, at the end of the story, the distance between Frog and Worm begins to blur. Visiting Katagiri at a hospital, boils begin to form on frog's body. These boils then burst, and from the ooze which emerges Katagiri sees "wormlike maggots" and other crawling creatures. One consequence of his battle with Worm, in other words, is that Frog has become more "wormlike" himself.

"all god's children can dance" is part of Murakami's response to Aum. The question he asked himself in the aftermath of the Aum attack is what he, as a writer of fiction, could offer people who are looking for something more—something beyond what secularized Japan alone can offer (Murakami 2001, pp. 202–203). Yoshiya is a model of a young person on a spiritual quest who confronts the darkness within himself and turns it into something more positive. While the Aum attack has not yet occurred in the world Yoshiya inhabits, it is foreshadowed in the story, primarily in the detailed descriptions of train journeys. This begins with Yoshiya's commute to work. Yoshiya lives in Asagaya, and his commute takes him first to Yotsuya on the Chūō Line, and then from there to Kasumigaseki on the Marunouchi Line. He then transfers at Kasumigaseki, taking the Hibiya Line to his workplace in Kamiyachō (literally God Valley Town). It is on the reverse commute, again at his transfer at Kasumigaseki, that Yoshiya spots the man he believes could be his biological father, and he follows him onto the Chiyoda Line and into the suburbs of Tokyo and beyond. Katō Norihiro points out the way these detailed directions, while likely meaningless to the average English reader who has never visited Tokyo, will remind at least some Japanese readers of the Aum attack, which occurred on three of the train lines Yoshiya uses—the Chiyoda, Hibiya, and Marunouchi lines (Katō 2004, p. 108). In all three attacks, the intended target was Kasumigaseki (the same station where Yoshiya spots his "father"), a station close to many government buildings and not far from the Japanese Diet building. The aim of the Aum attack, in other words, was to strike at the heart of Japan's political center. What Yoshiya's train route is thus foreshadowing is the existential stakes involved in his search for the "father," and the consequences which can follow when it is not managed well.

What Yoshiya's spiritual journey also demonstrates is how the discovery of a "God within" can compensate for the loss of a "God without." This discovery of the "God within" is highlighted primarily by the circular motions

Yoshiya begins to make in his dance on the baseball mound. As will also be discussed later in relation to the short story "Cream," the circle is a central symbol in Jungian thought for what I have been calling the "God within," or what Jung also called the Self. Jung's ideas about the Self or "God within" came from many places, but one symbol he was particularly fond of for explaining and exploring this psychological phenomenon was the mandala. Jung had found himself spontaneously producing mandalas in a time of great mental distress, and he soon came to realize that the symbols he was producing for himself had historical precedents, including in religious iconography. As Jung writes, "The Sanskrit word *mandala* means 'circle'" (Jung 1981, para. 629), and he continued to draw and explore such mandala over his lifetime, personal circles that for him were a symbol of the unconscious drive for individuation and wholeness. While Jung tended to express his inner mandala primarily through drawing, he recognized that there are other forms in which a spontaneous expression of the "God within" might emerge, including in dance. In *The Secret of the Golden Flower*, Jung writes that,

> Among my patients I have come across cases of women who did not draw *mandala* symbols but who danced them instead. In India this type is called *mandala nrithya* or *mandala* dance, and the dance figures express the same meanings as the drawings. My patients can say very little about the meaning of the symbols but are fascinated by them and find them in some way or other expressive and effective with respect to the subjective psychic condition represented. (Wilhelm and Jung 1957, 97–98)

Yoshiya's dance on the baseball diamond is a mandala dance. The circles he spontaneously forms with his flaying arms are an expression of an unconscious drive to connect with the "God within." The Father God Yoshiya's mother had offered him (the religious story) had not helped him in any meaningful way, including with his desire to catch fly balls in baseball, and the story of his biological father (the medical or scientific story) had not filled this void either. But here, on the pitcher's bound of a baseball diamond, Yoshiya has discovered a God within (the personal story that connects him with his own unconscious) and a message that all God's children can dance. This is part of Murakami's response to Aum and to religious fundamentalism more broadly. It is an approach which acknowledges both the need for spirituality in contemporary society and the dangers of placing religious authority in others. Instead, what the story advocates for is the finding of spiritual authority within.

1Q84

One thing the novel *1Q84* shares with "all god's children can dance" is a view that God may be "out there" but simply too cold or emotionally distant to bother getting involved in human affairs. This view is most dramatically expressed by Tamaru, the bodyguard who works for a woman known as the dowager, and who, in a scene near the end of the novel, executes a private detective called Ushikawa who has been hired by a religious cult to hunt down the assassin of their leader. Before killing this man, Tamaru tells him a story about the stone home (nicknamed the Tower) which Carl Jung built by hand in Bollingen, Zurich, after his wife died. Jung had called the Tower "a confession of faith in stone" (Jung 1983, p. 250). In his story, Tamaru calls the Tower a "three-dimensional mandala" (Murakami 2011, p. 871). The Tower, in other words, was an outward expression of Jung's search for the "God within." Over one of the doors within the Tower Jung had then engraved the Latin phase *Vocatus atque non vocatus, Deus aderit,* which is often translated into English as "Called or not, God is present" (the same phrase was carved over the front door of Jung's home in Kusnatcht and was also engraved on his tombstone). Tamaru gets this part of his story wrong, mistakenly explaining that the phrase was carved on a stone near the entrance to the Tower, and he also gets the quote wrong, explaining to Ushikawa that what Jung had carved were the words "Cold or not, God is present" (Idem.).

Shimizu Yoshinori has noted this misquote and argues that it is likely intentional black humor on Murakami's part (Shimizu 2006, loc. 2703). In my 2019 interview with Murakami, I asked him directly about this point, and he explained that he had originally misheard the quote and written it in his novel, but that this was pointed out to him before the novel was published at the stage of producing the galleys, and so he could have corrected the quote from "Cold" to "Called" if he had wanted to. In the end, he decided that he liked the quote as it was. Murakami visited Bollingen Tower in 2008 with his wife, spending an entire day there with the Japanese ambassador to Switzerland and his wife, so that may have been the time when he first heard (or actually misheard) the quote (Kawai and Murakami 2016, p.10). Murakami's decision to keep the quote as he originally wrote it in *1Q84* is an interesting one. It suggests that there was something intrinsically appealing about the idea of a "cold God" rather than a "called God" that he wanted to keep in the text.

For Tamaru, this conception of God as something cold but present is both in keeping with his experience of religion in general and an idea which he finds strangely comforting. He explains this to Ushikawa:

> I don't know why, but I've been drawn to these words for a long time. I find them hard
> to understand, but the difficulty in understanding makes it all the more profound. I don't
> know much about God. I was raised in a Catholic orphanage and had some awful experi-
> ences there so I don't have a good impression of God. And it was always cold there, even
> in the summer. It was either really cold or outrageously cold. One or the other. If there is
> a God, I can't say he treated me very well. Despite all this, those words of Jung's quietly
> sank deep into the folds of my soul. Sometimes I close my eyes and repeat them over and
> over, and they make me strangely calm. (Murakami 2011, p. 872)

What Tamaru seems to have found is a kind of mysterious mantra that expresses his mixed feelings about God. Like Yoshiya before him, he is not
denying the existence of God, but he is protesting His lack of warmth. At the
end of his story about Jung's Tower, Tamaru has Ushikawa repeat the phrase
twice: Cold or not, God is present. He then places a plastic bag over Ushikawa's head and suffocates him to death.

Along with Tamaru's cold God in *1Q84*, however, is the unconscious
God of another character called Aomame (the female assassin already mentioned). This is a God which slowly emerges in Aomame's life, despite her
conscious objections. Aomame, like Yoshiya, is someone who grew up in a
strongly religious household (a group modelled in the novel on the Jehovah's
Witnesses) but who left her family's faith at a young age. Despite leaving her
childhood religion behind, however, she finds herself reciting the rote prayers
she learned in times of stress and eventually she comes to realize that despite
her rejection of the God of her parents, she has always "believed in a God
outside of the conscious realm." This is not necessarily a God found in any
particular religious tradition, but a personal God she has come to know
through direct experience. Revealing Aomame's thoughts, the narrative reveals, "This is not a God with a form. No white clothes, no long beard. This
God has no doctrine, no scripture, no precepts. No reward, no punishment.
This God doesn't give, and doesn't take away. There is no heaven up in the
sky, no hell down below. When it's hot, and when it's cold, God is simply
there" (Murakami 2011, p. 743).

Like Tamaru's God, Aomame's God is connected to temperature, but
can be present in both heat and cold. This God outside of the conscious
realm is not without its benefits. Standing with a gun in her mouth and ready
to take her own life at the end of Book Two (of what is three books in the
original Japanese), Aomame is looking for something to hold onto, and she
finds her answer in God. "Nobody can hear what I am saying, I'm sure. But
so what? As long as God can hear me. The important thing is that God is
watching you. No one can avoid his gaze. Big Brother is watching you" (Ibid.

p. 575). Having God see her and hear her in her time of greatest need is what allows Aomame to live another day. When Yoshiya had been dancing on his baseball mound, he had likewise felt like someone was watching him, and though he couldn't determine who this someone or something was (perhaps his biological father, perhaps his spiritual father, or perhaps someone else altogether), in the end, he decides that it doesn't matter. Whoever they are, let them look: "all god's children can dance." For Aomame, the God who sees and hears her is something similar—a mystery that she cannot begin to make sense of consciously, but which supports her regardless.

Reviewing *1Q84* for the magazine *First Things*, Franklin Freeman argues that:

> Murakami sees the world from a sort of Gnostic dualism. But he rises above this by what seems to be the opening of a door in his work to the reality of God. It is not a Judeo-Christian God, although there are favorable references to such in the novel, but more of a Jungian God. Murakami believes in God, it seems, but he's afraid of the zealotry and madness of fanatics and so he draws back from defining God in too detailed a way. (Freeman 2012)

Jung was a student of Gnosticism, and much of his approach to the "God within" can be understood in Gnostic terms. For much of *1Q84*, Aomame wrestles with a phrase she has inherited from her childhood about the coming kingdom of God, but what she slowly appears to realize is that the vision of the kingdom she continues to pursue may be something closer to what Jesus offered in one of his more Gnostic quotations found in Luke 17:21: "the kingdom of God is within you." Again, a Murakami character learns to find their spiritual authority, not in a God out there, but in a God within.

Cream

"Cream" is the story of a young man who is invited by a childhood acquaintance to a piano recital in the hills of Kobe. When he gets there, though, the venue is locked, and has seemingly not been in use for some time. Nobody is around. He checks his invitation again and begins to wonder whether this was a prank, though he cannot work out who might have been behind it (his best guess is that, without realizing it, he may have done something in the past to hurt the girl who invited him to the concert). Not knowing what to do, he then retreats to a small park where he experiences "stress-induced hyperventilation." This is not the first time this had happened to him, and he does what he always does on such occasions—waits it out. When he eventually calms down and looks up, there is an old man sitting across from him who, without any introduction, offers him a mysterious message about a circle with many centers and no circumference. The narrator of this story, who is now much older and who is recounting his story to a younger man, confesses early on in his account that he has never been able to draw much of a conclusion from this episode. When pushed by the younger man for his interpretation though, he replies:

> In my life, whenever an inexplicable, illogical, disturbing event takes place (I'm not saying that it happens often, but it has a few times), I always come back to that circle—the circle with many centers but no circumference. And, as I did when I was eighteen, on that arbor bench, I close my eyes and listen to the beating of my heart.
> Sometimes I feel that I can sort of grasp what that circle is, but a deeper understanding eludes me. This circle is, most likely, not a circle with a concrete, actual form but, rather, one that exists only within our minds. When we truly love somebody, or feel deep compassion, or have an idealistic sense of how the world should be, or when we discover faith (or something close to faith)—that's when we understand the circle as a given and accept it in our hearts. Admittedly, though, this is nothing more than my own vague attempt to reason it out. (Murakami 2021, p. 25)

When Murakami was asked about the meaning of this mysterious circle in an interview for *The New Yorker*, he answered, "I think it corresponds to a kind of faith. This doesn't have to be a particular religion, though" (Treisman 2019). So what kind of faith is this?

The description of a circle with no circumference and many centers is one with a long history in Western thought (it has been traced back to numerous figures including Alain of Lille and Pascal and appears frequently in the work of Jung) and is usually taken as a paradoxical description of the nature of God, though Murakami claimed to be unaware of this history when I questioned him on the matter. I offer the relevant part of my interview below:

> **Jonathan Dil**: In your recent short story "Cream" you write about a circle with many centers and no circumference. This is an idea with a long history. It's an idea you can find in Jung's work. You can find it in lots of places. I think Joseph Campbell writes about this circle with many centers and no circumference. Usually, it's taken as a mystical description of the nature of God. Most people read this image in that way. What was your reference for the image—for the circle? Where did you get the idea from? Where did you read it?
> **Murakami Haruki**: Circle?
> **JD**: The circle in the short story "Cream." This is a famous image or idea that's been used for centuries and centuries normally referring to God. Where did you come across the idea?
> **MH**: I don't remember. I wrote about a circle right, yes.
> **JD**: Yes, a circle with many centers and no circumference. This is in Jung's work. It's in Joseph Campbell's work. It goes back hundreds and hundreds of years. Many people talk about it.

> **MH**: Really?
> **JD**: Yes, [its'] very famous. Very well known.
> **MH**: Really, it's very well known?
> **JD**: Very well known. Well not super well known, but when you look it up it has a long history.
> **MH**. When I was writing it, I thought it was a Zen kōan. It looked to me like a kind of Zen kōan.
> **JD**: What about a mandala? Did you think of a kind of mandala image?
> **MH**: It's kind of an oriental thing in my impression. But it's famous in Jungian …?
> **JD**: Well Jung quotes it in a couple of books, but it goes back many many years.
> **MH**: Maybe I read that somewhere in the past, but I don't remember what it is, and I have no [memory].

Here, Murakami presents the mysterious circle as something like a Zen kōan, a strange paradox you are invited to struggle with for years that may one day lead to a kind of *satori* or enlightenment. Like Tamaru, who could not understand what it meant that "Cold or not, God is present," but who found himself drawn to these words regardless, or like Aomame, who finds herself believing "in a God outside of the conscious realm," there is a sense here that God (a circle with many centers but no circumference) cannot be grasped by rational means, but that, like a Zen monk sitting in zazen day after day wrestling with a riddle that has no logical answer, it is possible for us to find meaning in things we do not fully understand. What makes the particular "kōan" Murakami has chosen for this story significant is that is comes from Western speculations about the paradoxical nature of God—not the God of mainstream Christianity, necessarily, but something close to the Jungian God or God within.

Like the other two stories already examined in this essay, this "God within" in "Cream" is explicitly contrasted with a "God without." Retreating to the small park, what the narrator had originally heard was a voice coming from a vehicle's loudspeaker preaching a Christian message of hell and the possibility of salvation through Jesus Christ: "But all those who seek salvation in Jesus Christ and repent of their sins will have their sins forgiven by the Lord. They will escape the fires of Hell. Believe in God, for only those who believe in Him will reach salvation after death and receive eternal life" (Murakami 2021, p. 13). The narrator welcomes this voice, more for its conviction than for its message, but the voice soon disappears, leaving him alone again. While he does not directly take this Christian message of sin and judgment to heart, his thoughts do turn to the girl who invited him to the concert, and he starts searching his memory for things he may have done to hurt her in the past. This rumination then causes him to lose his mental stability and to start hyperventilating. It is after this experience that the mysterious old man appears and offers his message.

So what is the meaning of this "kōan" offered to the narrator by a wise old man and which he, now in turn, is passing on to a younger acquaintance? What is the Jungian God within? Jung would at times speak confidently on the question of God in a way that invited misunderstanding. In a famous interview with the BBC, for example, when asked whether he believed in God, he answered, "I *know*. I don't need to believe. I know" (Quoted in Dyer 2000, p. 4). In his writing, however, Jung was usually more careful to distinguish between God as a psychological and God as a metaphysical reality. When he says he knows that God exists, what he is saying is that he knows from firsthand experience that God exists as a psychological reality, but as a scientist, he is agnostic about what this means for the metaphysical question of God. In his book *Symbols of Transformation*, for example, Jung writes,

> I am therefore of the opinion that, in general, psychic energy or libido creates the God-image by making use of archetypal patterns, and that man in consequence worships the psychic force active within him as something divine. We thus arrive at the objectionable conclusion that, from the psychological point of view, the God-image is a real but subjective phenomenon. (Jung 1976, para. 129)

Writing elsewhere, Jung puts it even more simply: "God is an archetype" (Jung 1980, para. 15). When Jung speaks of his first-hand knowledge of God then, what he is really talking about is the "God-image," the reality of God as a psychological phenomenon, or the idea of God as an archetype. Jung's appeal to this inner, psychological, archetypal God fits with the descriptions of the inner God in Murakami's fiction.

The God archetype takes many names and forms in Jung's writing and is central to understanding his life's work. Perhaps the most common name Jung gives the God archetype is simply the self, and it is opening up to this archetype which provides the aim of individuation. Jung writes, "The self … is a God-image, or at least cannot be distinguished from one" (Jung 1979, para. 42). Elsewhere he writes, "Intellectually the self is no more than a psychological concept, a construct that serves to express an unknowable essence which we cannot grasp as such, since by definition it transcends our powers of comprehension. It might equally well be called 'the God within us'" (Jung 1972, para. 399). Murakami, like Jung, appears to be open to this "God within us," not as a metaphysical claim, but as a psychological reality. This "God within," his fiction suggests, can be the antidote to the God without, a father in heaven who may or may not be there, but who is too cold and distant for it to matter either way.

Early in his career, in a conversation with Kawamoto Saburō, Murakami was explaining his writing method and the emphasis he places on spontaneity above all else. Kawamoto then pointed out to him the parallel of this improvisational approach to the jazz playing of pianist Keith Jarret. Murakami quickly countered that he doesn't believe in God though, explaining how Jarret believes he is being guided in his improvisational performances by a higher power. Considering the comparison some more though, Murakami continued, "Of course, I don't believe in the existence of God, but I must believe in some power like that in the human system" (Kawamoto 1985, p. 65). Murakami, we might conclude, believes in God in the same way that Jung believes in God—as a direct experience with the deepest parts of himself. While Jung was more open to the possibility of the metaphysical God—the God out there—than Murakami appears to be, when it comes to the inner God, they are speaking the same language.

Conclusion

In his book *Partial Faiths: Postsecular Fiction in the Age of Pynchon and Morrison*, John McClure makes the case for a postsecular turn in contemporary American literature. The body of literature McClure is interested in is postsecular, he argues, for three main reasons:

> because the stories it tells trace the turn of secular-minded characters back toward the religious; because its ontological signature is a religiously infected disruption of secular constructions of the real; and because its ideological signature is the rearticulation of a dramatically "weakened" religiosity with secular, progressive values and projects. (McClure 2007, p. 3)

As is implied in this last reason, postsecular fiction does not reflect a return to traditional religious faith. McClure explains that these "narratives affirm the urgent need for a turn toward the religious even as they reject (in most instances) the familiar dream of full return to an authoritative faith" (Ibid. p. 6). Instead, what postsecular fiction provides are works which draw "from a whole range of religious discourses and produce new, weakened and hybridized, idioms of belief" (Ibid. p. 4).

The three stories discussed in this essay are postsecular fiction as defined by McClure. They offer, not a return to "authoritative faith," but "new, weakened and hybridized, idioms of belief." What is interesting in Murakami's case is how this idiom of belief is juxtaposed against a God who seems loosely

Christian in its conception. Christians make up less than 1% of the population of Japan, though the cultural impact of Christianity on Japan is greater than this number alone would suggest. And yet it still seems slightly odd for Murakami, who comes from a line of Buddhist priests but who is not religious himself, to be wrestling so directly in his fiction with a God/father who sits high up in the heavens (even if He is an absentee father in many respects). Yoshiya was told that he was a special child of God, and Aomame grew up in a religion that is loosely modelled on the Jehovah's Witnesses. The narrator of "Cream" receives a message of Christian judgment just before his encounter with a mysterious man and a message about a circle with many centers and no circumference. In each of these stories, the coldness of the God without is juxtaposed with a mysterious God within which is seen as the answer to existential anxieties. As Murakami explains, this God within represents "a kind of faith" but not an appeal to "a particular religion."

Perhaps what Murakami's juxtaposition of these two Gods represents is his position as a global writer. Though he is writing stories about spiritual crises and breakthroughs set in Japan, these stories are simultaneously intended as responses to the rise of religious fundamentalism worldwide and are appeals to resist closed religious certainty in favor of open spiritual uncertainty. What is interesting about this response, however, is that it is less Japanese than we might expect. Instead, as I have argued in this essay, Murakami's response to the spiritual crisis of our age is deeply informed by Jungian thought and is deeply Gnostic in nature. The kingdom of God is within you; the spiritual answers you need to live your life with "a kind of faith" can be found inside you. Or perhaps it is fairer to call Murakami's response a new hybrid of Japanese and esoteric Western sensibilities. What he has done is to take a mysterious description of a cold God who is there whether He is called or not, or of a God who is a circle with many centers and no circumference, and turn them into something like Zen kōans. Like any good kōan, there are no logical solutions to the puzzles Murakami offers his readers. Instead, like Yoshiya, we are more likely to grasp their meaning in dance or in other representations of the mandala or circle. As Jung would put, God is an archetype—in fact, the archetype of archetypes—and thus is an object or force worthy of a lifetime's questing and contemplation. At the end of such a lifetime, will one find *satori* or not? Murakami's postsecular fiction, the work of a self-proclaimed atheist, suggests that we just might.

References

Bates, Alex. 2017. "Nature and Disaster in Murakami Haruki's after the quake." In Ecocriticism in Japan, edited by Hisaaki Wake, Keijiro Suga, and Yuki Masami, 129–155. Lanham, MD: Lexington Books.

Düker, Ronald. 2004. "Es gibt nicht nur eine Realität." *Zeit Online* (January 9). https://www.zeit.de/2014/03/haruki-murakami?utm_referrer=https%3A%2F%2Fwww.google.com.

Dyer, Donald R. 2000. *Jung's Thoughts on God: Religious Depths of the Psyche.* York Beach: Nicholas-Hays.

Endō, Shūsaku. 2006. *Watashi ni totte kami towa (What God is to me). Tokyo: Kōbunsha.*

Endō, Shūsaku. 2009. *Endō Shūsaku bungakuronshū shūkyōhen* (Literary Essays from Endō Shūsaku: The Religious Edition). Tokyo: Kōdansha.

Freeman, Franklin. 2012. "A Review of 1Q84." *First Things* (October 2). https://www.firstthings.com/web-exclusives/2012/10/a-review-ofq84.

Gabriel, Philip. 2006. *Spirit Matters: The Transcendent in Modern Japanese Literature.* Honolulu: University of Hawai'i Press.

Granqvist, Pehr. 2020. *Attachment in Religion and Spirituality: A Wider View.* New York: The Guilford Press.

Irving, John. 2018. *The World According to Garp.* New York: Dutton.

Jung, Carl. (trans. R. F. C Hull). 1972. The Collected Works of C.G Jung, Volume 7, *Two Essays in Analytical Psychology.* Edited by Herbert Read, Michael Fordham, Gerhard Adler, and William McGuire. Princeton, NJ, Princeton University Press.

Jung, Carl. (trans. R. F. C Hull). 1976. The Collected Works of C.G Jung, Volume 5, *Symbols of Transformation: An Analysis of the Prelude to a Case of Schizophrenia.* Edited by Herbert Read, Michael Fordham, Gerhard Adler, and William McGuire. Princeton, NJ, Princeton University Press.

Jung, Carl. (trans. R. F. C Hull). 1979. The Collected Works of C.G Jung, Volume 9, Part 2, *Aion: Researches into the Phenomenology of the Self.* Edited by Herbert Read, Michael Fordham, Gerhard Adler, and William McGuire. Princeton, NJ, Princeton University Press.

Jung, Carl. (trans. R. F. C Hull). 1980. The Collected Works of C.G Jung, Volume 12, *Psychology and Alchemy.* Edited by Herbert Read, Michael Fordham, Gerhard Adler, and William McGuire. Princeton, NJ, Princeton University Press.

Jung, Carl. (trans. R. F. C Hull). 1981. The Collected Works of C.G Jung, Volume 9, Part 1, *Archetypes and the Collective Unconscious.* Edited by Herbert Read, Michael Fordham, Gerhard Adler, and William McGuire. Princeton, NJ, Princeton University Press.

Jung, Carl. (trans. Richard and Clara Winston). 1984. *C.G. Jung: Memories, Dreams, Reflections*. London: Flamingo.

Katō, Norihiro. 2004. *Murakami Haruki Ierōpēji Part 2* (Murakami Haruki Yellow Pages: Part 2). Tokyo: Arechi shuppansha.

Kawai, Hayao, and Haruki Murakami (trans. Christopher Stephens). 2016. *Haruki Murakami Goes to Meet Hayao Kawai*. Einsiedln: Daimon.

Kawamoto, Saburō (1985) "Monogatari no tame no bōken" (An Adventure for Story), *Bungakukai* August, 34–86.

Kirkpatrick, Lee A. 2005. *Attachment, Evolution, and the Psychology of Religion*. New York: The Guilford Press.

Shimada, Hiromi. 2009. *Mushūkyō koso Nihonjin no shūkyō dearu* (The Religion of the Japanese is 'No Religion'). Tokyo: Kadokawa.

Shimizu, Yoshinori. 2006. *Murakami Haruki wa kuse ni naru* (Murakami Haruki is Additive). Tokyo: Asahi shinbun shuppan.

McClure, John A. 2017. *Partial Faiths: Postsecular Fiction in the Age of Pynchon and Morrison*. Athens: The University of Georgia Press.

Miller, Laura, and Don George. 1997. "Haruki Murakami." *Salon* (December 16). https://www.salon.com/1997/12/16/int_2/.

Murakami, Haruki. 1981. "Shika to kamisama to seiseshiria" (Deer, God, and Saint Cecelia). *Waseda Bungaku* (June), 6–10.

Murakami, Haruki. 2001. *Underground: The Tokyo Gas Attack & the Japanese Psyche*. London: The Harvill Press.

Murakami, Haruki. 2003. *after the quake*. New York: Vintage International. Kindle.

Murakami, Haruki (trans. Philip Gabriel). 2005. *Kafka on the Shore*. New York: Alfred A Knopf. Kindle.

Murakami, Haruki (trans. Jay Rubin and Philip Gabriel). 2011. *1Q84*. New York: Alfred A Knopf. Kindle.

Murakami, Haruki. 2016. *Uten enten* (Come Rain or Shine). Tokyo: Shinchōsha. Kindle.

Murakami, Haruki. 2019. "Abandoning a Cat: Memories of my father." *The New Yorker* (September 30). https://www.newyorker.com/magazine/2019/10/07/abandoning-a-cat?utm_source=NYR_REG_GATE.

Murakami, Haruki. 2021. *First Person Singular*. New York: Alfred A. Knopf.

Roemer, Michael. 2009. "Religious Affiliation in Contemporary Japan: Untangling the Enigma." *Review of Religious Research*, Vol. 50, No. 3, March, pp. 298–320.

Treisman, Deborah. 2018. "Haruki Murakami on Parallel Realities." *The New Yorker* (August 27). https://www.newyorker.com/books/this-week-in-fiction/haruki-murakami-2018-09-03.

Treisman, Deborah. 2019. "Haruki Murakami on Asking the Right Questions." *The New Yorker* (January 21). https://www.newyorker.com/books/this-week-in-fiction/haruki-murakami-01-28-19.

Wilhelm, Richard, and Carl Jung. 1957. *The Secret of The Golden Flower: A Chinese Book of Life*. London: Routledge & Kegan Paul Ltd.

Tomoki Wakatsuki & Matthew C. Strecher

Rebels With a Cause:
A Cosmopolitan Examination of Haruki Murakami and Kazuo Ishiguro

Abstract: *This paper discusses the cosmopolitan outlook found in common between Haruki Murakami and Kazuo Ishiguro. As contemporary novelists, they share the pursuit of memory as a subject matter that is inherently connected with the issue of identity and belonging. It is notable that they resist conventional categorization not only as writers but also as individuals. By examining comparatively the careers of these two authors in what Nigel Rapport calls the "cosmopolitan world" (2012), we argue that memory, for both Murakami and Ishiguro, is key to understanding their cosmopolitan principles and commitment, how these relate to their family histories of war experience, and how this in turn establishes their work as part of a wider global literature.*

Keywords: Haruki Murakami, Kazuo Ishiguro, cosmopolitanism, history, memory, Japaneseness, identity, belonging, global literature, Haruki phenomenon

Introduction

As long as there have been novelists, there have been critics attempting to categorize them, and as long as there have been literary categories, there have been novelists trying with all their might to avoid being placed into them. Contemporary writers Haruki Murakami (b. 1949) and Kazuo Ishiguro (b. 1954) are two such novelists. In the case of the British Ishiguro, owing to his Japanese birth and heritage, attempts have been made to mark him as 'post-colonial,' presumably in the most general sense of Western hegemony vs. Asian periphery, since Japan has never been anyone's colony. Ishiguro, of course, denies being post-colonial, and emphasizes the fact that any vestige of Japan that remains within him, other than what he absorbed while being raised by two Japanese parents, is purely imaginary. Similarly, efforts to politicize his early novels, the first of which is set in Nagasaki (his birthplace as well as site of the second atomic bombing, August 9, 1945) tend to fall flat; Ishiguro is more interested in personal than collective memories, and his novels interrogate how individual identity is constructed and maintained.

Murakami is an even trickier case, for critics have attempted, at various times, to place him into many categories, and ultimately have never succeeded in placing him into any. Many saw in his use of magical realist settings a nod toward the postmodernist craze that coincided with his meteoric rise to success; others sought traces of the postwar political writer. Some dismissed him as "light," and others as "fantasy." If anything, Murakami is best understood as a storyteller who will not be limited in what he writes, though his works do frequently play on the tension between the physical and metaphysical—the conscious and unconscious—worlds in which we function from day to day. As with Ishiguro, Murakami's stories tend to explore identity formation and, perhaps even more than Ishiguro, the threat posed to that identity by state-sponsored, collective ideologies.

This, however, is not all these two authors have in common, nor is it necessarily the most important thing. Rather, the fixation on identity might be seen as a symptom of something bigger: a cosmopolitan urge to belong, while at the same time protecting individual autonomy. Both Murakami and Ishiguro demonstrate ways of living and working that transcend dichotomies such as East and West, nationalism and cosmopolitanism, or the "us vs. them" divide, engaging the world through a form of cosmopolitanism that Hannerz describes as "a state of mind, or—to take a more processual view—a mode of managing meaning" (Hannerz 1990: 238).

In the pages that follow we will explore how these two writers express what we term "everyday cosmopolitanism," which entails a conscious sense of openness toward the Other, a desire for belonging within ever-widening circles of community (local, national, global), while at the same time maintaining a strict sense of individual freedom, of selfhood that is, however, always ready to be acted upon by the Other.

Much of this operation with regard to Murakami is discussed in Wakatsuki's volume *The Haruki Phenomenon: Haruki Murakami as Cosmopolitan Writer* (2020; Springer), a brief summary of which follows. By reviewing the substantially cosmopolitan nature of the Haruki Murakami phenomenon (Murakami Haruki *genshō*) we will establish the tools and basis, but also the limitations, for the wider comparative discussion of Murakami and Ishiguro to follow.

The Haruki Phenomenon: A Case Study

The Haruki Phenomenon is focused on one very simple, yet pervasive question: why is Haruki Murakami so popular around the world, and why is his readership so diverse? How has a writer who was largely rejected by the Japanese literary establishment risen to such heights that he has been a top bet to win the Nobel Prize in literature for more than a decade? This vexing question, approached from a purely literary perspective, has led to assertions that Murakami's so-called *mukokuseki*[3] (nationality-less) written style is somehow appealing to readers across borders; others have argued that the author's deployment of magical realist elements is what draws readers. Some have noted the subtle yet discernible presence of political allegory within the Murakami fictional universe. And for still others, the answer lies in the mythological tropes visible within the Murakami narrative structure.

No doubt Murakami's popularity resides in the combined strength of these various aspects of his writing, but it does not tell the full story. While acknowledging literary aspects of Murakami's remarkable rise as a global writer, *The Haruki Phenomenon* also attributes this global success, from a cultural sociological perspective, to Murakami's cosmopolitan identity, which seeks belonging within the wider global community, while at the same time tenaciously preserving the autonomy of the individual self amidst the pressures of socially and culturally constituted national identities. Cosmopolitanism, in brief, gains its name from the Cynic philosopher Diogenes of Sinope (ca. 412/404–323 BCE), who famously declared himself to be *kosmopolitês*, a "citizen of the world," in defiance of the convention in the ancient Greek world of subordinating to one's city-state. Was Diogenes indicating his belonging in the whole world, or merely declaring himself an outsider to all human society? Either way, we see a similar gesture on the part of Murakami, who seems to have gone out of his way *not* to follow the "normal" path for young Japanese entering society: choosing *not* to join the workforce after completing his university degree, he opened a jazz bar; choosing *not* to become a conventional Japanese novelist, he invented his own style of writing and narrative. Achieving immense fame after publishing *Noruwei no mori* (1987; Norwegian Wood), he chose to live abroad. Noting that "novelists are a special breed" in his 2009 Jerusalem speech,[4] he reconfirms his commitment to breaking with convention and relying on his own experiences and instincts. It is an act of resistance, of rebellion against the power of social

---

3   The term *mukokuseki*, literally "without nationality," refers to the lack of culture and language-specific markers in Murakami's prose that would identify it as Japanese. In practice, it means that, while Murakami writes using the Japanese language, his Japanese is not considered standard in the strict literary sense. While his stories generally take place in Japan, there is nothing in the narrative that would specifically require this to be so. The term *mukokuseki* has been used by a number of critics (cf. for instance, Kim 2009, Strecher 2014, 2017) to acknowledge the sense of otherness in Murakami's prose.

4   Acceptance speech for the Jerusalem Prize for the Freedom of the Individual Society in 2009. See Murakami (2009).

systems that define identity for the individual, an issue that remains endemic to all societies, and is particularly pronounced in Japan. Murakami demonstrates through his life and his work his openness to influencing and being influenced by the cultural Other in defiance of a social and cultural system that, much like Diogenes, chooses rather to define itself in terms of its difference, its separateness, from the Other. In contrast with the "us vs. them" mentality, the true cosmopolitan sees only "all of us."

Such a strategy no doubt worked, historically speaking, in the era in which Murakami emerged and made his name as a writer, for his rise coincided with the rapid advancement of globalization in the spheres of politics, economics, transportation, and particularly, communications. It is no accident that a novelist like Murakami should achieve global success in the same era that brought about the rise of the Internet, laying open the entire world to instant scrutiny. Nigel Rapport (2012) argued a decade ago, correctly, we believe, that it was time for us to confront the fact that we were living in a cosmopolitan world, referring to the effects of globalization and its ensuing transnational and transcultural shifts. Murakami's global popularity owes much to such shifts, for he employs settings, characters and situations that transcend the local/national and become easily transferrable across national/cultural boundaries.

Such transnational and transcultural shifts are not without resistance, and globalization in Japan has been accompanied by an equal and opposite urge to define what is "truly Japanese" and what is "Other." In contrast to the openness and belonging of "everyday cosmopolitanism," which *The Haruki Phenomenon* describes as a frame of mind that is nurtured and practiced through the everyday lives of people, this sense of being "truly Japanese," expressed in Japan as *Nihonjinron* ("theory of Japaneseness"), emphasizes the uniqueness and exclusivity of Japanese culture and society. That same impulse to separate Japan from the Other also grounds the literary establishment in Japan, which valorizes *and defines* "pure literature" (*junbungaku*) as literature written in Japanese by Japanese, for Japanese, and about Japanese.[5] Given his inclination towards the cosmopolitan mindset, it comes as no surprise that Murakami and the literary establishment did not take to one another from the start.

---

5   For more on the relationship between "pure literature" and *Nihonjinron* see Strecher 2017.

Murakami and Ishiguro: A Tale of Two Novelists

Whereas *The Haruki Phenomenon* seeks to explain the rise of Haruki Murakami as a cultural phenomenon by focusing on his cosmopolitan tendencies, the present essay has more modest goals. Here we propose to explore in a comparative manner cosmopolitan tendencies in Murakami and recent Nobel laureate Kazuo Ishiguro. This will not be easy, as from a purely literary standpoint, Murakami and Ishiguro are not all that similar. Murakami writes in a determined plainstyle that defies literary convention, while Ishiguro's prose is formal and proper, thoroughly English. Murakami is well known for his consistent use of a magical realist structure, and thematically he fixates on the tension between the individual and the State; Ishiguro, by contrast, is eclectic, working in a generally realist mode in his early works (*A Pale View of Hills*, *An Artist of the Floating World*, *Remains of the Day*), surrealism (*The Unconsoled*), detective (*When We Were Orphans*), and drifting into something between fantasy and science fiction in later ones (*The Buried Giant*, *Never Let Me Go*, *Klara and the Sun*). And while both novelists have an abiding interest in memory, particularly as it relates to the Second World War, Murakami concentrates on the recovery and protection of memory, while Ishiguro interrogates the tendency—and sometimes, the desirability—willfully to forget.

Yet there *are* meaningful similarities between Haruki Murakami and Kazuo Ishiguro. Both were born into a postwar Japan that was struggling to overcome the physical and emotional impacts of a disastrous war, though neither of them was old enough to remember those struggles, nor the war that occasioned them. Both grew up at a time when the youth of the world seriously questioned the moral and ethical correctness of their parents' generation and way of life (though Ishiguro was a little too young to have participated in the worldwide student protests of the 1960s). And most important of all, both are deeply concerned with identity, particularly the identity of those who feel somehow misplaced within their own surroundings. And thus, both chose to rebel against the demands placed upon their identities, as people and as novelists.

To make pronouncements such as these is admittedly risky, yet not especially far-fetched. Murakami, for instance, grew up with not one but *two* parents who taught grammar and Japanese literature; it might therefore be expected that the young Haruki would grow up sharing their interest in Japanese literature. And while he probably did, he spent his youth instead reading contemporary American writers like Truman Capote and John Irving, in their original English. And although he did eventually become a novelist, Murakami did all in his power to distance himself from the professional *literati* of his day, as we have already noted. Upon achieving an enviable level of success as a novelist, again as noted above, Murakami eschewed the common practice of making himself available to a public eager to meet him; he did not even make the rounds of the television talk shows after *Norwegian Wood* became a "million seller;" instead, he fled the country. While older contemporaries like Kenzaburō Ōe and younger ones like Ryū Murakami worked diligently to explore social problems specific to Japan, Murakami spent his time writing *mukokuseki* texts about something as ephemeral (and vaporous) as the human soul. In a society that expects its writers to be intellectual leaders, Murakami frequently denies knowing much about anything, stating only that he has his own opinions, and others may listen or not, as they choose.

Ishiguro, for his part, was born in Nagasaki, but brought by his parents to Surrey, southwest of London, at the age of five. Because this was intended to be a brief stay rather than a permanent move, Ishiguro's parents continued to speak Japanese to him at home, though he went to ordinary English schools and in time grew bi-cultural, but probably a good deal more English than Japanese. His first two novels, *A Pale View of Hills* (1982) and *An Artist of the Floating World* (1985), are set in Japan, but no attempt is made to be accurate in his depictions; rather, the Japan in his novels is almost completely imaginary, based on the fragmentary memories of a five year-old child (Ishiguro did not visit Japan as an adult until 1989). As he noted to an interviewer in 1986 about *An Artist of the Floating World*, "I just invent a Japan which serves my needs. And I put that Japan together out of little scraps, out of memories, out of speculation, out of imagination" (Ishiguro and Mason 1989, 341). Describing himself as "very much of the Western tradition," he admits to being "amused" when reviewers try to compare him to Japanese writers (Ibid). We see in this "amusement" also an urge to rebel against the determined efforts of some critics to force Ishiguro into the neat category of "Japanese" writer, or at best, of "international" writer, and Ishiguro has a bit of fun with this as well. Rebecca Suter notes that, in his early works, "Ishiguro plays the role of 'Japanese writer' with some irony at the expense of the reader … the irony appears mostly in the descriptions of landscapes and settings that appear somehow deliberately artificial and stereotyped" (Suter 2020, 27).

These invented versions of "Japan," ironic or not, betray both a sense of displacement and of ambivalence. In his 2017 Nobel Prize lecture he calls Japan "a place to which I in some way belonged, and from which I drew a certain sense of my identity" (Ishiguro 2017), and yet he described himself to Kenzaburō Ōe in 1989 as "a kind of homeless writer … I had no clear role, no society or country to speak for or write about," for "I wasn't a very English

Englishman, and I wasn't a very Japanese Japanese either" (Ishiguro and Ōe 1993, 169). His ambivalence manifested, by his own account, as something approaching hostility to the idea that he should know the country of his birth. In the same Nobel speech he admits that, in his youth, "[h]ad you mentioned Japan, asked me about its culture, you might even have detected a trace of impatience enter my manner as I declared my ignorance on the grounds that I hadn't set foot in that country—not even for a holiday—since leaving it at the age of five" (Ishiguro 2017).

We make here two very simple points that are true of Murakami and Ishiguro alike: first, that both men felt displaced (or displaced themselves) from the surroundings in which they were raised, in which they perhaps even fancied themselves "aliens" of a sort; and second, that both men rebelled— and in some ways continue to rebel—against being what others expect them to be. To an extent this last is common to all, particularly in childhood and adolescence; as children and young adults we all delight in confounding ex- pectations, in surprising others. But only an extraordinary (and extraordinarily brave) few, in our estimation, dare to continue their "rebellion"—let us call it resistance—in both public and private spheres (work and home), into adult life. This may well be a quality of the intellectual mind; Kenzaburō Ōe, argu- ably the most intellectual Japanese writer of the twentieth century, is well known for resisting definition as a "Japanese writer" during *his* Nobel ac- ceptance speech, in which he pointed to "the wide discrepancy between how the Japanese actually appear to others and how they would like to appear to them" (Ōe 1995, 122). Or perhaps this rebellious nature is merely an aspect of the creative mind—the novelist's or the artist's—as it seeks out new modes to express the inexpressible. Ishiguro hints at this in 2017 when he states that "we must widen our common literary world to include more voices from beyond our comfort zones of the elite first world cultures. We must search more energetically to discover the gems from what remain today unknown literary cultures ..." (Ishiguro 2017). Whatever else it may be, it is a crucial part of the cosmopolitan mindset, which determinedly resists the demands of local identity, of national narratives and social codes, looking beyond these to what is universally *human* in *all* cultures.

Individual Memory versus Collective Memory
Culture is memory. It is built upon a collective memory of who we are, of where we come from, perhaps even a hint of where we are going. We noted above that Murakami and Ishiguro share a common interest in memory, how it is preserved, recovered, or let go. Both writers, as noted earlier, have

demonstrated particular interest in the Second World War, memories of which are complex for Japan as a nation, which occupies positions both as victim (of strategic bombing, of nuclear attack) and perpetrator (as aggressors, invaders, colonizers). The question of responsibility always lies at the back of any discussion of the Second World War. This is not the place for us to go into specific historical issues of war responsibility, but we should address the effect of collective war memory on the generation of Japanese who did not participate in the war, but merely heard about it from their elders. For these memories passed on from the older generation to the younger in some ways proved nearly as traumatic as they did to those who experienced it.

Looking at Ishiguro and Murakami, we see that no matter how grand the historical narratives they confront, ultimately they will insist upon an intensely individual approach to those narratives. The war memories to which both writers relate are, in fact, those of their families. For Murakami this related to his father, who served in the Japanese Imperial Army in China during the war. Murakami writes in the afterword of a 2019 essay—his first time writing about his father—that war "profoundly and significantly transforms the life and spirit of a person—a nameless, ordinary citizen" (Murakami 2020, 99).[6] It is not lost on Murakami that, had things turned out differently for his father in China, he himself might never have existed, and in this sense "history does not belong to the past" (Ibid). Yet, Murakami is not concerned solely for his own fate; one of the things he learned from his father at a very early age—perhaps only seven or eight—was that his father's transportation unit had been involved with murdering Chinese prisoners of war. Whether his father participated in these atrocities or merely observed them, even Murakami professes not to know for certain. Nevertheless, the author notes, "some part of this thing that weighed so heavily on my father's heart for so long—today we would call it trauma—was passed along to his son, to me" (Ibid. 52). Traumatic or not, Murakami betrays a sense of responsibility to preserve—if not actually recover—his father's memories, for this is the duty of later generations, to maintain the memories of their ancestors, even the things we might prefer not to see. "However unpleasant the contents, however much we might like to turn away, we must accept a part of it into ourselves. If not, then where is the meaning in history?" (Ibid. 52–53).

---

6   The essay "Neko o suteru—chichioya ni tsuite kataru toki ni boku no kataru koto [Throwing out the cat—what I talk about when I talk about my father]" first appeared in *Bungei Shunjū* 97.6 (June 2019 special issue): 240–267. This essay was published in 2020 as *Neko o suteru—chichioya ni tsuite kataru toki* with an afterword. All translations from the Japanese are by the authors, unless otherwise stated.

Ishiguro admits to a similar sensation in being the son of a *hibakusha* (atomic bomb survivor), for his mother was in Nagasaki on August 9, 1945. As he told an interviewer in *The Guardian* in 2000, "[i]f I had been born 10 years earlier, I would have been alive when the bomb was dropped" (Ishiguro and MacKenzie 2000). He goes on to relate how his mother, upon his emergence as a writer, urged her son to use his public position as a writer to share her memories of the bombing. "I remember my mother saying, 'You are in the public realm now, you have some power. There are certain memories that should not die with me'" (Ibid). It would be difficult to express more explicitly the pressure felt by the youthful writer to re-claim and re-present the narratives of the past—narratives in which he played no part, of which he has no direct memory. Here, too, we see the "meaning in history" noted by Murakami, but also a powerful urge to achieve belonging, for both writers aspire to locate narratives that go beyond over-arching, collective narratives, and both are in search of their own belonging through inheritance of the narrative of *the nameless ordinary citizen*, as Murakami states it. It is this process of confronting collective memories of past tragedies, of stirring the imagination through activation of suppressed *individual narratives*, that deflects social amnesia and denotes the cosmopolitan quality of belonging to the world. Murakami's claim for the significance of *the nameless ordinary citizen* reconfirms the spirit of "everyday cosmopolitanism," to engage the people regardless of their attachment.

Perhaps because of this, Ishiguro sets his first novel, *A Pale View of Hills*, in Nagasaki, yet in no way addresses the atomic bombing that occurred there. His interest lies less with the sublime narrative of the atomic bomb, the widely shared experience of destruction and suffering, than with the question of individual memory and experience. Ishiguro's mother was knocked unconscious by the blast, and thus was spared seeing much of the immediate aftermath. It would be excessively simplistic to insist that this is why Ishiguro's interest as a novelist lies in *missing* memories, absences and gaps; yet this surely is what occurs in his early novels, as characters struggle to determine which of their memories are real and which are invented; which memories they wish to recall, and which they are at pains to repress. These omissions in the memory are not of traumas by which they and others were afflicted, but of *personal* actions for which they cannot quite absolve themselves.

Others have argued that the setting of *A Pale View of Hills* reflected the author's attempt to reconnect with his "Japaneseness," and in the same gesture, to resist it. Erica Aso, for instance, argues that the work seeks to refute misconceptions and stereotypes of Japaneseness, particularly the Western myth that Japanese are more prone to suicide than people in other cultures (Aso 2010, 62). Suter picks up on the same issue, noting that "the alleged Japanese instinct for suicide recurs in other works by Ishiguro … although always with the same intent of subverting stereotypes" (Suter 2020, 24). Suter goes on to construct a useful and clever argument in which she notes that emphasizing certain Japanese customs, such as removing shoes when entering a home, or eating with chopsticks, "connotes [the text] as written from, or for, a Western eye, emphasizing the foreignness of these elements" (Ibid. 28).

While repudiating these myths and cultural stereotypes might have been one of Ishiguro's motivations, what he actually achieves in many of his works is a palpable resistance to stereotyping essentialism, that is, the ideological notion of culture as "innate, tacit, taken-for-granted, unconscious, implicit, irrevocably habituated" (Rapport 2012, 532), and that imposes collective cultural identity as a result. For Ishiguro, as for Murakami, culture and principle are not to be imposed, still less to be simply accepted, but should rather develop organically through the combination of countless individuals' personal and unique experiences. This is perfectly logical, for neither Ishiguro nor Murakami fits into the mold of the "typical" Englishman, Japanese, or even novelist. Both, in fact, defend the right to be weird more or less to the death, and they want their determination to be visible to the reader.

We see this clearly enough in Ishiguro's third novel, *The Remains of the Day*, in which he constructs a vision of England that is altogether *too* English. As he noted to an interviewer in 1990, "With *The Remains of the Day* it's like a pastiche where I've tried to create a mythical England … as a kind of shock tactic of the relatively young person with a Japanese name and a Japanese face who produces this extra-English novel …" (Herzinger, Ishiguro, and Vorda 1991, 138–39). Many writers, especially those in the early phases of their careers, do seek to shock their readers, sometimes to carve out their personal space in the literary world, and other times to declare their right to exist.[7] Ishiguro's imaginative conception of Nagasaki in *A Pale View of Hills* and of his imaginary Japanese city in *An Artist of the Floating World* bespeaks an identity that is both Japanese and not-Japanese, connected to his heritage and yet breaking free of it. Similarly in *The Remains of the Day*, he declares himself to be both "too English" and at the same time, because the England of Mr.

---

7   In the former regard we might think of Ryū Murakami's debut novel *Kagirinaku tōmei ni chikai burū* (1976; Almost Transparent Blue); in the latter, sexuality in J.D. Salinger's *Catcher in the Rye* (1951), or the use of illegal narcotics in William S. Burroughs' *Naked Lunch* (1959).

Stevens the butler *is* wholly imaginary, "not English at all." Like his settings, Ishiguro's identity is 'somewhere in-between,' or 'nowhere to be found.'

Exclusion and Belonging

This could suggest that Ishiguro belongs to neither world—that he is excluded from the Japanese world (because he was raised abroad) and from the English world (because of his racial background) alike. We contend, however, that Ishiguro's true strength lies in his ability to exist between his two worlds, and belong to both, yet only to the extent he chooses. That is, one who has been raised bi-culturally, as Ishiguro clearly was, might choose to cast his lot with one culture or the other; Ishiguro, by contrast, has achieved a degree of fluidity in his identity and his self-identification that strikes us as cosmopolitan.

This kind of self-identification does not necessarily go unchallenged. Early in his career Ishiguro met his share of critics who seemed intent on forcing him into his role as a Japanese writer, and others who would exclude him from that role. This desire to categorize, as we noted at the beginning of this essay, seems irresistible in the critical world. "To begin with, readers want to find out whether the author is male or female, how old, and to ascertain their country of origin as well as cultural background" writes Megumi Arai (Arai 2008, 108). Suter notes how he "complained about being stereotyped as a 'Japanese writer'" (Suter 2020, 10) and Ishiguro himself recounts with some chagrin in multiple interviews how critics would probe relentlessly for something "Japanese" in his novels, often to his bewilderment. By contrast, Japanese novelists and critics, perhaps not surprisingly, seem to take the opposite tack. During the aforementioned 1989 conversation between Ishiguro and Kenzaburō Ōe, the latter, no doubt seeking to reassure Ishiguro, tells him that he was "described [by Japanese critics] as a very quiet and peaceful author, and, therefore, a very Japanese author. But from the first, I doubted that" (Ishiguro and Ōe 1993, 169). Yet Ōe's point here is not to exclude, but rather to define the "international author," and so he tells Ishiguro, "rather than being an English author or a European author, you are an author who writes in English" (Ibid. 171). Only a page later he comments similarly about Murakami that "Murakami Haruki writes in Japanese, but his writing is not really Japanese. If you translate it into American English, it can be read very naturally in New York" (Ibid. 172). The distinction is subtle but important; there are some writers, Ōe suggests, whose linguistic medium supersedes their cultural medium. Yet we see this as a double-edged sword: Ishiguro and Murakami may well be writers who simply exist and write in a certain language, but the implication is that being "international"—belonging any-where—could also mean belonging nowhere.

If the reigning Nobel laureate of Japan declares Ishiguro "not Japanese," while English critics refuse to accept him into the circles of English writers, then where *can* Kazuo Ishiguro exist? His strategy of rebelling against catego-rization—"Like any writer I resist being put in a group" (Herzinger, Ishiguro and Vorda 1991, 135), he told interviewers in 1990—becomes literally an act of self-preservation, then; by maintaining a fluid identity in which he moves freely between two cultures—Suter, in fact, has dubbed Ishiguro a "two-world author"—he manages to find belonging *in* both, while wholly belong-ing *to* neither.

A similar impulse drives Haruki Murakami in his bid to be different, both from other Japanese, and from other Japanese writers. This is perhaps most clearly expressed, as we stated earlier, in his attitude toward the Bundan, or "literary guild," Japan's literary establishment, and against its model for what is called *junbungaku*, or "pure literature." Since the final decade of the nineteenth century *junbungaku* has been a key component of modern (post-1868) Japanese literature and through most of the twentieth century it stood as a means of expressing Japanese identity, what Strecher calls "Japan's ver-sion of a national literature, produced by, for, and about Japanese culture and society" (Strecher 2022, 261). Even in the latter half of the twentieth century and into the twenty-first, *junbungaku* and the Bundan have largely defined what Japanese literature is, and what a novelist should be: an artist, an intel-lectual, a public figure, a cultural spokesperson, and so on. "The purpose of literature," notes Kenzaburō Ōe, "is to create a model of a contemporary age … and a human model that lives in that age" (Ōe 1989, 193). Ōe speaks in general terms, but the same is surely true of Japanese "pure literature" on a culturally specific level. Criticism of Murakami's *mukokuseki* style stems, one imagines, from the deeply-seated belief among purists within the literary es-tablishment that authentic Japanese literature ought to be "rooted"—firmly grounded in the culture from which it emerges—for, in representing Japa-neseness, the text is considered one that *belongs* to the Japanese. It is against ready-made definitions such as these that Murakami rebels.

Rebels With What Cause?
If it is true, as we have contended, that Haruki Murakami and Kazuo Ishiguro are "everyday cosmopolitans" who strive both in daily life and daily work to preserve and develop individual identity, all the while seeking belonging in the wider world, then certain key conclusions may be suggested, both about

the two men and the wider world of global literature. Were we discussing Murakami alone, as in *The Haruki Phenomenon*, this might be expressed quite simply, as noted earlier, as a conflict between the exoticizing, exclusivizing, and above all, homogenizing doctrine of *Nihonjinron*—Japaneseness—versus the cry for individual autonomy. As Ishiguro is added to the mix, this simplistic model no longer works, or at least it does not work as well, for Ishiguro does not consider himself to be wholly Japanese.

This notwithstanding, we do believe that both Murakami and Ishiguro have faced pressure—perhaps inevitable pressure—to conform to certain models, or expectations, of what the contemporary novelist ought to be, each from within his own peculiar critical and cultural background. Murakami, coming from the tradition of "pure literature," of the intellectual novelist, the public cultural spokesperson, was expected to be a properly Japanese writer, and this did not suit him. Thus the Japanese literary establishment rejected him, and he rejected them. It was a classic "hate-hate" relationship.

And what of Kazuo Ishiguro? Few would be mad enough to expect him to be a "properly Japanese writer," despite brief, frantic attempts by the Japanese media to "claim" him in 2017 after he won the Nobel Prize for literature. Yet, Ishiguro faced equally insidious (if occasionally amusing) attempts to put him into a tidy little box. With the prevailing logic that British writers are Anglo-Saxon, and if you please, White, Ishiguro, with his Asian name and Asian face, was almost required to be "something else." Suter helpfully rehearses the various critical efforts to identify Ishiguro as (a) a Japanese author, (b) an English "ethnic" author, and (c) an international author (Suter 2020, 4–20).[8] And while Ishiguro himself seems comfortable enough settling, as we have said, in the liminal space between two cultures, we find it interesting that the simple designation of "British author" does not seem available. Instead, one has the impression of an *Igirisujinron* (Theory of Englishness) construct in play, one that accepts British "writers of color" such as Timothy Mo and Salman Rushdie, but is somewhat more comfortable with them when they are safely quarantined away from the Anglo-Saxon stock, preferably as "postcolonial writers."

It would seem that both Ishiguro and Murakami are unwilling to accept such labels, yet it is equally true that neither appears particularly concerned with being accepted into the mainstream of his own national literature. Kenzaburō Ōe may have hit most squarely upon the matter when he describes Murakami as someone who "writes in Japanese," and Ishiguro as a novelist

---

8   See Suter 2020, esp. pp. 4–20 for this in-text citation.

who "writes in English." Yet these two writers, in the final analysis, are neither a *Japanese* novelist nor an *English* novelist. Nor do they wish to be so. Instead, we must acknowledge that, woven into their identities as everyday cosmopolitans, and contemporaneous with their simultaneous urge for autonomy and belonging, is their role in the world as global writers.

We make this statement with some trepidation, for unlike "world literature," the concept of "global literature" is not particularly well defined in the field of literary scholarship. In fact, there are some who cannot tell the two apart. Here we have no wish to enter into that sticky and tricky debate, and will state only that the "global writer" is he or she whose work, potentially, speaks clearly, effectively, and provocatively to a global readership, regardless of cultural background, and is accepted by that readership, who communicate with the author in a space that transcends cultural localities.[9] Considering the great differences in writing style and approach between Murakami and Ishiguro, we must conclude that there are different paths to this end. Murakami achieves connection with his highly diverse readership through his Everyman protagonist, and his Anyplace setting; Ishiguro does so by navigating/negotiating the tortuous paths between cultures, through protagonists and settings that are hyper-defined, yet wholly imaginary; entirely fictitious, yet with every appearance of reality.

In a sense, this feels more like the beginning of the essay than its end; were we to continue in this line of inquiry, we might explore how Ishiguro's *An Artist of the Floating World* compares with Murakami's *The Wind-Up Bird Chronicle* in terms of recovering repressed memories. We might examine similarities and differences between Murakami's *Kafka On the Shore* and Ishiguro's *The Buried Giant*, and see how each handles the relationship between imagination, memory and responsibility. Or we might attempt to discern how identity construction, destruction, and *re*construction compare in, for instance, *Colorless Tsukuru Tazaki and His Years of Pilgrimage* and *Klara and the Sun*. For that matter, we might have had quite a lot of fun dissecting how the soul—the metaphysical part of *us*—can be separated out from the body. For Murakami it seems to be a matter of meditation, and occasionally the use of hallucinogenic narcotics; for Ishiguro, it is as simple as removing one "brain" and

---

9   In a fascinating homage to the power of Murakami's texts to reach audiences despite the linguistic "gap" that must arise in the act of translation, Ryūsuke Hamaguchi's 2021 film *Drive My Car*, based on three stories from Murakami's *Onna no inai otokotachi* (2015; Men Without Women) collection, depicts a production of Chekhov's *Uncle Vanya* using an international cast, all of whom deliver their lines in their own native language—including a mute "Sonya" who communicates in Korean sign language.

inserting another. And what is the ontological status of that soul, freed from its physical container and allowed to roam free?

That will be the subject of another paper.

References

Arai, Megumi. 2008. "Kazuo Ishiguro no shōsetu ni okeru 'kao no nai' katarite-tachi." *Suisei Tsūshin*, no. 26 (October/November): 108–115.

Aso, Erica. 2010. "Kazuo Ishiguro's Cosmopolitanism: Landscapes of the Atomic Bomb in *A Pale View of Hills* and *Never Let Me Go*." *Aoyama Gakuin Daigaku Bungakubu Kiyō*, no. 52: 57–76.

Hannerz, Ulf. 1990. "Cosmopolitans and Locals in World Culture." *Theory, Culture & Society* (7): 237–252.

Herzinger, Kim, Ishiguro, Kazuo and Vorda, Allan. 1991. "An Interview with Kazuo Ishiguro." *The Mississippi Review* 20 (1/2): 131–154.

Ishiguro, Kazuo. 1982. *A Pale View of Hills*. London: Faber and Faber.

Ishiguro, Kazuo. 1986. *An Artist of the Floating World*. London: Faber and Faber.

Ishiguro, Kazuo. 1989. *The Remains of the Day*. London: Faber and Faber.

Ishiguro, Kazuo. 1995. *The Unconsoled*. London: Faber and Faber.

Ishiguro, Kazuo. 2000. *When We Were Orphans*. London: Faber and Faber.

Ishiguro, Kazuo. 2005. *Never Let Me Go*. London: Faber and Faber.

Ishiguro, Kazuo. 2015. *The Buried Giant*. London: Faber and Faber.

Ishiguro, Kazuo. 2017. "Nobel Lecture by Kazuo Ishiguro." The Nobel Foundation. Accessed January 25, 2022. https://www.nobelprize.org/prizes/literature/2017/ishiguro/lecture/.

Ishiguro, Kazuo. 2021. *Klara and the Sun*. London: Faber and Faber.

Ishiguro, Kazuo and MacKenzie, Suzie. "Between Two Worlds." 2000. *The Guardian*, March 25, 2000. https://www.theguardian.com/books/2000/mar/25/fiction.bookerprize2000.

Ishiguro, Kazuo and Mason, Gregory. 1989. "An Interview with Kazuo Ishiguro." *Contemporary Literature* 30 (3): 335–347.

Ishiguro, Kazuo and Ōe, Kenzaburō. 1993. "The Novelist in Today's World: A Conversation." In *Japan in the World*, edited by Masao Miyoshi and H.DHarootunian, 163–176. Durham, NC: Duke University Press.

Kim, Y. 2009. "Kankoku ni okeru Murakami Haruki no juyō to sono kontekusuto" [Murakami Haruki's reception and its context in South Korea]. In *Higashi Ajia ga yomu Murakami Haruki* (Murakami Haruki as read in East Asia), edited by Shōzō Fujii, 7–34. Tokyo: Wakakusa Shobō.

Murakami, Haruki. 1987. *Noruwei no mori* [Norwegian Wood]. Tokyo: Kōdansha.

Murakami, Haruki. 1994–96. *Nejimakidori kuronikuru* [The Wind-Up Bird Chronicle]. 3 vols. Tokyo: Shinchōsha.

Murakami, Haruki. 2002. *Umibe no Kafuka* [Kafka On the Shore]. 2 vols. Tokyo: Shinchōsha.

Murakami, Hauki. 2009. "Of walls and eggs." (Jerusalem speech) Translated by Jay Rubin. *Bungei Shunjū* (April): 165–169.

Murakami, Haruki. 2013. *Shikisai o motanai Tazaki Tsukuru to, kare no junrei no toshi* [Colorless Tsukuru Tazaki and His Years of Pilgrimage]. Tokyo: Bungei Shunjū.

Murakami, Haruki. 2020. *Neko o suteru—chichioya ni tsuite kataru toki*. Tokyo: Bungei Shunjū.

Ōe, Kenzaburō. 1989. "Japan's Dual Identity: A Writer's Dilemma." In *Postmodernism and Japan*, edited by Masao Miyoshi and H.D. Harootunian, 189–213. Durham, NC: Duke University Press.

Ōe, Kenzaburō. 1995. "Japan, the Ambiguous, and Myself." Translated by Hisaaki Yamanouchi. In *Japan, the Ambiguous, and Myself: The Nobel Prize Speech and Other Lectures*. 105–128. Tokyo, New York, and London: Kodansha International.

Rapport, Nigel. 2012. "The Cosmopolitan World." In *The Sage Handbook of Social Anthropology*, edited by Fardon, R., 523–537. London: Sage.

Strecher, Matthew. 2014. *The Forbidden Worlds of Haruki Murakami*. Minneapolis: University of Minnesota Press.

Strecher, Matthew. 2017. "East Meets West, and then Gives It Back: Reinventing Japanese Literature in the Contemporary Age." *perspektywy kultury* [Perspectives in Culture], no. 19 (2017): 53–80.

Strecher, Matthew. 2022. "A False Peace: Literature in the Age of Heisei." In *Japan in the Heisei Era*, edited by Tina Burrett, Jeff Kingston and Noriko Murai, 261–271. London and New York: Routledge.

Suter, Rebecca. 2020. *Two-World Literature: Kazuo Ishiguro's Early Novels*. Honolulu: University of Hawai'i Press.

Wakatsuki, Tomoki. 2020. *The Haruki Phenomenon: Haruki Murakami as Cosmopolitan Writer*. Singapore: Springer.

Megumi Yama

Haruki Murakami, Novel as a Method: 'Memory' and his Creative Process

Abstract: In this paper, I discussed the creative process of Haruki Murakami from the perspective of depth psychology. Firstly, I considered Murakami's creative process focusing on the word 'memory' in the way that Murakami uses it in his work. Secondly, I explored the sources of his stories—his personal and collective memory. And thirdly, I explored Murakami's creative work through his words in interviews. In conclusion, I would like to argue that the stories Murakami tells resonate with what lies deep in the "soul" of his many disparate worldwide readers, who live with various backgrounds.

Key words: Creative process, Creative method, Memory, Personal memory, Collective memory, *Norwegian Wood*, Life and Death, Japanese classics

Introduction

Haruki Murakami's works, not only novels or short stories but also essays and conversations, have been translated into more than fifty different languages and have many enthusiastic readers around the world, Whenever I go abroad, I visit local bookstores, as it is always exciting for me to see a lot of books, even though I cannot understand the language they are written in. I often see special displays of books by Haruki Murakami, especially when a new novel comes out, and I also met people who say they are avid readers of Murakami. Of course, since I am Japanese, they may have been trying to flatter me, but even so, this phenomenon was interesting. Why does a story written by Japanese novelist Murakami touch the hearts of people in many countries where they have different histories and cultures?

In this essay, I would like to explore the creative process of Murakami from the perspective of depth psychology and psychotherapy.

Firstly, I will consider Murakami's creative process focusing on word 'memory' in the way that Murakami uses it in his work; what does 'memory' mean to Murakami? How is 'memory' depicted in his work? Secondly, I would like to explore the sources of his stories—his personal and collective memory. What are they and where do they come from? And thirdly, I would like to explore Murakami's creative work through his words in interviews.

Haruki Murakami and 'I'

Before going any further, a little explanation about the transition of my interest in Murakami's work is necessary. In the mid-1980s, I happened to read his novels, *A Wild Chase Sheep* (1982/2000), *Norwegian Wood* (1987/2000), and *Dance Dance Dance* (1988/1994). Since then, I have been an avid reader of his work. At first, perhaps like most other readers, I enjoyed the narrative through the unnamed first person 'I,' his comfortable writing style, his aphorisms that remain deep in my heart, and his wandering back and forth between 'this world' and 'the other world.'

In those early days, I was working at the University of Art and Design, and I had opportunities to listen to the narratives of art students, which spanned the entirety of their creative processes. Some of them used to visit me at my office and, as I do not specialize in art, but in-depth psychology, they seemed to feel free to talk to me about whatever they were thinking. Listening to their narratives carefully, gradually, I came to realize that some of the students were wrestling with fundamental, sometimes ontological, themes about human existence through their creative work. What was more, I saw them dealing with these themes not by referring to existing bodies of knowledge, such as in philosophy or psychology, but by confronting their own deep darkness, as if they were invited from within themselves. I felt that it was crucially important, especially in contemporary society where efficiency and results are overvalued. Around the same time, I was engaged in some clinical cases, where I had to go through deep and tough psychotherapeutic processes with my clients.

I would argue that Haruki Murakami has also been engaged in confronting his darkness through the creative work of writing. My experiences with my students got me interested in Murakami's process of writing as well as his works themselves. His novels can be regarded as the result of his creative work.

The Word 'Memory'

I have noticed that Murakami uses the word 'memory' repeatedly in his novels, interviews, and essays. In general, we forget what we see, hear, and experience, every day or even in every moment. This, however, does not mean that they all vanish completely. They remain and accumulate within us as memories, whether we are conscious of them or not.

Through my experience as a psychotherapist for nearly forty years, I have realized that the client's narrative of life consists of an accumulation of their memories. What does 'memory' mean to Murakami? We may be able to find some deep insights about his creative activity of writing in his novels and in his stories. When Murakami uses the word 'memory,' it does not always refer to remembering in the ordinary sense. In such cases, his word 'memory' seems to contain something very special and meaningful. Murakami (2015b) mentions that imagination is a combination of fragmental memories that lack connections. In a container named 'Haruki Murakami,' the fragments of memory accumulated inside him are likely to be combined and spun in various ways to create a story. By digging into the word 'memory' in a way that Murakami used in his work, I would like to explore his creative process.

Tactile Memories: When Murakami Became a Writer
Firstly, in order to explore the word 'memory' as Murakami uses it, I would like to refer to an anecdote about when he suddenly began writing novels at the age of twenty-nine. In *Wind/Pinball: Two novels* (1979, 1980/2015a), which contains his first and second works, *Hear the Wind Sing* (1979) and *Pinball, 1973* (1980), this anecdote is described in detail in the introduction, entitled The Birth of my Kitchen-table Fiction.

The author talks about his twenties. He decided to run a small jazz bar as he did not want to work for a company after graduating from university. He hated the idea of being involved in the system of Japanese society, but he had married while still a student despite his parent's strong opposition, and he and his wife did not have enough money to live on. He writes, "My twenties were … spent paying off loans and doing hard physical labor … from morning till night … Looking back, all I can remember is how hard we worked. I imagine most people are relatively laid back in their twenties, but we had virtually no time to enjoy the "carefree days of youth." We barely got by. What free time I did have, though, I spent reading. Along with music, books were my great joy." (Murakami, 2015a, ix).

One bright April afternoon in 1978, twenty-nine-year-old Murakami was watching a baseball game at Jingu Stadium in Tokyo, not far from where he lived. It was the Central League season opener, the Yakult Swallows against the Hiroshima Carp. Murakami was already a fan of the Swallows, a perennially weak team, which he describes as having little money and no flashy big-name players (Murakami, 2015a). Until this day, Murakami had written nothing and had no intention to do so.

Murakami (2015a, x) describes the day: "The sky was sparkling blue, the draft beer as cold as could be, and the ball strikingly white against the green field, the first green I had seen in a long while." At the moment when the first batter, Dave Hilton, a completely unknown skinny newcomer from America, hit a clean double, the idea, *I think I can write a novel* struck him from out of the blue. Murakami (2015a, x–xi) continues, "I can still recall the exact sensation. It felt as if something had come fluttering down from the sky, and I caught it clearly in my hands … I had no idea why it had *chanced* to fall into my grasp … Whatever the reason, *it* had taken place. It was like a revelation. Or 'epiphany' is a better word."

After the game was over, he bought a sheaf of writing paper and a fountain pen. He went home and began writing that very night. In the nights that followed, Murakami sat at his kitchen table after working at his jazz bar all day, working on *Hear the Wind Sing* until a few hours before dawn. He wrote a fragmental chapter each day. He started writing in the spring and completed the novel in autumn, when the Swallows won the championship for the first time in twenty-nine years. Murakami, himself twenty-nine, intuited that this coincidence was meaningful and that he should write. All of the Swallows players, including those who had already passed their prime, did their best, which inspired Murakami to do his best, too.

In Japan, where homogeneity is highly and unconsciously appreciated, people tend to aim to follow identical careers, such as getting a job at a big company soon after graduating from university, although this tendency seems to be changing little by little. 'Outsiders' like Murakami may feel they are no longer young when they reach twenty-nine—on the verge of thirty—and this made his age seem even more meaningful.

In *The Christian Archetype,* regarding Mary's obedience to the divine call at Annunciation, Edinger (1987, 26) says, "Psychologically, this signifies the soul's acceptance of its impregnating encounter with the *numinosum.*" In Murakami's case, I would like to argue that he has experienced these seemingly coincidental series of events as the impregnating encounter with the *numinosum.* Everything seemed to have been meaningfully constellated. Such an experience will not produce anything if a person just passes through without accepting and trying to deepen it.

Murakami completed his first novel *Hear the Wind Sing* and submitted it to a literary contest. One sunny Sunday morning in spring, about a year after the fateful baseball game in Jingu Stadium, he received a call from the editor at the literary journal telling him that *Hear the Wind Sing* has been short-listed for the new writers' prize. He was surprised because by that time he had quite forgotten that he had sent his work to the contest. As he was not only surprised, but also still sleepy, he could not grasp the reality of what had happened. After Murakami went out for a walk with his wife, he found a wounded pigeon on the street, just as they were passing through an elementary school. He picked it up and carried it to the closest police station. He felt the warmth of the wounded pigeon in his hands. He felt it quivering. He describes the surrounding scene at that time as follows. "That Sunday was bright and clear, and the trees, the buildings, and shopwindows sparkled beautifully in the spring sunlight" (Murakami, 2015a, xvi). At that moment, the idea hit him that he was going to win the prize and become a novelist who would enjoy some degree of success. We are well aware that his intuition at this time came true. Murakami writes about his memory of a series of experiences of those days when he became a writer as follows:

> I can still remember, with complete clarity, the way I felt when whatever it was came fluttering down into my hands that day thirty years ago on the grass behind the outfield fence at Jingu Stadium; and I recall just as clearly the warmth of the wounded pigeon I picked up in those same hands that spring afternoon a year later, near Sendagaya Elementary School. I always call up those sensations when I think about what it means to write a novel. Such tactile memories teach me to believe me in that *something* I carry within me, and to dream of the possibilities it offers. How wonderful it is that those sensations still reside within me today. (Murakami, 2015a, xvii)

In a modern society full of information, we tend to experience a lot of things as something transient that passes by quickly before our eyes. I would like to argue that it takes a special talent to be able to retain and cherish a memory of such experiences deep in the psyche for a long time. I think the memory of what he caught in his hands at the Stadium and the warmth of a wounded pigeon in his hands are what Murakami calls 'tactile memory,' which gives us the energy to live in a true sense. Later, I will explore how Murakami developed such talent by delving into the layers of history of his memory.

A Memory of Intimate Warmth: Tengo and Aomame in *1Q84*

I would like to show one of the examples of how the 'tactile memory' is beautifully depicted in *1Q84* (2009, 2010/2011). Tengo and Aomame, who are two protagonists in *1Q84*, have been forced to live lonely and repressive lives since their early days. One day, when they were ten years old, Aomame tightly grasps Tengo's hand in an empty classroom after school. After that, they are separated and encounter many difficulties. They have to go through tough lives on their own. The intimate warmth they felt when they were ten years old, however, eventually brings them salvation. In the novel, it is expressed as follows.

> … his (Tengo's) fingers retained the touch and the warmth of her (Aomame's) little hand. *This warmth will almost surely never fade*, Tengo thought, …
>
> Faint as it was, the warmth was surely there, conveying a promise like a lamp a traveler sees in the far distance.
>
> *I will go on living in this world*, Tengo thought … (*1Q84*, 738)

This is a beautiful depiction of 'tactile memory.' Murakami mentions, "After removing all the realistic (concrete) things, I will depict the scene again, relying only on the memories that emerge in my head" (1998/2012, 42, my translation). Murakami, it is felt, did not write his personal experiences as they were, but rather depicted them in the context of the life of Tengo and Aomame.

By removing the personal and concrete situation of Murakami, the novel has become a collective story of 'tactile memory of warmth' beyond individuals, which can be shared by many people. I would like to add here, as Murakami himself has often said, that such a creative process takes a long time because one has to go through it not only intellectually, but also using the physical senses to deepen the memory of the experience.

Norwegian Wood as a Story of Memory

Murakami left Japan in 1986, which he referred to as 'exile.' He began writing *Norwegian Wood* (1987/2000) on the island of Mykonos, Greece, completing it in Rome the following spring. I would like to understand *Norwegian Wood* as a splendid story of 'memory' for the following two reasons: 1) it depicts the memory of the loss experience, which is quite universal to humans, and 2) it is a story that developed when the protagonist sank the memory of his experience into the depth of the psyche.

I would like to argue that *Norwegian Wood* is a story that depicts a long process of engraving a memory of loss experience into the soul; that is, re-experiencing what happened in the past by exploring the memory using all physical senses. Although readers have different types of loss experiences, they may well discover that they have gone through the healing process after reading this novel. I must add, however, that most of the time this process takes place implicitly and unconsciously.

The story begins when thirty-seven-year-old Watanabe is about to land at Hamburg Airport. Thirty-seven is no longer young, but the protagonist still has some time before he is considered middle-aged. When he hears an orchestral cover version of the Beatles' *Norwegian Wood* that flows from the ceiling speakers, he is suddenly overwhelmed by memory and brought back to the fall of 1969, "… thinking of what I had lost in the course of my life: times gone forever, friends who had died or disappeared, feelings I would never know again" (*Norwegian Wood*, 3–4). There is no doubt that sometimes music has the power to shake our emotions and immediately take us back to the past. The plane reaches the gate and people are preparing to get off. The story unfolds with a first-person narrative, where Watanabe looks back on the past.

When 'I' (=Watanabe) was a high school student in Kobe, 'I' used to play with Kizuki and his girlfriend Naoko. However, one day in May, on the night after he and 'I' skip afternoon class and go play billiards, Kizuki suddenly commits suicide. 'I,' who enters a university in Tokyo the following spring, starts living in a dormitory and happens to meet Naoko on the train one Sunday in May for the first time in a year. Naoko is attending a women's college, also in Tokyo. They begin to meet on holidays and go on dates, but in April of the following year, Naoko, who suffers from mental problems, suddenly takes a leave of absence from college and goes to a sanatorium in the mountains in Kyoto. 'I' goes to see her there, but the following August, she also commits suicide.

In the novel, Watanabe looks back on the days when he started his new life in Tokyo, and says,

> There was only one thing for me to do when I started my new life in the dorm: stop taking everything so seriously; establish a proper distance between myself and everything else …
> It seemed to work at first. I tried to forget but there remained inside me a vague not-of-air kind of thing. And as time went by, the knot began to take on a clear and simple form, a form that I am able to put into words like this:
> *Death exists not as the opposite, but as a part of life.*
> … Until that time, I had understood death as something entirely separate from and independent of life … This had seemed to me the simple, logical truth. Life is here, death is over there. I am here, not over there.
> The night Kizuki died, however, I lost the ability to see death (and life) in such simple terms. Death was not the opposite of life. It was already here, within my being, it had always been here … (*Norwegian Wood*, 33–34)

Murakami has said that *Norwegian Wood* is a novel which he just attempted to write in a realistic style, and that he will not write a novel like it again. He thinks it is not a type of novel that he really wants to write.

In *Norwegian Wood*, Watanabe loses two irreplaceable intimate friends, Kizuki and Naoko, to suicide, which is, of course, a very special experience.

On the other hand, all of us inevitably have the experience of losing loved ones sometime in our life. In such a sense, a loss experience may also be understood as a collective experience, one which is shared beyond culture or nationality.

Over time, people tend to forget the vivid realistic sense they have in experiencing a loss. Murakami (2006, Question 251) says that he wrote *Norwegian Wood* as if he were clinging to it because he did not want to forget it.

Few people, including myself, know what really happened to Murakami when he was young. It does not matter at all, however, and is totally outside of my interest. It seems that Murakami tried to depict something that resides deep behind his personal and concrete memory, which I would like to call the reality of the soul. Murakami expressed it in the story in order to remain within himself, which would have brought him salvation, too. It seems that it was necessary for him to write this novel before moving on in his life.

Exploring 'Memory' in *Norwegian Wood* as a Keyword.
Norwegian Wood consists of eleven chapters. The first is about one-fortieth of the whole book, in which the important elements of 'memory' are expressed through the narrative of Watanabe. Let me return to the story again. In October, eighteen years before, Watanabe had gone to see Naoko at a sanatorium and walked in the meadow with her. Watanabe's monologue-like narrative goes on as follows:

> Memory is a funny thing. When I was in the scene, I hardly paid it any mind. I never stopped to think of it as something that would make a lasting impression, certainly never imagined that eighteen years later I would recall it in such detail. I didn't give a damn about the scenery that day …
> Now, though, that meadow scene is the first thing that comes back to me. The smell of the grass, the faint chill of the wind, the line of the hills, the barking of a dog: these are the first things, and they come with absolute clarity. I feel as if I can reach out and trace them with a fingertip. And yet, as clear as the scene may be, no one is in it. No one. Naoko is not there, and neither am I. (*Norwegian Wood*, 4–5)

The memory of the scenery of the meadow on that day is revived in Watanabe. It is a vivid memory through senses of sight, smell, touch, and hearing. In his creative process of writing, Murakami always stays in the scene he is depicting and tries to feel with all his senses, using his power of imagination.

In an interview in 2017, Murakami talks about when he wrote *Kafka on the Shore* (2002/2005). It is the story of a fifteen-year-old boy who runs away from his father to escape an Oedipal curse. Murakami says that he has vivid memories of when he was fifteen years old. There are physical things, such as what kind of smell there was, what kind of air he was breathing, what kind of light he was exposed to. He says, "It was a lot of fun to write a story tracing such physical memories," (Murakami, 2017, 132–33, my translation) but he also mentions "Writing novels, to me, is basically a kind of manual labor" (Murakami, 2007/2008, 79). We can see from this that writing in his way is an extremely exhausting task that requires a lot of time.

Let's see how memories are depicted in *Norwegian Wood*:

> No one. Naoko is not there, and neither am I. Where could we have disappeared to? How could a such thing have happened? (*Norwegian Wood*, p.5)

> (Naoko said,) "I want you always to remember me. Will you remember that I existed, and I stood next to you here like this?" (I said) "I'll always remember" … "I will never forget you," I said, "I could never forget you." … Even so, my memory has grown increasingly distant, and I have already forgotten any number of things. (*Norwegian Wood*, 11–12)

A long time before, Watanabe tried to write about Naoko, when his memories were far more vivid than they are now, but he could not produce even a line. I think that makes sense. When the concrete memory is still real and vivid, it is difficult to articulate it. That is because the task of writing requires an objective perspective with some distance.

> The more the memories of Naoko inside me fade, the more deeply I am able to understand her. (*Norwegian Wood*, 12)

It will take a much longer time than is generally thought to deepen a memory, as Watanabe suggests in the story. Murakami (1999) states in an interview that maturation (maybe for ten years) is necessary to provoke physical reactions. The concrete memory of an event goes away over time and recedes into the background. Only then, however, can something like the reality of the soul emerge from the depths. We should not run away from this. Murakami probably wrote what took place inside him during the process, which is considered to be very important.

In this novel, everything seems to be condensed into the phrase '*Death exists, not as the opposite but as a part of life,*' which seems to have come from within Murakami after a long period of creative work. Such an experience may fundamentally change our view of the world, and the way of life and may continue to exist deep in our hearts.

I would like to argue that *Norwegian Wood* is a story of loss, that is, a story of presence and absence in the guise of a romance novel. Next, I will discuss why Murakami had to write it as if he were clinging to it.

In the Deepest Layer of Murakami's Memory

1.   *Murakami's earliest memory*

I would like to go down to the deepest layer of Murakami's memory. Murakami (1985, 23–24, my translation) recounts his earliest memory: "When I was two or three years old, I fell into the river. I drifted away. I was almost swallowed up in a culvert when I was found and rescued. I remember the darkness at the time. It's my earliest memory, an unpleasant memory." He says that he remembers looking up at the water surface from the bottom of the river.

From my experience in psychotherapy, I have learned that how early memory is incorporated in the context of our life has important implications for shaping our worldview. That is why I pay attention to a person's early memories, especially, their earliest memory.

I am not sure how much Murakami really approached death at that time, but that is not the point. What matters most is the fact that his memory of falling into a river, that is water (= unconscious), and catching a glimpse of unearthly darkness remains real inside him for decades, as vividly as when he experienced it. The darkness reminds me of the resonant phrase, "How can those who live in the light of day possibly comprehend the depths of night?" in *Hear the Wind Sing* (1979/2015a, 101). Elsewhere, I have also referred to his grandfather's tragic death in a railroad accident when he was nine years old. In an earlier book, I mentioned that this experience of death along with his early near-drowning gave Murakami an unusual taste of death, darkness, and mortality (Yama, 2016).

2.   *Life and Death, Presence and Absence*

I would like to present one more important experience Murakami had in his early childhood. Exploring old newspapers and *The History of the City*, Inoue (1999) found some articles about a six-year-old boy who fell into a river and drowned. The boy was Murakami's friend, and they were the same age. Murakami has not mentioned anything directly about his friend's death, but the short story titled Gogatsu no Kaigansen [*A Coastline in May*] (1981) seems to have something to do with this event. The protagonist (narrator = I) returns to the city where he used to live when he was a child for the first time in a long time. It was to attend his friend's wedding. He is deeply immersed in his memories of the past. Standing on the coastline, which has disappeared now due to land reclamation, he remembers what happened twenty years before. His old memories are recollected one after another, as if each memory wakes the association of the next. When the protagonist's association reaches Neil Sedaka's song, *Breaking Up is Hard to Do*, he gradually seems to remember what happened so long ago. And the narration goes as follows.

> Drowned bodies were launched on the shore several times a year, too … One of them was my friend. It was a long time ago, when I was six years old. He died after being swallowed by a river flooded by torrential rain. On a spring afternoon, his corpse was rushed offshore with a muddy stream, and three days later it was washed ashore alongside driftwood.
> The smell of death.
> The smell of a corpse of a six-year-old boy being burned in a hot furnace.
> The chimney of the crematorium towering in the cloudy sky of April. And gray smoke.
> Disappearance of existence. (*A Coastline in May* 1981, 109, my translation)

Although Murakami once fell into a river, he had just a glimpse of the darkness before returning to 'this world.' On the other hand, his friend who also fell into a river, passed away after being swallowed up by water, and his existence vanished completely from "this world." The boundaries between life and death decisively separated Murakami from his friend. It is assumed to be an experience of being hit by the fact that 'I' (Murakami) am alive (=present) but he (my friend) is dead (=absent).

Elsewhere, I have noted that "presence and absence" is one of Murakami's central themes in his novels (Yama, 2019). I would like to argue that his memory of intense experiences in childhood lies in the basis of his creative work. Symbolically, the coastline is thought to be a boundary between water and land, by which Murakami and his friend had to be separated. Now it has disappeared after being reclaimed. It seems that this short story suggests some important themes in his work.

3.   *A Heritage of Memory from His Father*

Murakami, who had hardly ever talked about his family until then, mentions his father in his acceptance speech, entitled the *Wall and the Egg* (2009), for the Jerusalem Prize, which follows.

> My father died last year at the age of 90. He was a retired teacher and a part-time Buddhist priest. When he was in graduate school, he was drafted into the army and sent to fight in China. As a child born after the war, I used to see him every morning before breakfast offering up long, deeply-felt prayers at the Buddhist altar in our house. One time I asked

him why he did this, and he told me he was praying for the people who had died in the war.

He was praying for all the people who died, he said, both ally and enemy alike. Staring at his back as he knelt at the altar, I seemed to feel the shadow of death hovering around him.

My father died, and with him he took his memories, memories that I can never know. But the presence of death that lurked about him remains in my own memory. It is one of the few things I carry on from him, and one of the most important.[10]

Staring at his father's back every morning in those days, the memory of prayer for the souls of the dead may have been engraved deeply in Murakami's heart. Murakami did not actually experience the war in China, but having listened to his father's stories and using his own power of imagination, it is thought that Murakami accumulated within himself a kind of inherited memory. Murakami's father no longer exists in this world. However, as Murakami states, his memory was passed on to his son as a kind of inheritance. I would like to understand that what he inherited from his father was the deep sorrow of mankind, which is a memory of the soul in a collective sense. So far, I have only described Murakami's personal memories of death, but it is apparent that his view of the world has contained 'death' (=the other world) since he was a child. That is to say, the world does not only consist of 'this world.'

Influence from Japanese Classics

Murakami was born in 1949 in Kyoto. Both parents were teachers of Japanese literature and brought that into their daily life. His grandfather was a Buddhist priest, and his father was a part-time priest. Murakami was born into very traditional Japanese circumstances, but when he was two years old, his family moved near Kobe, a port city that has been deeply influenced by Western culture.

Murakami subsequently rejected Japanese literature and Japanese culture, which seems to have been in rebellion of his parents. He was deeply influenced by Western culture—its literature, movies, and music, especially jazz and classics. It was quite easy for Murakami to get paperback books in the city of Kobe during his high school days. In an interview he says, "I wanted to escape from this (Japanese) culture; I felt it was boring. Too sticky" (2004/2012, 212). As a schoolboy, he devoted himself to reading. He read a complete work of world history again and again, which seemed to expand his

---

10   For more information, please see: Haruki Murakami, "Always on the Side of the Egg" Israel News | Israeli Culture | Feb. 17, 2009, | https://www.haaretz.com/israel-news /culture/1.5076881

cosmology. His interest, however, is not in chronological history as enumeration of what happened in the past, but in "history as a collective memory," (Murakami, 2010, 26) what he calls a kind of inheritance [of image].

As I mentioned above, Murakami has been deeply influenced by Western culture through books and music since he was a child. After he became a professional writer, he lived in the United States and Europe for quite a long time. While Murakami has devoted himself exclusively to Western literature since childhood, he confesses that he can still recite some of the Japanese classics, all of which his father tried to make him memorize when he was a child. In Japan, it has often been said that Murakami is deeply influenced by American literature. However, I also recognize a traditional Japanese worldview in the foundation of his work.

I would like to briefly introduce some of the Japanese classics, which Murakami often refers to. They are 1) *The Tale of Heike*, 2) *Hōjōki*, and 3) *Tales of Moonlight and Rain*, which, he says, he continues to reread to this day.

1.   *The Tale of Heike*

The Tale of the Heike is an epic which depicts the struggle between Heike (the Taira clan) and Genji (the Minamoto clan) at the end of the 12th century. The story depicts the prosperity and decline of the Taira clan, as compiled from a collection of oral stories recited by blind traveling monks who chanted to the accompaniment of the *biwa*, an instrument reminiscent of the lute. In the story, narrated along with the sound of the melancholy *biwa*, is condensed a unique sense of impermanence (*mujō*). The famous opening paragraph begins as follows:

> The sound of the Gion Shōja bells echoes the impermanence of all things; the color of the *sāla* flowers reveals the truth that the prosperous must decline. The proud do not endure, they are like a dream on a spring night; the mighty fall at last, they are as dust before the wind.
> (*The Tale of the Heike*, Translated by McCullough, 1988, 23)

In Chapter 20 of 1Q84, there is a scene where a seventeen-year-old girl, Fuka Eri, who suffers from dyslexia chants a decisive part of the final sea battle in the *Tale of the Heike*, from memory. The following is a quote from a scene in *1Q84*.

> Listening to her recite the story with his eyes closed, Tengo felt as though he were hearing it the traditional way, chanted by a blind priest accompanying himself on the lute, and he was reminded anew that *The Tale of Heike* was a narrative poem handed down through an oral tradition. (1Q84, 320)

Then Murakami's view on memory seems to be uttered through Tengo, which is as follows. "Our memory is made up of our individual memories and our collective memories. The two are intimately linked. And history is our collective memory" (*1Q84*, 322). Murakami (1981, 124) mentions that he can still recite the whole *the Tale of Heike* from memory. Even though, as a child, he could not understand the difficult words, I suspect that the rhythms and tones of Japanese classics remain in the deep layers of Murakami's memory.

2. *Hōjōki*

Hōjōki is a short memoir that was written by a Buddhist monk, Kamo no Chōmei (c.1155–1216) at the beginning of the 13th century. Chomei recounts his life to withdraw from worldly affairs and live as a hermit in a tiny hut on the outskirts of Kyoto, the capital city. The work depicts the *mujō*, or the intransience, of human beings through descriptions of various disasters, such as an earthquake, a famine, a whirlwind, and a conflagration, that befall the people in Kyoto. The opening sentence of *Hōjōki* is very famous in Japanese classical literature as an expression of *mujō*:

> On flows the river ceaselessly, nor does its water ever stay the same. The bubbles
> that float upon its pools now disappear, now form anew, but never endure long.
> And so it is with people in this world, and with their dwellings.
> (*Hōjōki*, Translated by McKinney, 1212/2013, 5)

In his acceptance speech for the Catalunya International Prize (2011)[11], Murakami refers to *mujō* as a characteristic of the Japanese mentality. He explains *mujō* as follows, "… there is no steady state that will continue forever in life. All things that inhabit this world will pass away; all things continue to change without end. We cannot find permanent stability. We cannot find anything to rely on that will not change or decay. Although *mujō* finds its roots in Buddhism, the concept of *mujō* has taken on a significance beyond its original religious sense. This concept of *mujō* has been seared deeply into the Japanese spirit, forming a national mindset that has continued on almost without change since ancient times." Referring to cherry blossoms in spring, fireflies in summer, and red leaves in autumn as examples, he says, "We travel far to witness that moment of the natural phenomenon in its full glory. Yet it is not merely a matter of observing a beautiful locale. Before our eyes, evanescent cherry blossoms scatter, the fireflies' will-o'-

---

11   June 10, 2011. Catalonia International Prize Speech, Haruki Murakami. Full text of the
       Catalonia International Prize speech appealing for nuclear power plant elimination. Avail-
       able online: https://logmi.jp/business/articles/27598.

the-wisp vanishes, and the bright autumn leaves are snatched away. We recognize these events and we find in these changes a certain relief." All that remains is an empty landscape after the fleeting glory has passed.

In the first chapter of Norwegian Wood, all that existed on that day—Naoko and "I," the interaction between them, her facial expressions, etc.—receded from "my" memory. All except the scenery. There were Naoko and "I." But now everything is gone. What once was present is no longer there, where Haruki Murakami may feel some kind of beauty and relief. In the first chapter, there is also an interesting description of memory, which is "What if somewhere inside me there is a dark limbo where all the truly important memories are heaped and slowly turning into mud?" (*Norwegian Wood*, 12)

I would like to argue that Murakami picks up fragmentary memories from what he calls dark limbo' and embodies them. The memory given life in this way may be called an image. Murakami seems to spend a lot of time waiting for the story to develop spontaneously from the memories which were accumulated. In the undercurrent of Murakami's creative work, I would like to say that we can recognize a sense of mujō that is firmly engraved in a deep layer of his memory.

3.   *Tales of Moonlight and Rain*

Tales of Moonlight and Rain (*Ugetsu Monogatari*) is a collection of nine supernatural tales by the Japanese author Akinari Ueda (1734–1809), which was first published in 1776. Murakami (2003/2012) mentions that in the world of *Tales of Moonlight and Rain*, reality and unreality exist so closely that people tend to cross the boundary between them without any sense of incongruity. He points out that this characteristic has always resided in the Japanese psyche. It overlaps with Hayao Kawai's statement of "… for Japanese the wall between this world and the other world is … a surprisingly thin one" (1982/1996). I would like to argue that the state of the Japanese psyche is reflected here.

In Chapter 23 of *Kafka on the Shore* (2002/2005), there is a conversation about the tale of "The Chrysanthemum Pledge" from *Tales of Moonlight and Rain*. And in *Killing Commendatore* (2017/2019), the topic of Akinari Ueda and his works is dealt with, too. As I have mentioned above, Murakami sometimes incorporates Japanese classics in his works, but their influence tends to be evident in the worlds depicted in his works rather than a concrete or visible part of the stories themselves. In *Killing Commendatore* in the conversation with 'I,' Menshiki says "… sometimes in life we can't grasp the boundary between reality and unreality" (*Killing Commendatore*, 206), which reminds me of the world of *Tale of Moonlight and Rain* as mentioned by Murakami.

Murakami's Creative Method

1.   'Story' as Murakami Means It

Lastly, I would like to present some quotes from Murakami's interviews and conversations, which give us hints on how he creates his stories. Murakami has not appeared or spoken in public in Japan, as he used to feel distaste for the Japanese social system, Japanese culture, and the Japanese way of having relationships, from which he has tried to distance himself. However, he writes and talks a lot about his writing through interviews, conversations, and essays, and explains in detail how each novel was created and can be read as a long story of his creative process.

Murakami wrote *The Wind-Up Bird Chronicle* while he was at Princeton and Tufts from 1991 to 1995. Murakami (1995) himself has said that if this novel does not make any sense, his life itself may not make any sense. From this we see that *The Wind-up Bird Chronicle* seems to have a special meaning for him. Toru Okada in *The Wind-up Bird Chronicle* descends to the bottom of a well and finally passes through a wall. That is what Murakami experienced when he was writing the novel. Murakami went down to the depths and passed through an existing boundary using the power of imagery, which he says is the most important aspect of this novel. I would like to say that Murakami has reached the idea of Jung psychology, that is, people are connected at a collective level when they go to a deeper level of psyche. What is more important is that Murakami did not have any prior knowledge of Jungian psychology and reached that idea through his own experience.

In 1995, a conversation between Haruki Murakami and Hayao Kawai was held in the United States. Kawai is a Japanese Jungian analyst, professor emeritus of Kyoto University, and Minister of Culture for Japan from 2002 to 2007. The conversation was published the following year in 1996 under the title of *Haruki Murakami Goes to Meet Hayao Kawai* (1996/2016). Hinshaw, who edited the English edition, calls Kawai and Murakami Japan's foremost contemporary cultural spokespersons, an opinion with which I agree.

The following is a quote from Murakami in a footnote of the book:

> … writing novels is in large part an act of self-healing. Some people might set out to convey a particular message through a novel, but for me at least, this isn't the case. Instead, I write novels to discover the messages within me. In the process of writing a story, these messages suddenly appear out of the darkness—though in many cases, they are written in an indecipherable code. (Kawai & Murakami, 1996/2016, 62)

The essence of what Murakami calls a story is described above. If the writer has a message in advance and writes a novel to convey it to the reader, it is easy to understand. Murakami says, however, that this is not the case with him. He says that he writes a novel to find a message within himself. It is a message that is inside of him, but he is not aware of it yet. In other words, Murakami writes a novel as a way to find a message that resides in the unconscious of his psyche. Murakami continues.

> … The story has to be spontaneous. To me, it would be meaningless to systematically plot out every detail. So I spontaneously create a succession of things, and then finally I come to the ending … When I start writing, I don't have a rough sketch of the story or anything like that. I just immerse myself in the act of writing and then … [there's always an ending.] That provides a certain amount of catharsis. (Kawai & Murakami, 1996/2016, 63)

Murakami does not plan in advance when he creates a story. It is meaningful for him that the story tells spontaneously in the novel as a framework. It is important to leave himself to the flow of the story while being open to the unconscious. I see some similarities between his method of writing and his way of living. He did not plan to be a writer, but he suddenly started to write a novel as if he had received a revelation. For Murakami, the novel is the framework, the place for generation, and the method for that. Of course, nothing remains unless there is someone who articulates what happens there, so Murakami plays that role.

He further states, "I don't need to express myself if I use the context of a story. The story expresses itself instead … If my 'ego' is there, I sink it into the story. The most important thing is what the story communicates when my 'ego' hits bottom" (Murakami, 2003/2012, 116, my translation). First of all, I would like to pay attention to the fact that Murakami does not just say 'I sink my ego into the story,' but rather says 'If my 'ego' is there …' According to the idea of modern Western ego, the ego is something that exists without doubt. Murakami, however, seems to doubt its existence. His standpoint may have something to do with the fact that ego in the Japanese psyche is a much more ambiguous existence than in Westerners'. This then is what Murakami means by the word 'story.' It is an important concept in considering his creative activities.

2. *Descent*

Murakami explains his writing in the following quotes from interviews.

1)   "When I'm in writing mode for a novel, I get up at four a.m. and work for five to six hours. In the afternoon, I run for ten kilometers or swim fifteen hundred meters (or do both), then I read a bit and listen to some music. I go to bed at nine p.m. I keep to

this routine every day without variation. The repetition itself becomes the important thing; it's a form of mesmerism. I mesmerize myself to reach a deeper state of mind. But to hold to such repetition for so long—six months to a year—requires a good amount of mental and physical strength. In that case, writing a long novel is like survival training. Physical strength is as necessary as artistic sensitivity." (Murakami, 2004/2012)

2)   "Writing fiction is just a dream. You just experience the procedure of the dream. You cannot change the story line. You have to do what you have to do just to experience the dream, totally freely. We fiction writers can do that awake … We can continue intentionally to see those dreams as long as we want. When I concentrate on writing, I can dream as long as I want. I can continue dreaming the next day and the next day, intentionally. That is a great experience, but dangerous sometimes because we are descending deeper and deeper and darker and darker." (Murakami, 2005)

3)   "When I am writing a story, I go down to the dark places, to the deep places, like the bottom of a well or a basement. It's dark and it's damp and it's sometimes dangerous. You cannot tell what is in that darkness. But I have to enter that darkness because that is what I feel when I am writing fiction." (Murakami, 2005)

Murakami descends into the depths of his psyche, stays there, encounters his inner chaos and darkness, and describes with words what emerges there. Murakami (2009/2012) says that to write a novel, one needs to see the unhealthy, distorted, and dark sides of one's soul. This is not only a lonely, but also a dangerous task. The process in psychotherapy is often similar to Murakami's creative process, however, the big difference is that a client is accompanied by a therapist during the therapeutic process. Murakami, on the contrary, tackles this work totally alone. It is interesting that he describes writing fiction as dreaming while awake. It has something to do with how much one can be aware of what is in the unconscious, which is very similar to what is tackled in psychotherapy.

3.   *The Power of Murakami's Story*

Lastly, I would like to explore the power of Murakami's stories, which are created by descending to the depth of the psyche. Murakami says, "By writing, I'm digging into ground consisting of many layers. I always want to go deeper" (2003/2012, 164, my translation). And then he says, "If I can reach such a depth, I will be able to touch the collective base and communicate with my readers. If I do not go far enough, nothing will happen." (Murakami, 2003/2012, 164 my translation).

Murakami says that the task of creating a story in the dark varies from person to person. He continues as follows,

However, when I dig deeper and deeper and write a story about what I experience in the process, my story and the story of a person named 'A' should call and respond to each other, even though it is originally my story. 'A' has a potential story within to tell, but he can't articulate it as a story. My story and the potential story in 'A' call and respond to each other … I think it is empathy or a kind of responsiveness of the soul. If I am healed to some degree by creating a story, then it may also heal a person named 'A.' Such a thing could possibly happen." (2003/2012, 120, my translation)

I would like to argue that all the secrets of Murakami's creative work and the power of his story are expressed in his words above. Murakami says, 'It (the fact that his psyche is connected with his readers through stories) does not seem to have so much to do with the difference of nationality or generation.' This quote makes sense based on the fact that he has readers all over the world.

Conclusion

In this essay, I discussed the creative process of Haruki Murakami from the perspective of depth psychology. Firstly, I considered Murakami's creative process focusing on the word 'memory' in the way that Murakami uses it in his work. What does 'memory' mean to Murakami? How is 'memory' depicted in his work? Secondly, I explored the sources of his stories—his personal and collective memory. What are they and where do they come from? And thirdly, I explored Murakami's creative work through his words in interviews. To conclude, I would like to argue that the stories Murakami tells resonate with what lies deep in the psyche (I would like to call it 'soul') of his many disparate worldwide readers, who live with various backgrounds.

Funding

This research has been supported by a grant-in-aid from the Japanese Society for the Promotion of Science (No. 21KK0042).

References

Edinger, Edward F. 1987. *The Christian Archetype: A Jungian Commentary on the Life of Christ*. Toronto: Inner City Book.

Inoue, Yoshio. 1999. *Murakami Haruki to nihon no "kioku"* (Haruki Murakami and "Memory" of Japan). Tokyo: Sinchosha. (in Japanese)

Kamo no Chōmei. 1212. *Hōjoki*. Translated by Meredith McKinney. 2013. *Kenko and Chōme: Essays in Idleness and Hōjoki*. London: Penguin Books.

Kawai, Hayao and Murakami, Haruki. 1996/2016. *Murakami Haruki, Kawai Hayao ni ai ni iku* Tokyo: Iwanamishoten. *Haruki Murakami goes to meet Hayao Kawai.* Translated by Christopher Stephens. 2016.Einsiedeln: Daimon.

Kawai, Hayao. 1982/1996. *Mukashibanashi to Nihonjin no Kokoro.* Tokyo: Iwanami Shoten. *The Japanese Psyche: Major Motifs in the Fairy Tales of Japan.* Translated by Hayao Kawai and Sachiko Reece. CT: Spring Publications, Inc.

Kawakami, Mieko and Murakami, Haruki. 2017. *Mimizuku wa tasogare ni tobitatsu: Haruki Murakami A Long. Long. Interview by Mieko Kawakami.* (A Horned Owl takes off at Twilight: Haruki Murakami A Long. Long. Interview by Mieko Kawakami.) Tokyo: Shinchosha. (in Japanese)

McCullough, Helen C. 1988. *The Tale of the Heike.* Translated by McCullough, Helen C. California: Stanford University Press. The author is unknown.

Murakami, Haruki. 1979/2015a. *Kaze no uta o kike.* Originally published in *Gunzo.* Tokyo: Bungeishunjuu. "Hear the Wind Sing." In Haruki *Murakami Wind/Pinball Two novels.* Translated by Ted Goossen. New York: Alfred A. Knopf.

Murakami, Haruki. 1980/2015a. *1973 nen no pinbōru.* Originally published in *Gunzo.* Tokyo: *Bungeishunjuu. "Pinball,* 1973." In Haruki Murakami *Wind/Pinball Two novels.* Translated by Ted Goossen. New York: Alfred A. Knopf.

Murakami, Haruki. 1981/2014. "Gogatsu no Kaigansen." ("A Coastline in May") In a *collected work of Murakami Haruki* Vol.5, Short Stories, 1979–1989. 101–112. (in Japanese)

Murakami, Haruki. 1985. "Murakami Haruki Rongu intabyu." (Murakami Haruki's Long Interview) In *Shousetsu Shincho* rinji zokan '85 summer kojinteki iken. (*Novel Shincho,* special issue, 1985 summer, The Personal Opinion) 12–35. (in Japanese)

Murakami, Haruki. 1987/2011. *Noruuei no mori.* Tokyo: Kodansha. Translated by Jay Rubin. *Norwegian Woods.* London: Vintage Books.

Murakami, Haruki. 1988/2002. *Dansu Dansu Dansu.* Tokyo: Kodansha. Dance Dance Dance. Translated by Alfred Birnbaum. London: Vintage Books.

Murakami, Haruki. 1994–1995/2003. *Nejimaki dori kuronikuru.* Book 1–3. Tokyo: Shinchosha. Translated by Jay Rubin. *The Wind-up Bird Chronicle.* London: Vintage Books.

Murakami Haruki. 1995. Meikingu obu "Nejimakidori Kuronikkuru" (Making of Wind-up Bird Chronicle) *Shincho* Nov. issue. 270–288.

Murakami, Haruki. 1998. "Genjitsu no chikara/Genjitsu o koeru chikara" ("Actual power/Beyond actual power"). Originally in Complex Chinese in Jihoshukan. In *Murakami Haruki intabyuushuu 1997–2011 Yume o miru tame ni maiasa boku wa mezameru no desu*. In A collection of Haruki Murakami's Interviews 1997–2011 In order to have a dream I wake up every morning. Tokyo: Bungeishunjuu. 31–44. (in Japanese)

Murakami, Haruki. 1999. "A Story should always be spontaneous." Koukokuhihyou 231 1999 October issue. "Suputoniku no koibito o chuusinn ni" ("Focusing on *Sputnik Sweetheart*") In *Murakami Haruki intabyuushuu 1997–2011 Yume o miru tame ni maiasa boku wa mezameru no desu* (A collection of Haruki Murakami's Interviews 1997–2011 In order to have a dream I wake up every morning) Tokyo: Bungeishunjuu. 45–86. (in Japanese)

Murakami, Haruki. 2002/2005. *Umibe no kafuka*. Tokyo; Shinchosha. *Kafka on the Shore.*Translated by Philip Gabriel. London: Vintage Books.

Murakami, Haruki. 2003. *Umibe no Kafuka* o kataru (Talking about *Kafka on the Shore*). In *Bungakukai* 57(4) 10–42. (in Japanese)

Murakami, Haruki. 2003/2012. "Haruki Murakami: écrire, c'est comme réver evéille" Interviewed by Minh Tran Huy. Originally published in French, N° 421, Juin. "Kakukoto wa choudo mezamenagara yumemiruyouna mono." ("Writing is just like dreaming awake") In *Murakami intabyuu shuu 1997–2011 Yume o miru tame ni maiasa boku wa mezameru no desu* (When you want someone drink something, you have to be extremely kind in A collection of Haruki Murakami's Interviews 1997–2011 In order to have a dream I wake up every morning). Tokyo: Bungeishunjuu. 153–178.

Murakami, Haruki. 2004/2012. Haruki Murakami: The Art of Fiction CLXXXII interviewed by Wray, J. Originally published in English *The Paris Review*, 170. Translated in Nanika o hitoni nomaseyou to suru toki, anata wa tobikkiri sinsetsu ni naranakutewa naranai. In *Murakami Haruki intabyuu shuu 1997–2011 Yume o miru tame ni maiasa boku wa mezameru no desu* (When you want someone drink something, you have to be extremely kind in A collection of Haruki Murakami's Interviews 1997–2011 In order to have a dream I wake up every morning). Tokyo: Bungeishunjuu. 201–260.

Murakami, Haruki. 2005. "In Dreams Begins Responsibility; An interview with Haruki Murakami" Interviewed by Jonathan Ellis and Mitoko Hirabayashi. *The Georgia Review*, Vol. 59, No.3. Fall. 548–567

Murakami, Haruki. 2006. Question 251: A protagonist in *Norwegian Wood*. In *'Hitotsu Murakami san de yattemiruka' to seken no hitobito ga Murakami Haruki ni toriaezu buttsukeru 490 no shitsumon ni hatashite Murakami san wa chanto kotaerarerunoka?* (Can Murakami properly answer the 490 questions that people in the world ask Haruki Murakami: "I'll try to do it with Murakami?"). Asahi Shinbun Company. (in Japanese)

Murakami Haruki. 2007/2008. *Hashirukoto ni tsuite kataru toki ni boku no kataru koto*. Tokyo: Bungeishuju. (*What I talk About When I Talk About Running*.) New York: Vintage Books.

Murakami, Haruki. 2009. The Wall and the Egg. Jerusalem Prize acceptance speech. In *Zatsubunshu*. (A Collection of Essays) 2011.Tokyo: Shinchosha. (in Japanese)

Murakami, Haruki. 2009/2012. "Seicho o mezashite, nashitsuzukete" ("Aiming for growth, continue to grow") Interviewed by Hideo Furukawa. Originally published in *Monkey Business* vo.5. 2009 Spring Issue. Tokyo: Village Books. "<u>Rutsubo</u> no youna shousetsu o kakitai, *1Q84* zenya" ("I want to write a novel like <u>a crucible. *1Q84* Eve</u>"") In *Murakami Haruki intabyuu shuu 1997–2009 Yume o miru tame ni maiasa boku wa mezameru no desu* (When you want someone drink something, you have to be extremely kind in A collection of Haruki Murakami's Interviews 1997–2011 In order to have a dream I wake up every morning). Tokyo: Bungeishunjuu. 465–546. (in Japanese)

Murakami, Haruki. 2009, 2010/2013. *1Q84*. Tokyo: Shinchosha. 1Q84. Translated by Jay Rubin and Philip Gabriel. New York: Vintage Books.

Murakami, Haruki. 2010. Murakami Haruki Rongu Intabyuu in *Kangaeru Hito*, 33. 20–100. (Haruki Murakami Long Interviews in *Thinking Man*). Tokyo: Shinchosha. (in Japanese)

Murakami, Haruki. 2011. "Speaking as an Unrealistic Dreamer" Speech by Murakami Haruki on the occasion of receiving the International Catalunya Prize. Translated by Emanuel Pastreich. *The Asia-Pacific Journal* 9(29) 1–7.

Murakami, Haruki. 2015a. "The Birth of My Kitchen-Table Fiction." In *Haruki Murakami Wind/Pinball Two novels*. Translated by Ted Goossen. New York: Alfred A. Knopf.

Murakami, Haruki. 2015b. *Shokugyou toshite no Shosetuka* (A Writer as a Professional). Tokyo: Switch Publishing. (in Japanese)

Murakami, Haruki. 2017/2019. *Kishidancho Goroshi Part 1, 2*. Tokyo: Shinchosha. Translated by Philip Gabriel and Ted Goossen. *Killing Kommendatore*. London: Vintage.

Murakami, Ryu and Murakami, Haruki. 1981. *Walk, Don't Run Ryu vs. Haruki*. Tokyo: Kodansha. (in Japanese)

Ueda, Akinari. 1776. *Ugetsu Monogatari*. Translated by Anthony H. Chambers. 2007. *Tales of Moonlight and Rain*. New York: Columbia University Press.

Yama, Megumi. 2016. Haruki Murakami as Modern-Myth Maker. *Jung Journal Culture & Psyche* 10(1) 87–95.

Yama, Megumi. 2019. *Murakami Haruki, Houhou toshiteno shousetsu: kioku no kosou e* (Haruki Murakami, Novel as a Method: Descent into the Depths of Memory) Tokyo: Shinyosha. (in Japanese)

Ype De Boer

Ethics of a Split Existence: Murakami's *Hard-Boiled Wonderland and the End of the World* as a Poetico-Philosophical Experiment

Abstract: *This article philosophically develops one of the central themes in the fiction of Murakami Haruki: the experience of a split existence. Whether it takes place in the world surrounding them or rather internally, this split generally occurs when something unforeseen—the death of a loved one, an unexpected twist of fate, a resurging trauma or a new love—shakes their otherwise stable, routine, secure and comfortable lives to the core. Suddenly a world next to the one they know appears; suddenly they come face-to-face with living memories and parts of themselves that seem to operate autonomously. Reading Murakami's fiction in terms of what Italian philosopher Giorgio Agamben calls 'poetico-philosophical experiments'—texts that put the very mode of existence (ethos) of the writer and reader at stake—this article investigates 1) the way human existence is perceived from the perspective of a split inherent in it and 2) what mode of life becomes possible in response to this experience. Its main argument is that the ethical value of Murakami's fictional writing does not lie in the search for an authentic individuality, but in the exposure of the limitations of such a quest and the vital possibilities opened up by abandoning it. From this perspective, the article offers a close reading of Hard-boiled Wonderland and the End of The World. This intricate novel offers ample opportunity to explore the split nature of Murakami's narrative world and plays out different existential attitudes vis-a-vis this split. On the face of it, there seem to be only two options for its protagonist, either to hold fast even more tightly to his old, undivided identity or instead to resolve the split by creating a new one: a so-called more 'authentic' or 'true' self. However, this article argues that a third, more subtle option is at play, and that, moreover, this alternate option is the one Murakami's fiction leans toward as a whole. Instead of discovering or losing their true identity, the ethical transformation of the protagonist occurs when he abandons the very ideal of protecting or developing an individual identity and embraces the split nature of human life and the dynamic resulting from it. Outlining this third option allows this article to distance itself from prevalent pessimistic readings of Hard-Boiled Wonderland in particular and Murakami's fiction in general and proposes an alternative to the influential readings of* *it as a quest for individual identity and/or political and moral agency in an oppressive cultural environment. Beyond cultural critique, beyond the establishment of individual identity, Murakami's fiction tells of the deceptively simple aspiration of his protagonists to 'hear the wind sing,' as his debut novel titles.*

Keywords: Murakami; philosophy; split existence; Hard-boiled Wonderland and the End of the World; ethics; identity; Agamben; spirit

Introduction

> There's a kind of gap between what I think is real and what's really real. I get this feeling like some kind of little something-or-other is there, somewhere inside me … like a burglar is in the house, hiding in a closet … and it comes out every once in a while and messes up whatever order or logic I've established for myself. The way a magnet can make a machine go crazy. (*The Wind-up Bird Chronicle*, 236)

Kumiko, the lost wife from Haruki Murakami's *The Wind-up Bird Chronicle*, gives expression to an alienating experience of a split in her existence. Not only does she mention a gap dividing the so-called real world from the world as she experiences it, she also points to an unknown presence inside her—the split of her lifeworld is accompanied by an internal split. And this experience concerns not just some whim or caprice, for without her being able to put a stop to it, it eventually comes to dominate her existence. She develops a double life, divided between her calm and loving marriage with the book's protagonist Toru and another, sexually explosive one, until she cannot cope any longer and becomes entrapped in the mysterious 'hotel room 208.' And Kumiko isn't the only character in Murakami's fiction facing a split in her existence. We are dealing here with a theme present in virtually all of his stories. Guided by his double 'the boy named Crow,' the fifteen-year-old Kafka enters a village deep in a forest outside of time in *Kafka on the Shore*. The narrative in *1Q84* is set in one world with two moons and another world with only one. In the trilogy of the Rat (*Hear the Wind Sing; Pinball, 1973; A Wild Sheep Chase*), it is never really clear whether its protagonist is dealing with actual people or only with somehow separated parts of his inner life. Also, Murakami's short stories and even his more realistic novels testify in some way to a split existence, to an intriguing tension between an ordinary, structured dimension on the one hand and a mysterious, dreamlike dimension on the other which, however intimate to the protagonists, at first strikes them as alien and threatening.

This article aims to develop philosophically this central theme in the fiction of Murakami. Reading his literary writing in terms of what Italian philosopher Giorgio Agamben calls 'poetico-philosophical experiments'—texts that put the very mode of existence (*ethos*) of the reader (and writer) at stake—this article investigates 1) the way human existence is perceived from the perspective of a split inherent in it and 2) what mode of life becomes possible in response to it. My main argument is that the ethical value of Murakami's fiction lies not in the search for an individual identity, but in the exposure of the limitations of such a quest and the vital possibilities opened up by abandoning it. From this perspective, the article offers a close reading of *Hard-Boiled Wonderland and the End of The World* (hereafter, *Hard-boiled Wonderland*). This intricate novel offers ample opportunity to explore the split nature of Murakami's narrative world and plays out different existential attitudes vis-a-vis this split. Following the ethical modification its protagonist undergoes, allows the article to distance itself from prevalent pessimistic readings of *Hard-Boiled Wonderland* in particular and Murakami's fiction in general and to propose an alternative to the influential readings of it as a quest for individual identity and/or political and moral agency in an oppressive cultural environment.

Poetico-Philosophical Experiments

I am not the first to be struck by the philosophical value of Murakami's literary presentation of a fracture in human existence, and various interpretations of it already exist. At least since Matthew Carl Stretcher's influential reading in 1999 of Murakami's fiction as a quest for identity in a consumerist, postwar Japan (Stretcher 1999a, 269; 1999b, *passim*), most prominent in this regard are analyses interpreting this fracture culturally, psychologically, and politically or morally. Such analyses focus on the struggle of the Murakami-protagonists with a 'system,' the exact nature of which seems intentionally left open in most of Murakami's stories; sometimes it indicates a capitalist and consumerist network, other times a totalitarian government sectarian ideology, and most of the times an undetailed combination these. The parallel worlds of Murakami's fiction are taken to represent modernity in its cultural and political darkness, laying bare at a symbolical level the repression of individuality effected by such apparatuses, structuring his stories psychologically in terms of jaded individuals searching for a sense of individual identity. Building on similar diagnostics of a conflict between culture and individual, various morally and politically oriented analysis interpret Murakami as investigating new modes of struggle and responsibility (Welch 2005, 56; Dil 2009,

102; White 2012, 69). Also, analyses of the split that do not emphasize this conflict per se tend to stick to the cultural level. Rachel Stewart, for instance, reads Murakami's *1Q84* through the promising lens of 'worlding,' arguing that "the role of duplicity if not multiplicity of world views [is to] alter the characters' ability to navigate themselves through city spaces" befitting of contemporary globalization and cultural hybrid-cities such as Tokyo (2015, 147). Yet beyond its socio-historical embeddedness, what is the nature of such a 'navigation' allowed for by a splitting of worlds? What role does it play in human existence? Taking a different route than those above formulated above, my reading is to uncover an ethical concern in Murakami's fiction beyond (or perhaps before) identity, culture, politics, or morality. As I shall argue, the enigmatic space for navigation constitutes the space of *ethics* for Murakami: the space from which we develop an attitude towards the totality of existence: a way of dwelling within it. In order to do so, I will treat his fiction as a poetico-philosophical experiment. What does this entail? In an essay on Herbert Melville's *Bartleby, the Scrivener*, Agamben delineates a peculiar type of experiments conducted by thought and poetry. Such experiments:

> … do not simply concern the truth or falsity of hypotheses, the occurrence or nonoccurrence of something, as in scientific experiments; rather, they call into question Being itself, before or beyond its determination as true or false. These experiments are without truth, for truth is what is at issue in them. (Agamben 1999, 260)

Experiments conducted in regular science concern the verification or falsification of a hypothesis measured against the backdrop of a certain view of nature, knowledge, and method. They aim to "establish the truth of a theory or the existence of an entity," but to this end already presuppose a notion of truth and existence (Van der Heiden 2019, 48). In a similar way, what Agamben calls 'morality' knowingly or unknowingly takes its departure from an unquestioned 'metaphysical' background—that is, a certain idea of what is, of humankind's nature and what it is capable of, of the good, the just, the true and/or the desirable, which ultimately forms the horizon from which moral judgements and acts become meaningful and events can be normatively evaluated. In contrast to those of science and morality, the experiments Agamben has in mind question precisely the 'background,' the way Being (and life and man) is viewed and becomes meaningful in the first place. Such poetico-philosophical experiments, as one might call them, are thus not experiments that 'measure' a certain action, judgement, or idea against an already established way in which Being is perceived and presupposed, *but experiment with these presuppositions and perceptions themselves.* They experiment with the images, concepts, and ideals that constitute, so to speak, the limits of our mode of being in the world. They concern, for instance, whether one's existence and world are experienced as 'necessary' or 'contingent,' whether the human being is like a machine, or rather like an animal, or instead of a divine origin. Such meta-physical images and concepts, although empirically unverifiable or falsifiable, nonetheless decisively influence and structure our perception and evaluation of reality. Truth is thus still 'at issue in them': insofar as they are imaginings, visions of life, humanity or being that, were they taken (or experienced) to be true, our whole *ethos*, our whole attitude towards and in life would change, creating a new perspective on existence.

> Whoever submits himself to these experiments jeopardizes not so much the truth of his statements as the very mode of his existence; he undergoes an anthropological change that is just as decisive in the context of the individual's natural history as the liberation of the hand by the erect position was for the primate or as was, for the reptile, the transformation of limbs that changed it into a bird. (Agamben 1999, 260)

Since poetico-philosophical experiments concern being and (potentially) modify our mode of existence, the truth at stake in them concerns a sort of truth of existence. Not a truth about something *within* existence, but regarding the nature of existence as a whole. As they concern the *totality* of existence, there are no criteria outside it by which to verify or falsify it. Yet this does not mean they are beyond reason or arbitrary. Their truth and reasonability can still be tested, but only by attempting to live it; that is, by undergoing its effects, letting it modify the totality of (one's) existence. While the word 'ethics' isn't mentioned in Agamben's brief exposé, I take them to be profoundly ethical as they put humankind's very mode of existence, its *ethos* at stake.

A well-known example from western philosophy is Nietzsche's eternal recurrence of the same. *The Gay Science* §341 presents this metaphysical, experimental idea not in the form of an argument but of a whisper, spoken by a demon in *your loneliest loneliness* challenging one's attitude towards existence. One can resent and curse the demon (and its 'truth') or view him a divine messenger: "you are a God and never have I heard anything more divine" (2001, 194). Whether everything that happens and will happen will recur forever, cannot be verified or falsified in a scientific or empirical manner. Yet such an idea concerning the nature of human existence beyond what can be empirically established about it nonetheless modifies the way we experience our lives, how we act, what we see and what we miss, how we feel and so forth. It is an experiment that introduces a new 'weight' to existence, challenging one's attitude toward life, testing whether one truly has overcome all traces of resentment, has truly become able of saying yes to life in its totality, dwelling in it affirmatively, beyond political or moral considerations: *amor fati.* Importantly, such experiments are not limited to philosophy. As in the Nietzschean example, poetico-philosophical experiments intimately involve poetic imagination. Accordingly, insofar as artworks, poems, or literary figures experiment with ideas concerning the nature of reality, with perception and ways of life, they too form an essential part of this type of ethical discourse.

Recapitulating the above in relation to Murakami's fiction, more specifically *Hard-Boiled Wonderland,* one gets the following methodological vista: In what way does it 1) call into question being and 2) (potentially) modify our mode of existence? This lens will allow for a positive rather than negative appraisal of the fate of its main protagonist and, moreover, bring into view an as of yet underappreciated thematic of his fiction: the life of the mind. In addition, it forms an alternative to dominant cultural, political, and psychological readings. Analyzed from a socio-cultural perspective, Murakami can be read as dealing with a specifically contemporary conflict between the system and the individual. Psychologically, this may take the form of bringing to light one's 'core identity' and the assertion of an authentic individuality. Morally and politically, it concerns taking responsibility against oppressive and exploitative structures. The ethical perspective developed here leads to a different conclusion. Murakami's fiction concerns not the dying breath of authentic identity vis-à-vis overwhelming structures, nor the (failed) awakening of moral or political activism, but the attempt to move beyond the conflict between cultural-individual, act-counteract, right and wrong. Yet, as I shall argue, this does not necessarily mean escapism. Shedding itself of the identity-ideal that keeps one within this vicious circle of recognition, it invites one to enter an open space that is none other than simple, everyday life but now lived in an ethically modified manner.

Reading a text as a poetico-philosophical experiment means taking it to its limit. Within a text, it searches for the point inviting to be developed philosophically (Agamben 2009, 8). Thus, while developing its argument on the basis of the concrete situations, protagonists, conversations, and images of Murakami's fiction, this article endeavors to find within it a point that leads beyond it. This problematic is that of 'spirit' or 'mind,' which I believe is the unpolished gem hidden at the core of Murakami's literature. Neither consciousness or unconsciousness, individual or cultural, it concerns a point of non-coincidence with them, allowing for a spiritual receptivity toward existence. Beyond cultural critique, beyond the establishment of individual identity, Murakami's fiction tells of the deceptively simple aspiration of his protagonists to 'hear the wind sing,' as his debut novel is titled.

Calling into Question Boku's Status Quo

> I can distinguish between myself and another as beings of two different realms. It's a kind of talent. (*The Wind-Up Bird Chronicle*, 78)

Before diving into *Hard-Boiled Wonderland*, first some remarks on the mode of existence of Murakami's protagonists at the beginning of his stories. Whether it concerns Tengo from *1Q84*, the student-life of Watanabe in *Norwegian Wood*, the narrator from the Rat-trilogy, Toru from *The Wind-up Bird Chronicle*, or Hajime from *South of the Border*, they all live a highly regular, shielded existence, where the days blend in with each other. They are calm, individualistic people that have organized their lives in a self-sufficient manner, not needing or burdening anyone else. Averse to all institutes that could meddle with their lives, they try to stay clear of religion, group ideology or political activism. To enable such a life, they find a working environment that doesn't require great ambition and offers them a lot of space: they become freelance tutors, start a translation company, or open a jazz-bar. Overall, they "take a convenience-sake view of prevailing world conditions, events, existence in general" (*Hard-Boiled Wonderland*, 4). They do household chores, cook food, regularly enjoy a beer, prefer disappearing into novels over making friends, do their job, and now and then find themselves in bed with someone. All attachments—especially emotional attachment—are considered a threat to their autonomy and independence. Concerning this point, it makes little difference whether they are married or single, as the protagonist from *Hard-boiled Wonderland* shares:

> I had five years of marriage, but now I can hardly remember what it was like. It seems as if I'd always lived alone. … Two people can sleep in the same bed and still be alone when they close their eyes. (*Hard-boiled Wonderland*, 377; 388)

Notwithstanding this distance between himself and his wife, he found "married life [to be] great" (*Hard-Boiled Wonderland*, 388). Put more strongly, it is precisely within such a distance toward other people (and events) that Murakami's protagonists are most at ease. They pave their own path through life, mediocre as it may seem, and pride themselves for their individuality and autonomy.

Toward the things in life beyond their control, their attitude is one of acceptance and relativization. In addition to 'independence' and 'individuality' we can add 'equanimity': nothing is to threaten their stability. The affectional reward is comfort and peace of mind, experienced in solitude. Life need not be special for them. Happiness is of no true concern, contentedness is enough. The protagonists are quite self-conscious and have no trouble understanding (and accepting) that their lives might seem boring to others, yet they do not really care for this, not even if their mode of life ends up pushing others away. Everything occurring outside the borders (a wall, a garden hedge) of their existence potentially threatens their clear and orderly existence and cause only "useless troubles" (*The Wind-up Bird Chronicle*, 79). Everything seems to indicate that they are perfectly at home within their orderly existence. What they desire most of all is to continue living like this for as long as possible. Reflecting upon the way his uneventful has transpired, the protagonist of *Pinball 1973* muses: "A wonderful week," contemplating whether it "might stay that way forever" (*Pinball 1973*, ch. 18). They have attained autonomy, created a stable image of themselves and cultivated mechanisms to guard themselves against the upheavals of the soul and the pulsations of life. In short, what renders their ordinariness ideal, is the *self-preservation* they believe to guarantee through it.

For the most part, the protagonists succeed in communicating their mode of life as an ideal. They are, to speak with Jay Rubin, 'cool' in their normality. The typical first-person narrator, denoted as '*Boku*' (informal Japanese for 'I') is "polite and well behaved … is interested in girls and sex, but is not consumed by them, and he is gentile and considerate towards his bed partners. He is actually a kind of role model" (2012, 38). This characterization of Murakami's Bokus as role models is interesting and emphasizes the disarming effect they have on the reader. They have a charming and sobering way of reflecting on their own deficits and suffering. They are thoughtful, helpful, and considerate regarding others and their equanimity works as a kind of magnet for those seeking protection and shelter. In their serenity under dire circumstances one can experience comfort, consolation, and wisdom. Moreover, their one-person apartments, filled with books, music, cigarettes, whiskey and freshly encountered lovers, breathe a romantic atmosphere of freedom and ease. When the protagonists are married, one senses the very real shelter they find in their friendly and calm love and the power they draw from it. And also, the fear of losing their independence and equanimity is, to be sure, real and relatable. Every time Murakami's protagonists are forced to re-orient themselves, the threat of loss is prominent: at the borders of their everyday lives lurks, amongst other things, a confrontation with death. However, the characterization of Murakami's ordinary protagonists as role models is not generally shared. As briefly touched upon above, they have also been interpreted as nullified victims of modern isolation and indifference, induced by capitalism and consumerism or a governmental system that suppresses individuality and self-expression. As I have argued elsewhere, a fruitful way of interpreting their jaded way of life philosophically is through the diagnosis of modernity Walter Benjamin developed as a situation of *Erfahrungsarmut*, poverty of experience (Benjamin 2011 472–8; De Boer 2017, 46–50). Distinguishing between *Erlebnisse*, which concern experiences leaving one unaffected, unmoved, and unchanged and *Erfahrungen*, experiences that shape someone's character and view of life, Benjamin argued that, due to an overflow of spectacular experiences offered by modernity, modern man has become dulled into an indifference sterilizing every potential *Erfahrung* into an *Erlebnis*. Just as we moderns consume death, horror, violence, love, and passion on a daily basis from the safe distance of our sofa's, so the most fantastical of experiences tend to be digested in mere minutes by Murakami's protagonists.

However, whether one characterizes the everydayness, individuality, and self-preservation of Murakami's protagonists positively or negatively, such analyses remain one-sided if they do not take into account the crucial fact that, within Murakami's fiction, *they never succeed in maintaining this mode of life.* Just as constant as Murakami's point of departure, is his problematization of it. Contrary to what Carl Cassegard has argued, I do not believe that Murakami's protagonists are beyond the ability to be shocked (2002, 85). If one traces the way his characters unfold throughout a story, one sees that the harsh lesson they learn is that life—even modern life—ultimately does not comply with the self-preservation they seek. As counterpart to the nameless bed partners and short-lived affairs with married women, there are the women for whom the protagonists are ready to traverse the end of the world; opposed to the order and control of their routine, Murakami places the overwhelming power of fate; instead of eternal equanimity, the protagonists get to know the stormy motions of the spirit. An internal divide is brought to light, alternate dimensions of existence appear that do not follow the same laws as did their orderly, routinized lives.

The events laying bare this split existence are embedded in psychological and cultural contexts, but their implications are profoundly ontological and metaphysical, in the sense that they deactivate and re-arrange the mode of perception through which physical, psychological, and cultural existence is structured. Faced with love, death, fate, or their own demons, the identity they had all this time been cherishing now introduces itself as an *empty shell*, captivating them within a purely functional life. They discover a pricetag attached to their way of life: separation from others, a part of themselves and everything in general puts it at stake. What seemed an ideal way of life now appears as a self-designed solitary confinement (or a '*shoe box*' as Boku's future wife tells him in *Pinball 1973*): an insight accompanied by desperation and disorientation. They can no longer identify with their self-images, are no longer at home within their own existence; their mirror images, shadows, or memory-amalgams like the sheepman become separate characters. Using ontological vocabulary, we could term the stable and orderly life they had been cultivating up till this point—the image they have built of themselves, the customs they have developed, the things they have lived through, their memories, the defensive mechanisms surrounding them—the *actuality* of their existence. The other side of reality that imposes itself on them, is existence as *potentiality*. Not the potentiality *for* something concretely other, say the 'potentiality' to quit your job and finally become the movie star secretly hiding in you, but the potentiality *of* existence as it surpasses what you make it out to be: existence as it is gives itself without a pre-established user manual, without destiny.

'Calling into question Being,' the exposure of this disorienting divide jeopardizes the orderly mode of existence of Murakami's protagonists; however, they are not indicative of a normalized "multiple personality disorder" nor simply the result of modern times (Treat 2015, 106–107), but involve events and experiences that are part and parcel of human existence in general. Moreover, although this divide can be stifling and demolishing—indeed, like Kumiko, one risks losing oneself in the abyss opened up by it—it ultimately marks a positive turning point in Murakami's stories. For the non-coincidence with their actuality also means opportunity. Their cocoon cracked, his protagonists finally glimpse vital possibilities they were closed off from. As Gitte Hansen has argued in relation to Murakami's *Sleep*, namely that what is at stake for its protagonist is her 'awakening' from a pending reification in search of a vitality beyond her ordered existence as a housewife (Hansen 2017, 127–131), counts for his other protagonists as well. No longer merged with their actuality, a certain space around it becomes visible, allowing them to re-engage (navigate) anew their memories, identity-images, loved ones. No longer able to rely on their previous mode of existence, life itself demands of them to undergo an ethical modification if they are not to end up as empty shells. In order to grasp this ethical modification, I now turn to *Hard-Boiled Wonderland.*

Ethics in Wonderland

Hard-Boiled Wonderland tells of a divorced thirty-five year old who works as a 'calcutec,' coding information for a big security company: a well-paid job allowing him to lead an independent life which, or so he hopes, after some fifteen years has yielded him enough to spend the rest of his days drinking cocktails, playing cello, and reading books in a mountain cabin. Until then he works as much as possible, now and then orders a call-girl, drinks whiskey, and reads a book or watches a movie in bed. He has no friends and has stopped reading the newspaper yet is not embittered. He is happy to find his mailbox empty and his solitary way of passing the time is "[a]s precious to [him] as a beautiful sunset or good clean air" (*Hard-boiled Wonderland*, 67). Interestingly, the sci-fi meets fable type book not only describes life as the protagonist lives it consciously and at the surface, but also what it looks like at an unconscious, symbolical level. As the result of a brain surgery undergone for his work as a Calcutec, the narrator seems to live in two worlds. The first storyline, denoting the protagonist with the formal Japanese for 'I,' '*Watashi*,' takes place in a quasi-futuristic Tokyo. The second storyline tells of the protagonist's—here '*Boku*'—integration into a mysterious place called the 'Town' or 'End of the World,' enclosed by a giant, unsurpassable wall, which protects the citizens within it from the surrounding woods. The only beings regularly moving in and out are the Gatekeeper and the mysterious golden beasts under his care. The Town is marked by a utopian perfection: "everything you need … it will set before you" and

> … no one hurts each other here, no one fights. … They work, but they enjoy their labor. … There are no complaints, no worries … no internal conflicts … no growing old, no death, no fear of death. (*Hard-boiled Wonderland*, 333)

In it, each citizen has its specific place and function, and alongside the Gatekeeper we also meet a Librarian girl and a Colonel. Escaping time and history in an eternalized functionality, at its center stands a clocktower that "has long forfeited its original role as a timepiece" (*Hard-boiled Wonderland*, 38).

Reading this second storyline, as the novel itself suggests, not as a different world but as a way of perceiving the surface life of Watashi, the symbolism is clear: Watashi has built a wall around his orderly existence, shielding it from whatever might threaten it. As he himself states: out of "self-preservation" he has built an "emotional shell" (*Hard-boiled Wonderland*, 192). Within these walls nothing can harm him and nothing can meddle with the order of his existence. Personal contact is kept to a minimum because the Townsfolk address each other only in terms of their function. Like most of Murakami's protagonists, Watashi starts out quite content with this way of life and dreams of continuing it forever, optimizing his routinized, withdrawn existence as pensionado by retreating to a mountain cabin as his own private utopia.

However, as mentioned above, such idealized everydayness never holds in Murakami's stories. The Town has a peculiar entrance fee. Citizens need to part from their shadows, such is the integration policy safeguarding its purity and perfection: "Either you lose the shadow or forget about coming inside" (*Hard-boiled Wonderland*, 62). But one need not mourn one's shadow, the Gatekeeper assures Boku, for shadows are "useless anyway. Deadweight" (*Hard-boiled Wonderland*, 63). For the Town, the human shadow thus constitutes an as of yet undefined inner excess, which threatens its utopic way of life, which can only exist by ridding its citizens of it. As long as the shadow lives, citizens remain internally divided, capricious, unstable and mutable. Yet this separation is not an easy procedure. Although cut off from his shadow early on in the novel, Boku is not immediately integrated. Fighting till its last breath, his cut-off shadow lives on as an autonomous character attempting reunification until the very last pages. In this storyline, the narrator's internal division is thus externalized, allowing for a confrontation between the separated parts. Cut-off from his shadow, Boku is thrown into doubt: should he let his shadow die and become Townsfolk or find some way of saving his shadow and attempt to move beyond the walls. If life without 'internal division' is possible only by cutting off a part of human existence, should he then live life *with* or *without* internal division?

As I remarked above regarding Murakami's fiction as a whole, *Hard-Boiled Wonderland* in particular has been interpreted as a critique of contemporary Tokyo, leading to analyses of the conflict between system and individual and the loss of authentic individuality, represented by the repression of the shadow (Strecher 1999b, 270–285; Dil 2009, 104–7). Read in this vein, there seem to be only two options for its protagonist in confronting his split, either to deny the fracture and hold fast even more tightly to his old, undivided identity or instead try to sow it back together and establish a new identity which is presumably more 'authentic.' And since the protagonist in the end chooses not to reunite with the shadow, *Hard-Boiled Wonderland* is consistently interpreted as a book about failure (Stretcher 1999b, 280; Cassegard 2001, 83; Dil 2009, 106; Dehoux 2012, 285; Stewart 2015, 152). However, looking beyond this socio-cultural problematic to focus on the more abstract ethical plane of developing an attitude toward human existence as a whole, I will argue that a third, more subtle option is at play. Murakami's fiction doesn't reiterate the modern adage of wholeness or 'finding your true identity.' On the contrary it points to an ethical transformation that occurs when the protagonist *abandons* the very ideal of an 'authentic identity'—be it cultural or individual—and embraces the split nature of human life and the spiritual dynamic resulting from it. Interestingly, this allows for a positive appraisal of the ending of the novel. For the sake of brevity, I focus mainly on the second storyline, returning to the first only in establishing some effects of the ethical transformation he undergoes.

Shadow and Mind

First, what does Boku's internal divide consist of? What have the Townsfolk abandoned or ignored in rejecting the shadow? What is this inner excess, this threat to the walled circle of order, comfort, and functionality? Despite the trivializing remark from the Gatekeeper, we immediately sense that with the shadow something real and important is at stake. It has to do with Boku's memory, his (earlier) identity and his 'mind,' all three of which cannot exist without it. The shadowless Townsfolk are without history, personal identity, and mind, and the weaker Boku's own shadow gets, the more he becomes like them. Along with his shadow, he loses his name: "From now on you are the Dreamreader. You no longer have a name" (*Hard-boiled Wonderland*, 39). Symptomatic of his imminent mindlessness are the loss of sight upon which his Dreamreading is conditioned and the confusion he experiences when performing this task. Preparing him to read 'old dreams' every night as part of his integration process, the Gatekeeper 'marks' Boku's eyes by piercing them with a special blade, rendering them incapable of enduring daylight. Presented with the object which he is to dreamread, he becomes confused, for it is the strange white skull of an unknown animal. And although the explanation of the Librarian is simple enough—all he needs to do is lay his hands on the skull and follow with his fingertips the sparks of light that it will emit—he experiences great difficulty in deciphering the dreams. The lights form a "busy current, an endless stream of images" but never a coherent picture and instead "dissipate" into the air (*Hard-boiled Wonderland*, 61; 336).

Eventually, we learn that the skulls belong to the golden beasts, whose function is the absorption of the sparks of mind of the Townsfolk and take them beyond the wall. When they die, traces of mind remain in their skulls which the Dreamreader is to "skim off" (*Hard-boiled Wonderland*, 335). The Town never intended Boku to make sense of these traces, on the contrary, he was to let them disappear into nothing. If he succeeds in doing so, that is, when he has become accustomed to Townlife to such a degree as to become indifferent to the upheavals of spirit, his integration is complete. Yet what should we take 'mind' to mean here? What type of sparks and upheavals does idealized actuality not allow? According to the professor from the first story-line—a kind of scientific wizard responsible for Watashi's brainsurgery—the mind concerns a inexplicable 'spontaneity,' irreducible to the memory structure. It has to do with memories and personal identity, with consciousness and unconsciousness, but they are not synonymous with each other. "Nobody's got the key" to the unconscious and in answer to the question of what constitutes the spontaneity of mind "nobody can come up with a decent answer. … Freud and Jung and all the rest of them published their theories, but all they did was t'invent a lot of jargon t'get people talking" (*Hard-boiled Wonderland*, 257). Despite this indefinability, there is a strategy that allows us to interrogate its meaning in the novel. Since the Townsfolk are explicitly characterized as mindless, the effects of the absence of mind can teach us something about its meaning and value. Moreover, since Boku's shadow and mind are still alive, he can be contrasted with the mindless Townsfolk.

Mind does not equal consciousness: the shadowless Townsfolk still talk, act, and have thoughts. Apparently, mindful or mindless denote not so much doing or thinking, but the *way* in which one relates to or lives one's actions and thoughts. They are attitudes towards existence, distinguished by a subtle yet crucial difference. In one of the first conversations Boku has with the Librarian a tension appears between these different attitudes.

> [Girl:] "To tell the truth, I do not know this thing called 'mind,' what it does or how to use it. It is only a word I have heard."
> "The mind is nothing you use," I say. "The mind is just there. It is like the wind. You simply feel its movements." (*Hard-boiled Wonderland*, 61)

Boku and the mindless Librarian seem to speak different languages. Her ignorance regarding the mind has to do with the way she approaches it: that is to say, from the ideological Town-attitude. She tries to grasp it instrumentally as an object of use and thereby misses it completely. Because the spirit is not something one uses, from her instrumental, functionary perspective it appears an empty word. Boku answers the Librarian in another vocabulary, namely that of presence, sentiment, and movement. This dissonance between mindful and mindless is further problematized in a conversation with the Colonel, who tells Boku that

> Kindness and a caring mind are two separate qualities. Kindness is manners. It is superficial custom, an acquired practice. Not so the mind. The mind is deeper, stronger, and, I believe, it is far more inconstant. (*Hard-boiled Wonderland*, 170)

The Colonel warns Boku not to overvalue the kindness offered him: it is courtesy and custom. Although friendly and pleasant company, his assistance serves mostly to smooth Boku's integration; Boku shouldn't feel the need to change anything and just patiently accustom himself to Townlife: "lay down your mind and peace will come. A peace deeper than anything you have known" (*Hard-boiled Wonderland*, 318). Likewise, regarding the Librarian, he advises Boku not to fall in love with her, for her mindlessness renders her unable to requite his feelings: "You are fond of the girl and I believe she is fond of you. Expect no more" (*Hard-boiled Wonderland*, 170). Love requires something "deeper, stronger, and … far more inconstant" than behaving well: the mind (*Hard-boiled Wonderland*, 170). In conversation with his shadow Boku learns that along with love also sadness, happiness, despair, faith, and solidarity disappear with the demise of the shadow. According to the care-taker of the Town's powerhouse, no-one cares for anything anymore. That is to say, all intensity of desire is reduced to everyday needs. What remains is life as an 'empty shell' or a 'phantom-life'—the negative orientation point of Murakami's ethics.

To conclude, the difference between a life with and a life without mind concerns the presence of intimacy, emotion, meaning, and desire. The Town recognizes only basic needs, and Townlife consists in managing them. Precisely insofar as it is that within us which cannot be reduced to our everyday needs and customs, doesn't align with inclinations toward stability and identity (sameness), but instead involves mutability, spontaneity, direction, and sense beyond self-preservation (faith, despair, happiness, love, intimacy etcetera)—that is, *potentiality* rather than *actuality*—mind is an enemy of the Town. Playing with the limits of things, of what they could be beyond their superficial presentation, mindfulness makes life unpredictable, risky, full of troubles, and renders suffering and disappointment real possibilities. With the disappearance of mind, love becomes courtesy and action becomes doing ones duty in an endless *status quo*. There are thus two modes of life at stake in Murakami's story. One stable, orderly, and content but jaded and mindless. The other dynamic, affectional, and mindful but insecure and transient. Whereas, from the point of view of Townlife, the life without internal division, cares, and desire appears a perfect life, from the perspective of mind and potentiality, the Townlife is revealed in its malaise. The idealized preservation of a stable, orderly, and comfortable life is at the same time the death of everything that enables change, growth, affection, and vitality. This is the dark side of idealized everydayness, of life without internal division. Self-preservation and overemphasized individual identity are exposed as roads toward self-destruction, for they demand the mind as sacrifice and entrap the human being within a self-designed eternal repetition of the same. It constitutes the reduction of human existence to its structured actuality, 'skimming off' all potentiality.

Life in the Woods
Now that the stakes in *Hard-Boiled Wonderland* are clear, let us return to the narrative: what mode of life will the protagonist choose? Despite discouragements (from the Colonel, the Librarian and the Gatekeeper, the professor and his daughter) stating that it is impossible to reunite with his shadow, it is precisely such a patching of the divide that Boku considers when he becomes aware of his loss of identity and separation from actuality. Following the plan of his shadow, he intends to mislead the Gatekeeper, leave the Town, and retrieve his former life and identity. Up until the last pages of the novel, one is led to believe that this is precisely what Boku will do. The story would then have a simple schematic structure: due to some trauma or intense event existence is split, resulting in an alienation which is to be resolved by healing the fracture and retrieving an original unity or wholeness. Yet can such a schema render intelligible the ending of *Hard-boiled Wonderland*? Boku assists his shadow in escaping the Town but ultimately decides not to reunite with him and instead start a life with the library girl in the Woods. What happens here? Wasn't it the case that Boku would lose his identity and his mind—and thus the possibility for love—if he would fail to reunite with his shadow? Has Boku, by retaining a distance to his former self, in the end chosen a mindless life? But then, how is it that his mind survives without such a reunion? Is *Hard-Boiled Wonderland* truly a book about failure?

When we consider the internal divide and existential split between Boku and his shadow the problem, then yes, one might reach that conclusion. When we measure Boku's success by whether or not his old identity and old life are restored, then yes, Boku's choice seems testimony to his failure. However, if we instead understand Boku's split existence not as a to-be-resolved problem, but as the very condition of possibility for a dynamic, mindful life, then suddenly his choice appears in a different light. Instead of opting for one pole of the conflict between a life according to an oppressive system or ideology or an 'autonomous' individuality, he has found *a way out* of this false dilemma. False because it was not simply an external oppressive system (consumer culture, Orwellian government) but at the same time his own exaggerated need for self-preservation and autonomy that captivated him. Both lead to the same result: mindless phantom life. "How can I be sure that self [his former identity, YdB] is worth returning to? Or that world?", Boku reflects near the end of the novel (*Hard-boiled Wonderland*, 333). If my interpretation of Townlife as the symbolical representation of Watashi's *ethos* is correct, then Boku's alienation from his old existence and former identity constitutes not so much a negative moment but a positive one. Boku has slowly begun to realize that it was precisely this former existence and identity that led him to the Town, that led him to building its wall. In order not to become a phantom-being, Boku is not to *restore* his former world, but instead *let it go*, because it was on the verge on solidifying and eternalizing beyond possibility of escape into Townlife. It is precisely this former self that 'skimmed off' sparks of spirit, removing all threats to his way of life: no desire transcending his orderly life, no intimacy, no openness. Instead of disappearing into his own routinized and apathetic existence, he needs to open himself up to the spontaneity of the spirit and transgress his self-built walls. Boku/Watashi does not re-unite with the shadow but instead sets it free, allowing the distance he has gained toward it do its work. Breaking the pattern of his past, the spontaneity of mind is released.

Crucial to this reading is that, despite not reuniting with Boku, the shadow *doesn't die*. On the contrary, "as if heavy shackles have lifted away, I see my shadow regain strength" (*Hard-boiled Wonderland*, 398). Moreover, the divide is not total: "I won't forget you" Boku tells it, which suggests he will stay in touch with his past, with the memories bound to his shadow, yet without *coinciding* with it. In this non-coincidence a new way of life is enabled. Aside from the possibility of turning into a mindless, empty shell *or* subjecting the mind again to his old self, Boku discovers a third option, which does not seek to rectify the existential split: life in the Woods. "Shadows that do not die here can only leave behind incomplete deaths. You'd live out all eternity in the embrace of what's left of your mind. In the Woods'" (*Hard-boiled Wonderland*, 335).

We do not learn much about life in the woods, aside from the fact that the Townsfolk speak warily of the Woodsfolk due to them retaining mind and being internally divided, leading imperfect lives. From their point of view, this makes sense. Because of their internal division, Woodsfolk never precisely know who they are, develop all kinds of desires, undergo transformations through experiences of love and death which all involve risks of suffering, sadness, and disappointment. Yet the Woods are full of life, apple trees, plants, flowers, and food. When Boku takes a walk through the woods

> … there unfolds a mysteriously peaceful world. Infused with the life breath one sense in the wild, the Woods give me release. … Here the trees and plants and tiny living things partake of a seamless living fabric … All shades of misfortune soon dissipate, while the very shapes of the trees and colors of the foliage grown somehow more restive, the bird songs longer and more leisurely. (*Hard-boiled Wonderland*, 147)

Whereas the Town is marked by isolation and sterility, the woods are 'infused with the life breath' and living things 'partake' of the 'living fabric.' This stark contrast clearly suggests that opting for life in the woods is not a failure on Boku/Watashi's end, nor is it a compromise (Strecher 1999b, 280), but instead concerns an ethical modification that allows him to initiate a new, fertile mode of life partaking of a living fabric. If we take seriously what the Professor tells Boku, that the change he is about to undergo does not literally mean the end of the world, but another way of perceiving this very world, of his own actuality, of the very stuff of his life, then we are dealing here with a positive ethical modification. The jaded and isolated individuals become capable of partaking of the spirit of life, not by discovering their authentic individuality or militantly fighting ideological systems, but by becoming receptive and perceptive of the potentiality inhering in things: their ability to be otherwise than they are, to let them affect and move you. Appreciation of the split in existence as a source of vitality, self-preservation, and self-absorption make way for openness.

To support this reading, let me trace the development of Boku's relation with the Librarian girl. Doing so will show that 'what is left of the mind' after the 'incomplete death' of his shadow, is far more then Boku had ever experienced before.

Love and Awakening

> "Is there nothing else I can do for you?" she says, looking up unexpectedly.
> "You do so much for me already," I say.
> She stays her hand and sits facing me. "I mean something else. Perhaps you wish to sleep with me."
> I shake my head.
> "I do not understand," she implores. "You said you needed me." (*Hard-boiled Wonderland*, 225)

The task of the Librarian is to assist Boku in his role as Dreamreader. She polishes the skulls containing the dreams, cooks supper, turns on the heater, and serves tea. Immediately upon meeting her, Boku is attracted to her and in between his dreamreading tries to get to know her. Because the Librarian has lost her shadow as a child, she is so accustomed to Townlife that at first she doesn't know how to respond to Boku's solicitations. Falling in love with her, he searches for modes of contact that surpass her job description, but she is capable only of facilitation. Even when she proposes to share his bed, Boku senses that this is still part of her function. Were he to accept her offer, he would reduce their contact to the domain of servicing basic needs. This would be a way for the Town to "claim my mind" (*Hard-boiled Wonderland*, 225). When she says she doesn't understand Boku's rejection, she uses the word 'need' in a different manner than Boku. Here the difference between mindlessness and mindfulness is again testified: within the boundaries of Townlife, their contact can only be a friendly service (as by a call-girl), whereas outside of it, it may become something else, namely love. Despite the librarian's closed state of mind, however, Boku doesn't give up and eventually discovers a way to reach her by talking about her mother and playing music. When finally she confesses a certain desire to retrieve her mind, Boku gains enough hope that her mind is still there and their love thus still stands a chance. This is the decisive event leading to his choice for a life in the Woods alongside her.

The effects of this event are narrated beautifully. After a long period of disorientation, a dwelling in darkness so deep as to have rendered the light of day unbearable, he succeeds, inspired by his love for the Librarian girl, to reopen his mind. Boku's vision is restored and his confusion as Dreamreader makes way for an intense receptivity: the otherwise dark and gloomy magazine holding the skulls in the library is illuminated by sparks of spirit:

> Clear as starlight, yet a light not from the heavens. It is the room that is aglow ... An ancient fire that has lain dormant in them is now awakening. The phosphorescence yields pure to the eye; it soothes with memories that warm and fill my heart. I can feel my vision healing. Nothing can harm these eyes anymore. ... It is a wonderous sight. Quietude itself. Countless flecks of light fill the space. ... There is your mind, I say. (*Hard-boiled Wonderland*, 369)

Precisely in choosing an open, risky and unpredictable life in the woods, that is, in letting potentiality rather than dry actuality affect him, Boku's eyes are healed and he becomes receptive not only to the upheavals of his own spirit, but also those of the Librarian. Does this mean that now he has a new plan, a new purpose, destiny, or identity? Does he now know who is, healing his fractured existence to finally become whole? No. He retrieves some of his memories, but is not restored to his former self. He wants to lead a life with the Librarian girl, but has no way of knowing what this life will look like. Neither does he know what will happen to his shadow; that is, he doesn't know what relation he will develop toward his past. But by taking leave of his old way of life, a different one is opened up: different in its mode of dwelling. Instead of trying to mend the split, he recognizes it as a vital aspect of human existence, precisely by creating a distance toward his former self and walled existence, a space (the woods) is opened up for life to transpire as potentiality.

In the first storyline, a similar modification takes place in relation to a library girl. Whereas normally Watashi sleeps with women only to fulfill some basic needs within the confines of his solitary existence, when at the end of the novel he finally becomes intimate with her, he awakens from it transformed. The following morning he looks at his clothes:

> These clothes. Up until a little while ago, they were part of me. But no longer. They're different clothes belonging to a different person. I don't recognize them as my own. … I'm not withdrawing into self-reflection. I feel as if I'm turning in on details, on the minute particulars of the world. Snails and the sound of the rain and hardware store displays, things like that. (*Hard-boiled Wonderland*, 374)

Watashi is not 'withdrawing into self-reflection,' meaning this bookend cannot be interpreted as a retreat "into an unconscious inner world" (Dil 2009, 106). Losing his identity, Watashi is instead opened by the spirit. Not to establish a new identity, again closing off potentiality in a well-demarcated 'more true' image of himself, but instead a life receptive of the potentiality inhering in things, of the 'minute particulars of the world.'

Conclusion: Pushing Murakami's Poetico-philosophical Experiment to its Limit

Reading Murakami's fiction as a poetico-philosophical experiment means posing the following questions: 'How does it call into question Being?' and 'In what way might it modify our mode of existence?' By consistently introducing in the relatable orderly, everyday lives of his protagonists experiences of a split in their existence, these lives are jeopardized to such a degree that they can no longer rely on their previous understanding and structuring of existence nor on their securely built and protected self-images. The first result is alienation, disorientation, and the fear of emptiness—a very real fear that might lead to despair and depression, but nonetheless part and parcel of any encounter with love, death, violence, and failure. In relation to this split existence, different modes of existence can be delineated. Firstly, the attempt to deny the experience altogether and stick with the mode of existence I dubbed 'idealized everydayness.' Secondly, the attempt to heal the fracture by rediscovering, reconstructing, or unearthing some sort of 'true self' or authentic individuality. Although most literature on Murakami seems to emphasize this second option—consequently interpreting most of Murakami's fiction as testimony to the failure of modern jaded individuals to establish an authentic or political individuality—this article instead argued for a third option: a mode of existence that neither denies nor heals the fracture, but instead embraces it and discovers through it a mode of receptivity, which we could call a mindful life or a life of spirit. Indeed, the Boku's talk about wanting to discover their true self, about destiny and individuality, and even Murakami himself expresses on multiple occasions his concern for individuality (Cf. Strecher 2014, 3). However, no such true individuality is ever found or formulated by the protagonists, no proper destinies discovered. Yet one should not deduce from this that Murakami's protagonists fail. What fails is only the very ideal of a true and authentic individual identity as the meaning of life. Jonathan Dil rightly questions whether Boku's choice in Hard-boiled Wonderland really concerns a deficit of character, and not rather a "realization that the modernist path, the path advocated by his shadow, is no longer possible?" (Dil 2009, 106). What the novel puts at stake, beyond the character of Boku, is the ideal of 'wholeness' and sovereign individuality itself. Taking this one step further, Murakami even presents an alternative to this ideal. The experience of an existential split makes his protagonists recognize the presence of something that cannot be reduced to their self-image yet intimately concerns them: the mind. Letting go of the modern ideal, potentiality is restored to their reified actuality and another mode of life appears. Beyond cultural or personal trauma's, reification forms the true enemy of Murakami's protagonists, making their partners leave them and turning them into empty shells.

The experience of a split thus constitutes a threat to any stability of human existence, but concerns always at the same time an invitation to initiate life anew: to 'navigate' through it differently. Shattering the certitudes of Murakami's Bokus, they are thrown into a disorienting darkness where the laws and values of their previous existence no longer hold, but only so they might revalue this darkness as the very potential for light—or movement, dance. In this sense, Murakami's fiction time and again speaks of ethical initiation, of the moment self-absorbed human beings recognize their reification, allowing the opportunity to engage life anew. The split existence of Murakami's protagonists, between what they know and what they do not know, between proper and improper, present and past, control and surrender is not the problem of their lives. On the contrary, it is the very *sine qua non* of intimacy, love, openness, joy, and vitality. Their internal divide should not be resolved, their identities need not be restored, they do not necessarily have to get back with their wives or husbands, the divide itself is to be embraced and their former identity let go. Not to become someone completely different, but precisely to let this existence be, to become receptive of what, in this existence, in this present, in these people I meet and desires that stir up within me, move me, affect me, and shape my life. The parallel worlds opened up by the split inherent to existence concern not other worlds, but the very same world, perceived in an indeterminate, unstructured manner, putting the limits of its actuality at issue. The inner split, living together with spirit, here appears as a principle of life: as the condition of change, movement, sensibility and growth. Independent of their political or moral activism, most endings of Murakami's novels are thus neither nihilistic nor escapist, for what is at stake is precisely the possibility of engagement. Whereas their jaded existences might indeed be termed escapist, not so the modification they undergo. And if it is true that in this "healthy distance," from the state of other socio-cultural apparatus that Murakami installs a "space of refuge," as Daniel White writes, then this refuge is found only by abandoning their earlier shell (White 2012, 69).[12] Inhabiting these worlds means inhabiting the open space of non-coincidence with one's actuality. Finally, they are enabled to engage with their memories anew, make contact with their loved ones beyond the ideas and structure—whether cultural or personal—they had encapsulated them within. Finally, they are allowed to experience life as without proper destiny and thereby partake in the 'stream of things,' to hear the wind sing, to feel the presence of spirit.

Some final remarks on this notion of mind. Insofar as the human is more than his conscious image, will and control, there is always a 'part' in him that does not coincide with this image, will and control. But this other part does not have any proper content. It is not 'the person you should have been' or your 'true voice.' We are not dealing here with some hidden essence, or 'core identity' that suddenly exposes itself, a truer but repressed or 'inaccessible' self that now finally lets itself be heard. What is essential is that spirit is *empty*. It has no content of its own and can, therefore, allow all kinds of things to fill it. Spirit marks the human as a being of *potentiality* rather than one that actualizes a destiny or plays out an identity:

---

12   Rebecca Suter also emphasizes a healthy distance installed in Murakami's fiction by questing the boundaries between real and fantasy, recognizing in it a subversive strategy toward ideological systems, which 'does not entail either escaping reality or addressing it through conventional forms of political commitment, but rather engaging it critically by relying on the subversive value of fantastic hesitation' (2016, 70). The 'hesitation' installs a room of non-coincidence rendering possible reflection, critique and change.

> To have all the building blocks of your life in place by that age was, by any standard, a real tragedy. It was as good as sealing yourself into a dungeon. Walled in, with nowhere to go but your own doom. (*Hard-boiled Wonderland*, 163)

Spirit is the open space of difference that exists in every human life between oneself and the content or actuality of one's life. If we would coincide perfectly with ourselves, there would not be space for desire surpassing custom, no room for affection, change, and modification. This may sound abstract but is in truth concrete and experienceable. When confronting death, situations beyond our control, big dilemma's, love—at these moments we sense that who we thought we were and what we thought life to be does not fit anymore, is too limited, one-sided, artificial or out of date in relation to what life now asks of us. Such events enable us to experience the non-coincidence between spirit and the identity-image we have shaped of ourselves. Ethics as ethos, self-relation, concerns at its core the way in which we allow this space to exist, the way we evaluate it and let it affect us. To end in Murakami-style with a phrase from a renowned pop-song:

> There is a crack, a crack in everything, that's how the light gets in.
> ('Anthem,' Leonard Cohen)

References

Agamben, Giorgio. 2010. *The Signature of All Things*, translated by Luca D'Isanto and Kevin Atell. New York: Zone Books.

—. 1999. *Potentialities*, translated by Daniel Heller-Roazen. Stanford: SUP.

Benjamin, Walter. 2011. *Gesammelte Werke II*. Frankfurt: Zweitausendeinds.

Cassegard, Carl. 2001. "Murakami Haruki and the Naturalization of Modernity." *International Journal of Japanese Sociology* 10: 80–92.

De Boer, Ype. 2017. *Murakami en het gespleten leven*. Amsterdam: AUP.

Dehoux, Amaury. 2012. "Murakami et la poétique du monde parallèle." *Poétique* 171: 277–290.

Dil, Jonathan. 2009. "Murakami Haruki's *Hard-boiled Wonderland and the End of the World*: An Allegorical Tale of a Writer's Dilemma in Late-Capitalist Japan." *Sōgōseisakukenkyū* 2(19): 97–107.

Hansen, Gitte M. 2017 "Not Just Asleep, Dead or Muted: Images of Women in Murakami Haruki." *The Japan Society Proceedings* 154: 122–137.

Heiden, Gert-Jan van der. 2019 "Literature as Experiment. The Ontological Commitment of Fiction" *Aesthetic Investigations* 3(1): 47–64.

Murakami, Haruki. 2003a. *The Wind-up Bird Chronicle*, translated by Jay Rubin. London: Vintage.

—. 2003b. *Hard-boiled Wonderland and the End of the World*, translated by Alfred Birnbaum. London: Vintage.

—. 2015. *Pinball 1973*, translated by Ted Goossen. New York: Penguin, epub.

Nietzsche, Friedrich. 2020. *Kritische Studienausgabe 3*. München: De Gruyter.

Rubin, Jay. 2012. *Haruki Murakami and the Music of Words*. London: Vintage.

Stewart, Rachel. 2015. "World Literature and Japan: Tokyo, Worlding and Murakami." *Literature Compass* 12(4): 146–160.

Stretcher, Matthew C. 2014. *The Forbidden Worlds of Haruki Murakami*. Minnesota: MUP.

—. 2002. *Dances with sheep: the quest for identity in the fiction of Murakami Haruki*. Michigan: Center for Japanese Studies.

—. 1999. "Magical Realism and the Search for Identity in the Fiction of Murakami Haruki." *The Journal of Japanese Studies* 25(2): 263–298.

Treat, John W. 2013. "Murakami Haruki and the cultural materialism of multiple personality disorder." *Japan Forum* 25(1) 87–111.

Welch, Patricia. 2005. "Haruki Murakami's Storytelling World." *World Literature Today* 79(1): 55–59.

White, Daniel. 2012. "Heteronomy, Autonomy, Soft Power, Escape: Murakami Haruki's Network Inside Out." *Pan-Japan. The International Journal of Japanese Diaspora. SE: Escaping Japan*, 48–67.

Amber A. Logan

Haruki Murakami's Non-Traditional Portrayals of Shadows and Doppelgängers

Abstract: *In the fiction of Haruki Murakami (most notably in his novel Hard-Boiled Wonderland and the End of the World), shadows and doppelgängers are generally portrayed positively. This tendency is noteworthy, as it places Murakami's portrayals at odds with the negative—or even evil—depictions of shadows and doppelgängers more commonly found in recent literature. In this article, I speculate why Murakami's depictions do not follow the more common Jung-influenced trend of characterizing shadows as negative entities, such as we find in Shūsaku Endō's novel Scandal. I examine three potential reasons: a lack of Jungian psychoanalytical influence on Japanese culture, a disinterest on Murakami's behalf in using pre-established symbolism in his work, and the vagaries of Japanese-English translation which affect how Murakami's conceptualisation of 'shadow' compares to that of English-language writers and readers. My research into each of these areas leads me to conclude that Murakami is aware of Jungian shadows, but chooses to diverge from more conventional portrayals because of his preference for Rorschach inkblot style symbolism—i.e. presenting images that can be defined individually by each reader— and because of the subtle connotations inherent in the Japanese word 'kage' that are not found in the English word 'shadow.'*

Keywords: Haruki Murakami, doppelgänger, shadow, Jung, symbolism, Japanese, translation

Introduction

Shadows and doppelgängers are common symbols of duality in literature, often representing the literalisation of metaphors involving duplication or division of a character's mental or physical state. As such, it is not surprising when works of literature involving shadows and doppelgängers become the subject of critical readings and analysis. The novels and short fiction of Haruki Murakami are no exception.

Haruki Murakami is often spoken of as a man of dualities: a Japanese author and a Westernised/international author, a highbrow (pure literature) creator and a lowbrow (mass literature) creator. Many dichotomies are present in his works, as well: reality/unreality, conscious/unconscious, magic/

commonplace, and East/West (Strecher 2002, 27). In addition, many of these concepts traditionally presented as dichotomies are instead presented as continuums in Murakami's stories; the line between reality and unreality or conscious and unconscious is rarely a stark divider in Murakami's work.

Some of the most pronounced examples of these dualities, dichotomies, and continuums are found in Murakami's explorations of the conscious vs. the unconscious. Murakami's novel *Hard-Boiled Wonderland and the End of the World* (1991) exemplifies these explorations, as the narrative structure is literally split between the 'real' world and the unconscious interior 'fantasy' world of the protagonist. Murakami's *Hard-Boiled Wonderland* also showcases his most profound and extended use of a shadow as an independent (and notably positive) entity. In this article, I will first compare Murakami's positive portrayal of shadows in *Hard-Boiled Wonderland* to Shūsaku Endō's sinister doppelgänger in his novel *Scandal* (1988), and then analyse three possible theories for why Murakami's portrayals of shadows differ from other Jung-inspired shadows in literature.

The Japanese author Shūsaku Endō was a contemporary of Murakami, but the two authors' portrayals of doppelgängers are strikingly different. Endō's novel *Scandal* (originally published in Japan just one year after Murakami's *Hard-Boiled Wonderland*) is reminiscent of the works of Ryūnosuke Akutagawa and Edogawa Rampo both in its blending of Western and Japanese themes and in its presentation of the doppelgänger. *Scandal* is the story of Suguro, a well-respected Catholic author unexpectedly accused of performing sinful deeds around town. Upon investigation, Suguro discovers an exact double of himself performing unsavoury actions while pretending to be him. This story is reminiscent of Akutagawa's "The Shadow," particularly after the reader learns that the doppelgänger is a manifestation of Suguro's suppressed emotions and desires. *Scandal* is also notable in that it references Freudian psychoanalysis and Jungian shadows in direct relation to the storyline, thus bringing together Western psychoanalysis with Japanese doppelgänger fiction. Toward the end of *Scandal,* Suguro comes to terms with the fact the doppelgänger is not just an imposter out to ruin his reputation, but a part of himself:

> Growing old, I have come to see sides of myself I never knew existed start to expose themselves. That hidden self began to appear in my dreams, then in phantom visions, and finally as the imposter you worried so much about—but no, it was not an imposter; it began to live inside me as a separate part of myself. It was my living ghost, a creature so foul I could never mention him to my wife. (Endō 1986, 248–49)

The Japanese-English translator of *Scandal,* Dr. Van C. Gessel (2020), confirmed in a personal correspondence that he did indeed translate "living ghost" in the above passage from Endō's original *"ikiryō,"* confirming that, even in a book with multiple references to psychoanalysis (and a doppelgänger that could serve as a textbook example of negative Jungian shadows), Endō still used a traditional Japanese explanation for his doppelgänger.[13]

Endō's combination of Freudian, Christian, and Japanese elements come together into a compelling story in *Scandal.* These factors are combined particularly masterfully in the scene when the main character, Suguro, is being interviewed on television about the way he portrays "sin" in his own novels:

> "I think there are two aspects of sin […] In order to live in our society, every day we suppress a variety of desires and instinctive urges. There is a sector of the heart that stores up those drives." He pointed to his chest. "It is the realm we call the unconscious […] These suppressed drives and instincts are not extinguished, but collect within the unconscious, waiting for the opportunity to spurt forth once again. When they spew out in some distorted shape, we often end up committing acts that I have chosen to label sins […] In this way, each day we compact our discontent and our resentment into the bottom of our hearts, but they don't just dissolve there. Suppressed passion never dissipates. In reality, these emotions are stored up in our hearts, where they smolder like embers in a hibachi."
> "That seems like a very Freudian view."
> "You could certainly regard it as Freudian […] Those smoldering embers can unexpectedly burst into flame. They can catch fire." (Endō 1986, 96–97)

Suguro is suggesting that, much like in Victorian-era doppelgänger narratives, sometimes it is the suppression of societally inappropriate desires that creates a doppelgänger. This explanation rings particularly true in a society such as Japan that emphasises politeness and collectivism, and which created the concept of *ikiryō,* the literal embodiment of strong emotions without an appropriate outlet.

In comparison to Endō's antagonistic doppelgänger in *Scandal,* Murakami's portrayals of doppelgängers are generally positive and therefore at odds with the negative, or even evil, portrayals of shadows and doppelgängers more commonly found in literature written after Jung's influential theories on shadows permeated the popular consciousness. The negative impression of shadows seems to come, however, from simplified interpretations of Jung's theories as compared to Jung's own words. When one digs deeper into

---

13   *Ikiryō,* usually translated to "living ghost," is a traditional Japanese concept describing a person's psyche separating from his or her body while the person is still alive, usually as a result of extreme emotions (such as love or vengeance).

Jung's theories, one realises that Jung disagreed with the simplistic view that all shadows are evil:

> If the repressed tendencies, the shadow as I call them, were obviously evil, there would be no problem whatever. But the shadow is merely somewhat inferior, primitive, unadapted, and awkward; not wholly bad. It even contains childish or primitive qualities which would in a way vitalize and embellish human existence, but convention forbids! (Jung 2013, 90)

In addition to denying the absolute evil nature of shadows, Jung leaves an opening for shadows to potentially be good, referring to "those rather rare cases where the positive qualities of the personality are repressed, and the ego in consequence plays an essentially negative or unfavourable role" (Jung 2013, 91). I argue that a less nuanced understanding of Jung's theories (as well as the relative rarity of positive qualities being suppressed) has led to a more generalised understanding of Jungian shadows as negative, dark beings in popular culture and fiction.

Another telling distinction between Endō's and Murakami's depictions of doppelgängers is the fact Murakami's characters who lose their shadows are seen as having lost some vital—and usually positive—part of themselves, rather than a repressed aspect of their personality. What Murakami's characters have actually 'lost' differs depending on the story (and, perhaps, on the reader's interpretation),[14] but I would argue that the loss is always painful, and is always some vital piece of self.

Murakami's *Hard-Boiled Wonderland and the End of the World* provides a profound example of this loss. *Hard-Boiled Wonderland* tells the story of a man living in a near-future, cyberpunk Japan who finds himself caught between two rival tech factions, and as a result has a fantasy world created in his unconscious. The story alternates between two narratives (one science fiction and the other fantasy) as the two worlds inevitably converge for the main character. In the fantasy world of his unconscious, the main character (as well as every other character in "the Town") has his shadow cut off and sent to fade away in a makeshift prison. While the main character seems content to stay in the Town, his shadow continually schemes to escape and return both himself and his master back to the 'real' world where they belong. Ultimately, the shadow escapes alone as the main character refuses to leave the fantasy world of his mind behind. Within the narrative it is suggested that the shadow retains all the master's memories and even his 'mind.' Professor of Japanese

---

14   What the character loses when he loses his shadow is somewhat dependent upon the translation, as I discuss below in "The Complexities of Translation" section below.

Studies Susan J. Napier (2005), however, argues that the characters in the fantasy narrative of *Hard-Boiled Wonderland* have lost their past, and suggests that this might be some socio-political commentary on Murakami's behalf regarding "life in modern Japan, a world where 'shadows' of the past are increasingly ignored" (214). Murakami scholar Dr Matthew C. Strecher suggests that Murakami characters who lose their shadows and "minds" have lost their sense of personal identity[15] (Strecher 2014, 49). Whatever the interpretation, the loss of a shadow in a Murakami story is tragic, but ultimately survivable.

But why are Murakami's portrayals different? Multiple potential explanations come to mind, including: a lack of Jungian psychoanalytical influence on Japanese culture, a disinterest on Murakami's behalf in other people's use of symbolism, and the vagaries of translation affecting how Murakami's conceptualisation of 'shadows' compares to an English-language writer.

Jungian Psychoanalysis in Japanese Culture

My first step in understanding Murakami's level of familiarity with Jung's theories was to search for references to Freud, Jung, or psychoanalysis in any of Murakami's works or interviews. Associate Professor of Foreign Languages Jonathan Dil suggests that Jung's influence on the cultural milieu of Japan in the 1970s was such that it would be difficult to assume his theories did not have some influence on Murakami's works[16] (Dil 2007, 71), and my own research supports this assertion. I found not only multiple references to Jung and psychoanalysis within Murakami's fiction, speeches, and interviews, but also quite the researcher's goldmine in a lengthy transcript (published in book form) of conversations between Murakami and Hayao Kawai, a trained Jungian psychoanalyst credited with introducing Jungian psychology to Japan. The book, aptly titled *Haruki Murakami Goes to Meet Hayao Kawai* (2016), documents conversations on topics ranging from marriage to translation to violence in society. While Murakami and Kawai do not engage with psychoanalysis directly, they do discuss psychotherapy and Murakami delves into the psychology of his own writing process.

In addition to finding Freud and Jung references in interviews with Murakami, casual mentions of the two famous psychologists appear in several of

---

15   Curiously, the characters in *Hard-Boiled Wonderland* are only considered to have fully "lost" their shadows when their shadows have literally died—and those who have merely been separated from their still-living shadows are in a strange limbo state.

16   The Jungian references in Endō's *Scandal* also support the assertion that Jung's theories were known in Japan in the 1970s and 80s.

Murakami's works, though often in a joking context. Murakami's most recently translated novel, *Killing Commendatore* (2018), alludes to psychoanalysis in a scene where the main character is viewing a painting and joking about how it might be interpreted:

> I shook my head and smiled a wry smile. I mean, how Freudian can you get? I imagined some egghead critic fulminating on the drawing's psychological implications: 'This black, gaping hole, so reminiscent of a woman's solitary genitalia, must be understood functionally, as a symbolic representation of the artist's memories and unconscious desires.' (Murakami 2018, 381)

In this scene, Murakami seems to be poking fun at psychoanalysis and overt symbolism, displaying an attitude consistent with his insistence that when he writes he does not use symbols with a specific meaning in mind,[17] preferring to leave interpretation up to the reader, as will be discussed in the section below.

Although my research made it clear Murakami is familiar with Jung and psychoanalysis, Murakami insists he does not take a Jungian approach to his conceptualisation of the unconscious. Murakami is firm in emphasising that he does not understand what his own stories mean—nor does he try to analyse them personally. Murakami has said that he does not set out to write a novel with a particular message in mind, but rather he writes novels "to discover the messages within me" (Murakami and Kawai 2016, 62).[18] Although Strecher (2002) maintains that Murakami's explorations of the conscious/unconscious divide are rife with opportunities for psychoanalysis, Dil points out that Murakami is known for downplaying any Jungian influences on his stories, stating "though he [Murakami] is more than happy to acknowledge his admiration for such Jungian inspired figures as Japanese psychologist Kawai Hayao and American mythologist Joseph Campbell, when it comes to Jung himself, he is much more guarded" (Dil 2007, 69). Dil also quotes Murakami as saying, "I certainly do not hold any sympathy for Jung's thought; in fact, I've hardly even read him" (Ibid.). Despite Murakami's protestations, Robert Hinshaw, editor of *Haruki Murakami Goes to Meet Hayao Kawai*, states in the

---

17   Translator Dr. Jay Rubin describes a Harvard class discussion illustrating this point: "When the students were asked what they thought the undersea volcano symbolised, Murakami interrupted to insist that the volcano was *not* a symbol: it was a volcano … and a lively debate ensued. Murakami's response was characteristically ingenuous: 'Don't *you* see a volcano in your mind when *you* get hungry? I do.' He was hungry when he wrote the story; hence, the volcano: it was as simple as that" (cited in Rubin 2012, 135).

18   For a man who eschews Jung's theories, this is a surprisingly Jungian approach to artistic creation—a concept I will discuss in my section on Murakami's Symbolism.

book's preface that after Kawai's death, Murakami's "interest in C.G. Jung led him to visit Küsnacht[19] and the Jung Institute" (Murakami and Kawai 2016, 10), suggesting an interest in the man's life, if not his theories.

Although Murakami denies intentional use of Jungian archetypal images or theories in his work, he has been known to employ Jungian terminology when discussing the confrontation with his own (notably Jungian) shadow as part of his writing journey:

> When I write novels myself, I encounter a totally unexpected vision of myself, which must be my own shadow. What's required of me then is to portray this shadow as accurately, and candidly, as I can. Not turning away from it. Not analyzing it logically, but rather accepting it as a part of myself. But it won't do to lose out to the shadow's power. You have to absorb that shadow, and without losing your identity as a person, take it inside you as something that is part of you. (cited in *Flood* 2016)

For a man who has said "I certainly do not hold any sympathy for Jung's thought" (cited in Dil 2007), these descriptions of an author confronting his own shadow—the dark, unseen version of one's self—are surprisingly Jungian. Murakami's willingness to discuss Jungian theories as they pertain to writing contrasts with his protestations about using Jungian theories and symbolism in his stories.

Murakami's Symbolism

> I don't read much Jung, but what he writes has some similarity with my writing. To me the subconscious is terra incognita. I don't want to analyze it, but Jung and those people, psychiatrists, are always analyzing dreams and the significance of everything. I don't want to do that. I just take it as a whole. (Murakami, cited in Miller 1997)

After uncovering proof of Murakami's familiarity with Jung, I decided to further investigate his use of symbols, returning to my postulation that Murakami's non-traditional portrayal of shadows is related to his tendency to utilise his own idiosyncratic symbols. This theory seems to hold true, particularly when considered alongside Murakami's rejection of Jungian interpretations of symbols. While some of Murakami's symbols (such as his use of wells)[20] are more conventional, others—such as his use of sheep, most notably in *A Wild Sheep Chase* (1989)—are designed for individualised interpretation.

---

19   The Swiss city where Jung's world-famous clinic was located.
20   When asked in an interview whether he had ever tried to sit in a well like one of the characters in his books, Murakami responded with: "No. But I've always been attracted by wells, very much. Every time I see one, I go over and look in" (cited in Miller 1997).

Murakami's translator Dr. Jay Rubin (2012) maintains that Murakami's idio-syncratic use of symbols is indeed purposeful:

> Murakami stubbornly insists that the images in his work are not symbols and that he him-self does not understand their 'meanings.' They come out of his unconscious, he says, almost like automatic writing, and any reader's interpretation is as valid as his own […] The very act of identifying a symbol and defining it, as far as Murakami is concerned, drains it of much of its potential power. He would prefer to leave it alone and let it do its work, undefined, in the mind of each reader. (Rubin 2012, 493)

This idea of artists mining their subconscious is itself a very Jungian concept; Jung (1978) argued that "it might well be that the poet, while apparently cre-ating out of himself and producing what he consciously intends, is neverthe-less so carried away by the creative impulse that he is no longer aware of an 'alien' will" and that "the poet's conviction that he is creating in absolute freedom would then be an illusion: he fancies he is swimming, but in reality an unseen current sweeps him along" (Jung 1978, 74). Even the idea that the author should not have to explain (or even understand) his own symbols is supported by Jung:

> Being essentially the instrument of his [the artist's] work, he is subordinate to it, and we have no right to expect him to interpret it for us. He has done his utmost by giving it form, and must leave the interpretation to others and to the future. A great work of art is like a dream; for all its apparent obviousness it does not explain itself and is always am-biguous. (Jung 1978, 104)

While Murakami denies any affinity for Jung's philosophies, his personal un-derstanding of his own artistic process appears very much aligned with Jung's ideas on the subject.

Despite Murakami's insistence that he does not use purposeful symbols in his work, there is no shortage of critics and scholars willing to analyse Mu-rakami's works—and Murakami's symbolism—today. Strecher remarks that when his first book studying Murakami's works came out in 2002, "many were skeptical that Murakami was worthy of such critical attention" but by the time his more recent *The Forbidden Worlds of Haruki Murakami* (2014) was published, the scholarly attention Murakami was receiving had greatly in-creased (cited in Flanagan 2018). According to Damian Flanagan (2018), con-tributing writer for the *Japan Times*, "these days, the diversity of critical re-search on Murakami is startling—you can read studies on the role of food in Murakami's stories (there are entire menus in Japan inspired by Murakami) or delve into research on the types of religious cults depicted in *1Q84*." As often happens in the world of literature, critics are ready to analyse

Murakami's work regardless of whether Murakami feels his books are appropriate for critical analysis.

Although I do credit Murakami's aversion to premeditated symbolism for some of his unconventional portrayals of shadows, one cannot discount the roles language and translation play in the interpretation of symbols, as will be discussed in the next section.

The Complexities of Translation

Another possible explanation for Murakami's unconventional portrayals of shadows is the differing connotations of several key words in Japanese (primarily *kage* and *kokoro*) versus their English counterparts. The fact that Murakami himself is a translator of fiction (from English to Japanese) is of note, as it suggests he is cognizant of how his own words might be translated into English, and how the differing connotations can affect reader interpretations. Dr. Jay Rubin remarks about the use of *kage* in the preface to his translation of Natsume Sōseki's Japanese classic *Sanshiro*, saying "Sōseki often uses the word *kage*, which can also mean 'image' or 'reflection' or 'the hidden side' of an object, to convey these dark hints almost subliminally. The English text employs the word 'shadow' somewhat more frequently than strictly idiomatic translation would require" (Sōseki and Rubin 2009, xlvii). Translator Charles Inouye, in his introduction to Kyōka Izumi's *In Light of Shadows* (2005, 3) also emphasises the varied spectrum of meanings the Japanese word *kage* can suggest: from shade (as in the shade of a tree), to light (as in *tsukikage*, "moonlight"). While the English word 'shadow' does have additional connotations beyond literal shadows cast by physical objects,[21] the Japanese word *kage* is arguably more nuanced.

The Japanese language contains many words without straightforward English equivalents. The term *kokoro* (generally translated into English as 'heart') is another great example.[22] As Murakami translator Ted Goossen remarks regarding *Hard-Boiled Wonderland* (originally translated by Alfred Birnbaum), "There, the hero loses his *kokoro* when his shadow is forcibly detached from his body [...] In English, however, the hero is trying to save his *mind*, a word that subtly alters the emotional and spiritual aspects of his dilemma" (Goossen 2013, 186). Also speaking about *Hard-Boiled Wonderland*, translator Dr. J. Philip Gabriel (2020), in a personal email, suggested that even the

---

21   It is interesting to note that "shadow" translates into Jung's native German as "Schatten"—a word whose definition does not differ significantly from the English.

22   Strecher (2014) points out that he has translated *kokoro* as "inner self" or even "soul" depending on the context (243).

precedent set by previous translators might affect how a translator handles specific words, stating that "Birnbaum translated the term [*kage*] as shadow in 'Hardboiled' so I think that influenced later translators such as myself, though I am not sure how else to translate *kage*." At the time of this writing, translator Jay Rubin is working on a new translation of *Hard-Boiled Wonderland* (Kosaka 2020). In a personal email (2020), I asked Dr. Rubin about the changes he would be making in this new *Hard-Boiled Wonderland* translation, and he informed me that in his version "*kage* is still 'shadow,' but *kokoro* is changing from 'mind' to 'heart,'" supporting Goossen's stance that "mind" does not adequately encapsulate Murakami's original intentions.

These vagaries of translation can affect how the reader perceives the text, as even slight word changes ('mind' vs. 'heart' vs. 'shadow') can greatly change the symbolism and therefore very meaning of a narrative. Strecher (2020), in a private email, explained his perspective on "shadows" as well as the use of *kage* and *kokoro*:

> My read of the image [...] has always been that the 'shadow' represents the metaphysical aspects of our identity, i.e., the non-physical [...] I have always believed that 'mind' would be a better word for Murakami to use, but somehow, the Japanese terms for this— *seishin* (emotion; psyche), *jiko* (self), and so on, just don't do the job. Murakami may have felt that *kage* was good when he wrote *Hard-boiled Wonderland* because it was abstract enough to make a good literary symbol. Perhaps he opted not to use *kokoro* (heart) because it might well be associated with Natsume Sōseki's much more famous novel by that title. Yet this would have been a good choice, because *kokoro* carries the 'baggage' of our memories, emotions, feelings, sensations—in short, 'mind.' Or maybe he felt it would simply not work. I mean, can you imagine the scene in which the shadow is removed in *Hard-boiled Wonderland*?[23] And how would you represent *kokoro* in this instance? It has no visible form. This may be why, while dissatisfied with the term *kage* in Japanese, it was just a little less bad than everything else.

I found Strecher's explanation of the differences between *kage* and *kokoro*[24] quite helpful in highlighting not just why Murakami likely chose to use *kage* in *Hard-Boiled Wonderland* but also the difficulties translators face when translating high-context words from Japanese to English.

The subtleties of translation between Japanese and English can create different understandings of a work, as a word in Japanese might have additional connotations not found in the English version. For example, Strecher

---

23   In *Hard-Boiled Wonderland* the main character's shadow is literally cut off with a knife.

24   Further blurring the lines between the concepts of *kokoro* and *kage*, Strecher (2014, 242) points out that Murakami has, in more recent years, moved away from using the term *kage* (expressing dissatisfaction with the English translation to "shadow") in favor of using *kokoro* or even *tamashii* ("soul").

(2014) points out that the Japanese pronounce "id" (Freud's term for the amoral, instinct-driven part of the brain) as *ido*—which happens to be a homonym for "well" in Japanese (72–73). Wells (along with other literal or figurative dark pits) are common in Murakami's narratives—most notably *The Wind-Up Bird Chronicle* (1997) and *Killing Commendatore*—usually as gateways to some liminal space between the real, conscious world and the "other" worlds of the unconscious (Ibid.). This subtle connotation behind the word *"ido"* in Japanese is not found in the English equivalent, which gives the English reader a subtly different experience than the person reading in the original Japanese. Understanding that the translation of a word can affect the interpretation of the entire work has led me to a greater appreciation of the difficulties facing Japanese-English translators, as well as a more nuanced understanding of why Murakami's *kage* deviates from more conventional portrayals of shadows.

Conclusion

My examination of doppelgängers in literature made me speculate why Murakami's shadows do not follow the conventional trend—in response to popular, yet superficial, understandings of Jung's original theories—of depicting shadows as purely negative. I came up with three potential reasons: a lack of exposure to Jung's theories, a reluctance to use pre-established symbolism in his work, and the vagaries of translation affecting the transmittal of ideas between author and reader. My research into each of these areas led me to conclude that Murakami seems quite aware of Jungian shadows, but chooses to portray his own shadows differently because he prefers to use Rorschach inkblot style symbolism—i.e. presenting images that can be defined individually by each reader (Rubin 2012, 34)—and because of the subtle connotations inherent in the word 'kage' that are not found in the English word 'shadow.' By analysing Murakami's use of shadows, one can better understand not just Murakami's singular writing style but also the complexities inherent in Japanese to English translation of literature.

References

Dil, J.P. 2007. *Murakami Haruki and the search for self-therapy.* Ph.D. University of Canterbury.

Endō, Shūsaku. 1988. *Scandal.* Translated by Van C Gessel. New York: Dood, Mead.

Flanagan, Damian. 2018. "Haruki Murakami: Literary Lightweight or Global Superstar?" Japan Times, March 24, 2018. https://www.japantimes.co.jp/culture/2018/03/24/books/haruki-murakami-literary-lightweight-global-superstar/#.XlljfihKjIU.

Flood, A. 2006. "Haruki Murakami cautions against excluding outsiders." *The Guardian*, [online] 1 November. Available at: <https://www.theguardian.com/books/2016/nov/01 haruki-murakami-hans-christian-andersen-prize-speech-outsiders> [Accessed 10.12.2019].

Gabriel, J.P. 2020. *Discussion on Murakami translation.* [email] (Personal communication, 22 February 2020).

Gessel, V. 2020. *Discussion on Shūsaku Endō translation.* [email] (Personal communication, 14 May 2020).

Goossen, Ted. 2013. *Haruki Murakami and the Culture of Translation.* Edited by Esther Allen and Susan Bernofsky. In Translation. Columbia University Press. https://doi.org/10.7312/alle15968.18.

Izumi, Kyōka, and Charles Shirō Inouye. 2005. *In Light of Shadows.* Honolulu, HI: Univ. of Hawai'i Press.

Jung, C. G. 2013. *The Essential Jung.* Princeton: Princeton University Press. https://www.jstor.org/stable/j.ctt46n45n.

———. 1978. *The spirit in man, art, and literature.* Princeton: Princeton University Press.

Kosaka, K. 2020. "Jay Rubin: an academic's path to translation." *The Japan Times,* [online] 22 August 2021. Available at: <https://www.japantimes.co.jp/culture/2020/08/22/books/jay-rubin-translator/> [Accessed 24 August 2020].

Miller, L. 1997. "Haruki Murakami." *Salon,* [online] Available at: <https://www.salon.com/1997/12/16/int_2/> [Accessed 1 October 2020].

Murakami, Haruki. 2018. *Killing Commendatore.* Translated by Philip Gabriel and Ted Goossen. New York: Alfred A. Knopf.

———. 1991. *Hard-Boiled Wonderland and the End of the World: A Novel.* Tokyo; New York: Kodansha International; Distributed in the U.S. by Kodansha America.

———. 1989. *A Wild Sheep Chase.* Translated from Japanese by A. Birnbaum. New York: Kodansha America.

Murakami, Haruki, and Hayao Kawai. 2016. *Haruki Murakami Goes to Meet Hayao Kawai.* Winsiedeln, Switzerland: Daimon Verlag.

Napier, Susan. 2005. *The Fantastic in Modern Japanese Literature.* Nissan Institute/Routledge Japanese Studies. Taylor and Francis. https://doi.org/10.4324/9780203974636.

Rubin, Jay. 2020. *Discussion on Murakami translation.* [email] (Personal communication, 12 January 2020).

————. 2012. *Haruki Murakami and the Music of Words.* London [England]: Vintage Books.

Sōseki, Natsume, and Jay Rubin. 2009. *Sanshirō.* London: Penguin Books.

Strecher, Matthew. 2020. *Discussion on Murakami translation.* [email] (Personal communication, 19 February 2020).

————. 2014. *The Forbidden Worlds of Haruki Murakami.* Minneapolis: University of Minnesota Press.

————. 2002. *Dances with Sheep: The Quest for Identity in the Fiction of Murakami Haruki.* Ann Arbor, MI: Center for Japanese Studies/University of Michigan.

Gemma Scammell

The Cityscape and Haruki Murakami's Despondent Characters: the use of magical realism in the creation of heterotopic space

Abstract: *Throughout his writing career, Haruki Murakami has continually provided us with characters that critique capitalism and suffer a sense of disillusionment with their immediate surroundings. These characters wander dark cityscapes, searching for spaces of refuge and resistance as they stumble through their quests. Using the novels, The Wind-up Bird Chronicle (1994), Hard-Boiled Wonderland and the End of the World (1985), and Dance Dance Dance (1988), I propose that these characters live on the outskirts of society. They exist in a state of despondence, living in various states of withdrawal, and struggle to find spaces of belonging. Trapped in cities that they fail to feel a part of, the characters seek out spaces that draw parallels to Foucault's heterotopia. This essay will propose that these spaces, such as the utopic town of Hard-Boiled Wonderland, the well in The Wind-Up Bird Chronicle, and the Dolphin Hotel in Dance, Dance, Dance, are heterotopias of resistance and refuge. Using Wendy B. Faris and Lois Parkinson Zamora's definition of magical realism, I shall explore how Murakami uses the magical in his depiction of heterotopic space. At the heart of these spaces is their reason for existing as a counter site to the dehumanising effects of mass consumerism capitalism.*

Keywords: cityscape, capitalism, consumerism, heterotopia, magical realism

Introduction

Haruki Murakami (b. 1949) has long been established as a serious writer whose works depict the negative effects of late capitalism on the individual. His books, of which there are over twenty (short story collections and novels), have been translated into over fifty languages and sold in their millions. His most recent publication, a short story collection, *First Person Singular* (2021), reached 11th on *The New York Times* best-seller list. Much of his work has been adapted into plays, TV and films. Last year, the film adaptation of the short story *Drive My Car* premiered at the Cannes Film Festival (2021), winning multiple awards. There is little doubt that his works, should he continue writing, will receive much well-earned attention. Yet his writing style, the technique he employs and his often nameless protagonist haven't really changed.

While there are some exceptions, such as Aomame (a female protagonist with a strong grip on her identity), the majority of Murakami's protagonists are young to middle-aged men suffering from varying levels of alienation and despondency. These characters live on the margins of society and continually feel as though they don't belong. While some are lured into a capitalist lifestyle, seduced by its glamour, ultimately, they find the price of such a lifestyle is the loss of their *shutaisei*.[25] These *Bokus*[26] are continually swept up in events out of their control. They are confused, hurt and lost. Yet readers keep turning the page and, for the most part, come away with a sense of Murakami's brilliance. His settings are realistic copies of Tokyo that are easily identifiable. Yet within his cityscapes are distinct pockets of alterity. These sites are heterotopias—a type of space that is radically different from the space surrounding it. Using magical realism, Murakami weaves the familiar with the impossible and creates distinctly other spaces.

Magical Realism

Wendy B. Faris and Lois Parkinson Zamora define magical realism as a mode of storytelling "suited to exploring—and transgressing—boundaries, whether the boundaries are ontological, political, geographical, or generic" (1995, 5). Faris outlines five key principles that define magic realist texts, separating them from works of fantasy. In her first and second principle, Faris emphasises all magical elements must be described in a realist way despite not being possible according to our understanding of reality (1995, 167–169). Thirdly, the reader may be subjected to doubt, and the distinction between reality and dream can become blurred as the reader tries to understand what the character has experienced (Faris 1995, 171). In her fourth principle, Faris states, "we experience the closeness or near-merging of two realms, two worlds" (1995, 172). Finally, "these fictions question received ideas about time, space, and identity [...]. Magical realism reorients not only our habits of time and space, but our sense of identity as well" (Faris 1995, 173–174). These principles resonate with Murakami's narrative style. He continually presents his readers with complex, impossible spaces as his characters cross into unknown worlds where their comprehension of time and reality is distorted. These characters

---

25   *Shutaisei* refers to one's core self or identity.
26   In multiple texts Murakami avoids naming male protagonists but refers to them as '*Boku*', the Japanese term for the first-person pronoun 'I'. Murakami also uses the term '*Watashi*', which is the more formal pronoun for 'I'.

either search out or stumble into these spaces as they embark on quests to establish their own sense of identity and find their place in society.

Magical realism originated in Europe during the Weimar Republic. It is largely credited to the German art critic Franz Roh, who coined the term to describe the return from abstract to realist painting. For Roh, these paintings expressed the mysteries of life through their "depictions of the material world" (Bowers 2005, 11). The term was later applied to literature and spread through Latin America. Writers such as Gabriel García Márquez, Alejo Carpentier and Jorge Luis Borges, to name but a few, are all credited with launching the term onto the global stage. Initially, the first depictions of magical realism in literature appeared in postcolonialism fiction, resulting in critics tying its definition to the genre and causing confusion. Critics such as Stephen Slemon have sought to clarify why magical realism is such a slippery term to define in literature. He argues:

> In none of its applications to literature has the concept of magic realism ever successfully differentiated between itself and neighbouring genres such as fabulation, metafiction, the baroque, the fantastic, the uncanny, or the marvellous, and consequently it is not surprising that some critics have chosen to abandon the term altogether. (Slemon 1995, 407)

As outlined by Slemon, magical realism transcends traditional genre boundaries. Magic realism has appeared in multiple works, regardless of whether its presence is highlighted. However, considering magical realism as a mode of writing rather than a genre permits writers to use "magical realist devices to enhance the expressive potential of their chosen genre" (Zamora and Farris 1995, 5). Magical realism has travelled the globe and crossed cultural divides as a mode of expression. While it is very popular in postcolonial works, I argue that magical realism is not limited to this type of fiction but transcends traditional genre boundaries. Magical realism is a crucial aspect of Murakami's writing style. As argued by Matthew Strecher, Murakami does not place the "political attachments that Carpentier and Flores would insist upon" in his depiction of magical realism (Strecher 1999, 269). But uses it to explore the "severe […] identity crisis among Japanese of Murakami's age and younger" (Strecher 1999, 265). Attributing the crisis to the economic boom that followed Japan's post-war years, Murakami explores the dehumanising effects of late-capitalism upon the individual.

Foucault's Heterotopia

Michel Foucault (1926–1984) was a French philosopher, historian and literary critic. Among his many interests was the formation of networks of power used to create and ensure social control. After appearing on a radio show about utopia, he was asked to give a lecture repeating his talk to a group of architects. The lecture resulted in the somewhat delayed publication 'Of Other Spaces' (1986), which is now the primary source of Foucault's heterotopology. Within the essay, Foucault outlines a space of alterity that forms in response to networks of power. This type of space opposes the dominant ideological and social order. These heterotopias are fundamentally different from the surrounding space. Since its publication, the spatial theory has successfully been applied to an array of disciplines, largely in part to the term openness resulting from unclarity on Foucault's part as to whether he meant the spatial theory to be a form of literary criticism or an urban concept. What can be said with certainty is that heterotopic spaces are sites of alterity.

I propose that heterotopias are sites born out of society's need for other space. These spatial pockets oppose the dominant social and ideological order making them primarily sites of refuge and resistance. Although heterotopology has been applied successfully to multiple fields, including urban studies and human geography, I am using it as a term of literary analysis. My application is similar to Foucault's, whose consideration of the space created in the fiction of magical realist writer Jorges Luis Borges triggered his thinking of other spaces. Borges' literary piece can be credited for initiating Foucault's heterotopology, so it seems fitting that I, too, am using the concept to consider a fellow magical realist writer.

Borges' fictional encyclopaedia, *Celestial Emporium of Benevolent Knowledge*, found in *The Analytical Language of John Wilkins* (1952), contained a list of the Emperor's animals that organised them in such a way that Foucault was profoundly unsettled:

> That passage from Borges kept me laughing for a long time, though not without a certain uneasiness that I found hard to shake off. Perhaps because there arose in its wake the suspicion that there is a worse kind of disorder than that of the incongruous, the linking together of things that are inappropriate; I mean the disorder in which fragments of a large number of possible orders glitter separately in the dimension, without law of geometry, of the heteroclite; and that word should be taken in its most literal, etymological sense so very different from one another that it is impossible to find a place of residence for them, to define a common locus beneath them all. (Foucault 1966, xix)

What Foucault first took to be merely amusing soon triggered a degree of uncertainty. Borges' encyclopedia altered the way Foucault thought about space, and he realised the natural order could be questioned within the realm of literature. The heteroclite allows other orders that can challenge our understanding of space and force us to realise that space is not a void but a complex entity that impacts our very being.

It's a hard-boiled wonderland at the end of the world

Murakami's *Hard-Boiled Wonderland and the End of the World* (1985) conveys a cityscape that is a possible future reality should mass consumer capitalism and technological advancements continue. In this futuristic city, two rival corporations are caught in a technological race to alter the human brain into the ultimate data storage device, effectively turning people's minds into hard-wired computer drives. The protagonist, Watashi, is a government employee known as a Calcutec who opted for a procedure to have a black box inserted into his brain so that he can store and transport confidential data safely. However, he is betrayed by the government and given to the Professor, the scientist in charge of the experiment who secretly continues his research beyond the initial procedure by altering Watashi's memories and inserting false ones.

Caught in a crisis of morality, the Professor confesses his actions and explains that Watashi was, out of the twenty-six test subjects, capable of operating two streams of consciousness. Effectively, he has been dividing his time between the two identities, "it's as if you descended to the elephant factory floor beneath your consciousness and built an elephant with your own hands. Without you even knowin'!" (Murakami 1985, 268). The creation of the town is Watashi's act of resistance to the harsh reality of life in the city. It is his heterotopia, a place that is different from the city on every level. In an attempt to redeem himself, the Professor tried to protect Watashi from the System, who now sought to remove the junctions and wiring inside his brain and use it as a blueprint for further research. But the destruction of his lab and theft of essential equipment leaves the Professor without the necessary tools. Watashi's consciousness will soon short-out and transfer him permanently to the other junction box. Watashi will no longer be able to return to his life in the city but will "enter another world" (Murakami 1985, 273). A dream world in the form of an archaic town.

Watashi's subconscious creates the town as a refuge from his life in the city. The town is his heterotopia, a space of compensation where he can experience a life devoid of capitalism. Within the city, Watashi leads a solitary life. He has no friends or interests and shows little remorse when his apartment is broken into and trashed. Other than a new acquaintance with a librarian, he has nothing tying him to the city. Like most of Murakami's protagonists, Watashi suffers from despondency and merely exists rather than actively lives. His disillusion increases upon learning that the Professor's experimental brain surgery altered his memories and created new ones leaving him to question who he really is.

The town, a small, impoverished and isolated community, presents as a haven from the city. It lacks any form of technological advancement operating with only minimal electricity provided by a small wind-power station. There is no system of government and no clear leader. There is also no clear ideology, and capitalism does not exist in the town. People work for the joy of working and not for monetary gains. The town could be considered a utopia in its complete opposition to the harsh, repressive city. However, instead of being located on an island that one must first undertake an arduous journey to reach (which is the classical Thomas More location for the utopia), the town exists within Boku's subconscious and blooms as an impossible space deep inside his mind. In doing so, it mirrors Foucault's theory on utopia, which he argued to be "sites with no real place" (Foucault 1986, 24). Within the town, Boku is cast into the role of the unenlightened visitor, which Alcena M. D. Rogan argues as "an important distinction because it signals an increasingly disenchanted worldview: these utopias do not encompass or constitute The World, but are rather one spatio-temporal zone located on the perimeter of a fallen contemporary world" (2009, 311). Watashi's increasing feelings of despondency make the town, with its complete lack of consumer capitalism which had infected every aspect of life in the city, all the more appealing. Within his mind, Watashi has created a society "in a perfected form, or else society turned upside down" by eradicating capitalism (Foucault 1986, 24).

Multiple utopian visions seek to either remove capitalism altogether or reduce its negative aspects. These works continually identify desire as the central aspect to be resolved before a functioning utopia devoid of the negative side of consumer capitalism can be achieved. Aldous Huxley's *Brave New World* (1932) achieves such a utopia. In Huxley's cityscape, the inhabitants are socially ranked whilst in the embryo stage. Alphas are the elite, upper class who hold the most respectable positions, whereas Gammas are tasked with cleaning and maintenance. Money is non-existent. People work because it is their place in society, and no one questions their placement. Huxley's society works because he has solved the problem of desire by controlling the populace with a highly addictive drug. People are "reduced to a servile condition by means of mass-suggestion, hypnopaedia and drugs, without any overt brutality or cruelty and without any conscious suffering" (Rees 1961, 116). While Huxley has removed the relentless pursuit of monetary gains, he has kept individuality and desire but controlled these aspects by making the populace addicted to soma.

Murakami also recognises the problem of desire. Within the city, the populace is controlled through mass consumerism capitalism. The System secretly splits, creating a pretend rival company called the Semiotecs. Together these corporations generate competition and drive consumer profits. The city's people are free to pursue their individuality because it is focused on consumerism. In the town, however, Murakami subverts the issue of individual desire by removing the inhabitants' individuality. Murakami uses his trademark magical realism to place the individual's core consciousness into their shadow. While the brain maintains bodily functions, the shadow holds the conscious mind. Without the shadow, the person is forced to function without a mind and unable to think or grasp concepts. In essence, they are reduced to blank slates.

The town is Boku's answer to the suffering he endured in the city as Watashi. He has removed capitalism, which, in the city, has created rival corporations whose war he had inadvertently become caught up in. Yet he has not removed the need to work completely and recognises that "work is no hardship. Better than having nothing to do" (Murakami 1985, 39). He has removed the need for violence by removing its root cause—emotion. He has created a society free from the tools of social control and the competitive demands of mass consumer capitalism that are associated with it. The town is, therefore, his space of compensation:

> No one hurts each other here, no one fights. Life is uneventful, but full enough in its own way. Everyone is equal. No one speaks ill of anyone else, no one steals. They work, but they enjoy their work. It's work purely for the sake of work, not forced labor. No one is jealous of anyone. There are no complaints, no worries. (Murakami 1985, 333)

By stripping the townspeople of their ego, Boku has effectively removed the horrors Watashi was subjected to in the city. Without the ability to feel, the townspeople have become robotic. In this sense, the town is more posthuman than the city. They "have no ego, no self," and therefore no will to compete, harm or endanger each other (Murakami 1985, 359). They live in harmony with each other because they cannot be any other way. Their lack of emotion is central to the town's ideological outlook. While the town presents itself as a utopia, it is not perfect, nor should it "be confused with the idea of perfection, one of its most recognisable traits is its speculative discourse on a non-existent social organisation which is better than the real society" (Vieira 2010, 7). The removal of violence and threat, which were a constant in the city in the form of Semiotic thugs and INKlings (fish-like monsters who kidnap people from the subway to eat them), makes the town a desirable alternative.

The only form of threat that exists in the town is the Gatekeeper and the shadows he has removed. To gain entry to the town, Boku must first surrender his shadow to the Gatekeeper who "produced a knife and deftly worked it in between the shadow and the ground. The shadow writhed in resistance. But to no avail. Its dark form peeled neatly away" (Murakami 1985, 62). Separated from his shadow, Boku's ability to think clearly and feel emotions is severely reduced. The Gatekeeper is further tasked with ensuring that no one within the town reunites with their shadow as doing so would jeopardise the town's harmony and threaten its social structure. The Gatekeeper keeps the shadows locked up and watches as they wither and die. By sacrificing their identities through the surrender of their shadows upon entering the town, the inhabitants effectively solve the issue of collective and individual desire.

Foucault stated that heterotopia has:

> a function in relation to all the space that remains. This function unfolds between two extreme poles […] their role is to create a space that is other, another real space, as perfect, as meticulous, as well arranged as ours is messy, ill constructed, and jumbled. This […] type would be the heterotopia, […] of compensation. (1986, 27)

The town is Boku's heterotopia of compensation. It is his counter-site to the harsh realities of life in the city as Watashi, where he was isolated, experimented on, betrayed, attacked and hunted by a rival corporation. The town, however, is his refuge, where he enjoys a peaceful life. He makes friends and forms attachments to people. He does not mind that they have no mind as he doesn't either. While he recognises that the town is not perfect and that there is still suffering within the town, he refuses to reunite with his shadow. Using Baudrillardian discourse, Burcu Genç views Boku's decision as reflective of his desire to establish an authentic self (2015, 8). Something he could not do in the city dominated by consumer capitalism. The town's freedom from capitalist ideology provides Boku with a chance to form a true self, and so he refuses his shadow's pleas for reunification, opting instead to remain in his heterotopia.

Using magical realism, Murakami places the core consciousness of the individual within the shadow and creates a character that can cut and peel shadows away, separating the person from their identity. In doing so, he raises the question of what life without the social control mass consumerism exhibits would be like and highlights the suppression of the individual that late-capitalist society demands.

Learning to Dance

Murakami's *Dance, Dance, Dance* (1988) is the final instalment of the Rat Trilogy. The series critiques late capitalism by presenting it as a tool of social and political control, used by the sheep—a supernatural creature set on world domination. Although the sheep was defeated in the previous book *A Wild Sheep Chase* (1982), Boku still finds himself in a capitalist society in which nothing has changed. He remains on the outskirts of society, suffering from isolation, acute loneliness and grief after losing his wife to divorce, his girlfriend who disappeared and his childhood friend, the Rat, who gave his life to stop the sheep. In an attempt to re-enter society and find a sense of belonging, Boku embarks on a quest to find his missing girlfriend, a nameless girl with magical ears who Boku believes is calling out to him in his dreams.

Boku returns to the Dolphin Hotel, a dilapidated building that is part hotel and part museum (it had previously been the Ovine Hall of records until the Japanese government disbanded its rearing of sheep program). The Dolphin was not a successful capitalist venture but a run-down building that barely took in guests. Yet when Boku returns, he is shocked and disappointed to find that it has been demolished. In its place stood a gleaming, art-deco creation of glass and steel "towering above everything else. Like the three wise men, I steered straight for the main attraction" (Murakami 1988, 31). The l'Hôtel Dauphin's grandeur is a testament to late capitalism: plush carpets, fresh paint, high-end rooms and five-star restaurants. There is no possible way for any remnant of the previous hotel to exist. Yet within its walls is a portal to the old Dolphin Hotel.

Murakami's other worlds operate rules that prevent certain characters from gaining entry and control how long a character can remain in the other. Generally, access to these spaces is often obscure. This Boku must proceed through "lacquer black darkness" (Murakami 1988, 73). The darkness is so intense that it forces him to question his understanding of reality: "my flesh had dissolved; my form had dissipated. I floated in space. […] I was adrift in the void. […] I stood. But I could not move. My arms and legs felt paralysed" (Murakami 1988, 74). Before Boku can proceed into the other world, he must first overcome his intense fear and retake control of his body.

Within Foucault's heterotopology, he listed six principles that denote heterotopic spaces. The fifth principle relates to the heterotopia's system of entry and is useful in understanding what Boku must face to be considered worthy of admission. Foucault stated:

> Heterotopias always presuppose a system of opening and closing that both isolates them and makes them penetrable. In general, the heterotopic site is not freely accessible like a public space. Either the entry is compulsory [...] or else the individual has to submit to rites and purifications. To get in one must have a certain permission and make certain gestures. (1986, 26)

Boku must conquer his fears by confronting the darkness and proceeding through the unknown before entry is granted. To overcome his fear, Boku first acknowledges that he is no longer in l'Hôtel Dauphin, "I had crossed a line and I had entered this world in limbo. I shut my eyes and breathed deeply" (Murakami 1988, 75). Accepting the existence of this impossible, magical space allows him to regain control of his body and proceed through the darkness.

Within the other world is the Sheep Man's room containing the many documents pertaining to the keeping and breeding of sheep in Japan that were previously stored in the old Dolphin hotel. For Boku, this room in the other world holds great emotional significance. Despite the musty carpets, dank furniture, and mouldy smell, this hotel, lacking in the most basic comforts, is important to him. The Dolphin hotel was the last place he stayed with his missing girlfriend and was instrumental in resolving his quest in the previous novel. Now it is his space of refuge where he can converse with the Sheep Man for guidance. Its ability to form inside the Avant-guard Dauphin denotes its qualities as a heterotopia of resistance because its presence defies the social order. It is not a space of luxury, consumerism and excess. It is an old, worn-out room filled with worm-eaten books and yellow stained papers.

Within this space, he meets with the Sheep Man, who acts "likeaswitchboard, weconnectthings" (Murakami 1988, 86).[27] Boku outlines his sense of disillusion with his work which he sees as nothing more than "collecting garbage [...] It doesn't matter whether you like it or not—a job's a job. For three and a half years, I'd been making this kind of contribution to society. Shovelling snow. You know, cultural snow" (Murakami 1988, 7). In addition to failing to find a sense of fulfilment in his role as a writer, he conveys his state of disassociation: "nothing touched me. And I touched nothing. [...] I'd lost track of what mattered. [...] I worked like a fool for things" (Murakami 1988,

---

27   **Editorial note:** The Sheep Man character's speech is intentionally rendered without spaces by the translator, Alfred Birnbaum; this is a stylistic choice which differs from the Japanese original.

83). Unable to establish a sense of connection with the society he inhabits, he actively seeks out the other world.

The other space in *Dance* has similar qualities to its previous depictions. It is dark, cold and the protagonist must face a trial of fear and trepidation before entry is granted. However, there are substantial differences in Murakami's depiction of the other world that reinforce its qualities as a space of resistance. Although the protagonist is on a quest to find his ex-girlfriend (who at this point in the narrative is deceased), this space has nothing to do with her, nor is it a space that incorporates the dead with the living, which is a reoccurring factor of Murakami's other world. Instead, the other world appears to be a portal into the past and returns Boku to the old Dolphin Hotel. Here, he can offload his problems and fully realise the extent of his disillusion with society.

Foucault claimed heterotopias have a "precise and determined function within a society" (1986, 25). For Boku, the heterotopia forms as a space of refuge from the dominant social order:

> 'Thisisyourworld,' said the Sheep Man […] 'Theplacewasputthereforyou. Special. Andweworkedspeciallyhardtogetyoubackhere. Tokeepthingsfromfallingapart. Tokeepyoufromforgetting.' (Murakami 1988, 84)[28]

The protagonist is advised to stop fighting society and find a way to belong, thus echoing the novel's title that he must learn to dance and become a part of society. The Sheep Man explains, "youlostyourway. Yourconnections-comeundone"[29] (Murakami 1988, 84). There is a strong sense of anti-capitalism within the text, yet the Sheep Man's advice seems contrary to this.

Throughout Murakami's oeuvre, there is a clear sense of social discontent rooted in political ideology. His characters routinely find themselves living on the outskirts of society, watching from the sidelines as other people form seemingly effortless connections and live as productive members of society. The protagonists struggle to find meaning in the capitalist society surrounding them and search out spaces of refuge and resistance. These characters have access to two worlds, the one over here, known as the *kochiragawa*, and the one over there, known as the *achiragawa*. Yet their time in these spaces is limited, and it is often dangerous for them to remain in the other for extended periods. Inevitably, they must return to the *kochiragawa*, so the role of the *achiragawa* is to aid them in resolving the issues that prevent them from

---

28   **Editorial note:** See note 27.
29   **Editorial note:** As above.

connecting with society. *Dance* is a novel that conveys this message. Boku has spent years failing to connect with society, and it has left him miserable and grief-stricken. The Sheep Man's message does not convey a way to resolve the very issues that Boku has with the capitalist lifestyle but tells him that he must overcome them and reconnect.

As part of his attempt to return to Japanese society, Boku reaches out to an old school friend who has become a successful actor. Gotanda is thrilled to hear from Boku, and the two begin a friendship. Through Gotanda, Boku experiences the highs and lows of participating in mass consumer capitalism. He is seduced by the glamour of Gotanda's lifestyle, participates in sexual gratification with multiple prostitutes, drives fast cars and dines at expensive restaurants. Yet the more time he spends with Gotanda, the clearer it becomes that Gotanda is miserable. By constantly pretending to be someone else, he has interrupted his hold on himself, and he can no longer discern himself from the roles he plays "it's like which is me and which is the role? Where's the line between me and my shadow" (Murakami 1988, 144). Gotanda realises that his lifestyle has become hollow. He no longer wishes to participate in mass consumerism, nor does he find fulfilment in his lifestyle of excess, waste, and meaningless sex. Now he desires a simple, quiet life with his ex-wife—the one thing he cannot have. The continuing denial of his happiness by the tools of capitalism (his manager, agent, fans, and his ex-wife's family), coupled with the societal expectation to conform, creates a gap between the image he portrays and his core self.

The compartmentalisation of Gotanda's true identity results in his state of crisis. He forms a heterotopia of resistance that he refers to as a "*dark world*. You know what I'm talking about? Not here in this one" (Murakami 1988, 356). Within this dark world, he attempts to kill his *shutaisei* so that he may fully embody the lifestyle and persona of the movie star version of Gotanda that society demands. He believes that killing his *shutaisei* will ultimately cure him of his deep-seated unhappiness: "I was strangling my *shadow*. I remember thinking, if only I could choke my shadow off, I'd get some health. Except it wasn't my shadow. It was Kiki" (Murakami 1988, 356). Gotanda's confession resonates with Boku, who has a unique understanding of the other world. He attempts to console his friend and assure him that he wouldn't really kill Kiki, but ultimately Boku fails. The realisation that Gotanda cannot separate from his *shutaisei* and that he is now a danger to the people he loves leads him to take his life.

The crumbling of Gotanda's identity represents the cost of late capitalism. It triggers Boku to return to the new Dauphin hotel and pursue his intense desire to form a relationship with Yumiyoshi. He realises that, unlike Gotanda, Yumiyoshi "existed in the real world. Her warmth and weight and vitality were real" (Murakami 1988, 381). He transfers the feelings of reassurance and comfort that he associates with the old Dolphin hotel onto Yumiyoshi, believing she holds within her the sole of the old hotel and that he can find true happiness with her.

When you need to get away from reality, go to the bottom of a well
Murakami's *The Wind-up Bird Chronicle* (1998) features two wells imbued with magical properties that become sites of alterity. The protagonist, Toru Okada, discovers a dried out well in the garden of an abandoned neighbouring property. He starts to visit the well, attracted by its location deep underground and soon finds that he feels truly separated from the city above him. The well becomes a refuge where he can temporarily escape his problems and consider why his wife left him. It is his sanctuary when his home no longer evokes the qualities of homeliness and, later, his site of resistance to the capitalist culture that dominates society above ground. The second well that appears in the narrative belongs to Lieutenant Mamiya, who, whilst on a covert mission into enemy territory during WWII, was forced to jump into it by Mongolian soldiers and left to die. Both characters have otherworldly experiences inside their respective wells despite the apparent differences.

Following his resignation as a white-collar worker, the novel begins with Toru in a state of retreat. He has withdrawn from society into the home sphere, effectively swapping traditional gender roles with his wife, Kumiko, who takes on the mantel of the sole earner. In this sense, Toru is significantly different from his male counterparts in the novel. He does not hear the wind-up bird's call, which Elmo Gonzaga takes to be symbolic for "the mindless compulsion to work which directs the members of Japanese consensus society" (2002, 53). Instead, Toru's apparent deafness separates him from:

> … those who hear its cry […]. In exchange for financial security, they surrender their individuality, and yet they only succeed in losing any definite sense of self. The relentless progression of time marked by the unwinding of the wind-up bird's spring is nothing but a slow countdown toward the destruction of their individuality. (Gonzaga 2002, 53)

Toru understands the negative effects of the white-collar lifestyle on his *shutaisei*, and so he withdraws in an attempt to reconstitute his core self. However, it is not just his identity he must relocate, but also that of his wife's Kumiko, who becomes increasingly alienated from him. After taking over the shopping and cooking duties, it becomes clear that he does not know his wife's tastes. He buys the toilet paper she doesn't like and makes her a meal she detests. Furthermore, he fails to realise the significance of this. Despite Kumiko's attempts to reconnect with Toru, he fails to recognise her voice at multiple points in the narrative, thus increasing their mutual sense of alienation.

The couple's swapping of domestic duties challenges the social order that places women in the household in positions of subservience to their husbands. Their defiant lifestyle draws the attention of Kumiko's brother, Noboru Wataya, an up-and-coming politician who views the couple's actions as an affront to society. Seeing it as his duty to correct his sister's lifestyle, Wataya separates the couple and assaults Kumiko by magically removing her black box, which holds her *shutaisei*. The loss of her identity renders Kumiko unable to fight or resist her brother's control. She is reduced to an object for men's sexual gratification by Wataya, who forces her into prostitution, thus reaffirming her role in Japanese society as subservient to men. Toru must find Kumiko and reunite her with her *shutaisei*. Although functioning without her identity, Kumiko is aware of how she can reunite with herself and escape her brother's control. She reaches out several times to Toru. Even going so far as to say: "You want to know my name, […] but unfortunately, I can't tell you what it is. I know you very well. You know me very well. But *I* don't know me" (Murakami 1998, 245). But Toru does not understand and fails to realise that the mysterious woman in the hotel room and on the phone is his wife asking him to reconnect with her. The reunification of Kumiko's identity is a central theme in the novel and the protagonist's primary quest.

The well is dramatically different from the types of space found within the city surrounding it. As Toru descends the rope ladder, he becomes aware of the silence, something he does not usually experience in his daily life in the city above him. Next, he encounters a sudden drop in temperature as he is surrounded by all-encompassing darkness. It is so dark that Toru beings to question whether he is still in Toyko or if he has passed into some other world. The strange atmosphere alters his comprehension of time, a factor of heterotopic spaces which are "linked to slices in time [… and] begin[s] to function at full capacity when men arrive at a sort of absolute break with their traditional time" (1986, 26). As he continues his descent, Toru's sense of time is disrupted, and beings to fear the well is bottomless.

Darkness is a crucial aspect of Murakami's otherworldly space. During his descent, Toru experiences a moment where he is forced to reconsider his understanding of reality brought on by the strange darkness: "the movement of my hand seemed to cause the darkness itself to shift, […] Staying very still

in the darkness I became less and less convinced of the fact that I existed"
(1998, 230). He loses his grip on reality and begins to think of the space as an
other world. Yet despite the fear involved in experiencing such darkness, he
continues to visit the well, actively searching out the other world in which he
can momentarily escape the Japanese consensus society he has fled. With
each descent, he refines his process of entry:

> There is no need for me to close my eyes, of course, down here in the darkness, but I do
> it anyway. Closing the eyes has its own significance, in darkness or otherwise. I take several
> deep breaths, letting my body grow accustomed to this deep, dark, cylindrical space. The
> smell here is the same as always, the feel of the air against my skin is the same […] with
> its mouldy smell and its trace of dampness […] down here there are no seasons. Not even
> time exists. (Murakami 1998, 392)

Within Foucault's heterotopology, he discussed "heterotopias that are entirely consecrated to these activities of purification—purification that is partly
religious and partly hygienic" (1986, 26). Toru's movements within the well
are ritualistic and deeply significant. The well has become such a crucial space
that he goes to extreme lengths to ensure his continued access, including taking on work as a spiritual healer as a part of a deal to secure the neighbouring
property that houses the well.

There is a fluidity to heterotopias that permits them to change according to
the needs of society. Foucault outlined this adaptability in his principles, stating:

> an existing heterotopia [can] function in a very different fashion; for each heterotopia has
> a precise and determined function within a society and the same heterotopia can, accord-
> ing to the synchrony of the culture in which it occurs, have one function or another. (1986,
> 25)

The well alters on a metaphysical level in response to Toru's desperate need
to find his wife. Its solid, circular walls change, allowing Toru to pass through
the wall and into the hotel that houses his wife's subconscious. Although
Toru appears confused as to how he passed through the solid wall, Kumiko
seems to understand how the heterotopia's system of entry and exit works.
She is instrumental in guiding Toru back through the well and to safety before
his presence inside the other is discovered:

> we slipped into the wall. It had the consistency of a gigantic mass of cold gelatin; I clamped
> my mouth shut to prevent it entering. The thought struck me: I'm passing through the
> wall! In order to go from one place to another, I was passing through a wall. And yet, even
> as it was happening, it seemed like the most natural thing to do. […] And I passed through
> the wall. When I opened my eyes I was on the other side of the wall—at the bottom of a
> deep well. (Murakami 1998, 246–247)

Murakami uses magical realism to reconnect Toru with his wife's core self, something the couple could not accomplish in the *kochiragawa*. Locating her *shutaisei* in the *achiragawa* is the first step in fighting for his wife and pivotal to his continued resistance to contemporary Japan.

Inside the hotel, Toru, like the majority of Murakami's protagonists, does not stop to question how he came to be there but merely accepts the magical transference of his consciousness and begins his search. The hotel is a site of alterity, a heterotopia in which Kumiko's consciousness is trapped. Toru manages to locate Kumiko's room but is hindered by yet another form of darkness that is "nearly opaque than that of the outer room. I stood in the doorway between the two and strained to see" (Murakami 1998, 244). Perhaps this darkness is indicative of the Lacanian unconscious other known as the "world of shade" (1978, 23). Particularly as Kumiko is aware that there is a linguistic structure to the space she inhabits, which she tries to explain to Toru by telling him, "all you have to do is remember it. If you can find my name, then I can get out of here" (Murakami 1998, 246). Despite her pleas, Toru fails to grasp what this mysterious woman, shrouded in further darkness, is trying to tell him.

The battle for Kumiko's *shutaisei* takes place in the *achiragawa*. In the *kochiragawa*, Wataya is a powerful man in the public eye, and Toru has no chance of beating him. But in the other world, Toru manages to defeat Wataya and break his psychological hold over Kumiko. Once Toru has completed his quest, the need for the portal and the well diminishes. Toru is transferred back into the well, and having fulfilled its purpose as both a site of refuge and resistance, it fills with water and returns to its original purpose.

Toru is not the only character to have an otherworldly experience inside a well. For Lieutenant Mamiya, the well is where he believes his *shutaisei* died, and he is left traumatised and in a state of extreme dissociation. During WWII, Lieutenant Mamiya was tasked to be a part of a covert mission into enemy territory. With the exception of Honda, a Corporal with a sensitivity that makes him seem as if he has psychic abilities, his team is captured by Mongolian soldiers. After witnessing the horrific torture of one of his companions, Mamiya is given the choice of either being shot or jumping into a dried-out well, perhaps to his death. He opts for the well, and although he survives the fall, he is badly injured. Instead of experiencing a slow, painful death trapped in the bottom of the well, he has an otherworldly and perhaps divine experience:

> The well was filled with brilliant light. A flood of light. The brightness was almost stifling: I could hardly breathe. The darkness and cold were swept away in a moment, and warm, gentle sunlight enveloped my naked body. Even the pain I was feeling seemed to be blessed by the light of the sun. (Murakami 1998, 165)

It lasts only momentarily, and he is soon returned to darkness, cold and pain. He realises that within that light, his "life's core were stiffening and dying bit by bit" (Murakami 1998, 166). Despite this, he comes to long for the light, and when it returns, he opens his hands in a welcoming gesture.

Murakami uses magical realism to convey dissociation, a psychological condition caused by extreme trauma that affects multiple characters. For Lieutenant Mamiya, the knowledge of Corporal Honda's prophecy, which declared that the Lieutenant would die in old age back in Japan, convinced Mamiya that he could not die. However, the trauma of being trapped within the well coupled with the atrocities he was forced to witness kills his *shutaisei*. Believing that the otherworldly light "burned up the very core of my life, until there was nothing left," the Lieutenant is left in a state of dissociation (Murakami 1998, 170). In addition to Lieutenant Mamiya, who embodies the trauma of WWII, Murakami uses Creta Kano's story to illustrate the objectification and abuse of women in Japan. Like Lieutenant Mamiya, she is left numb from her experience and unable to feel anything.

To summarize, Murakami uses magical realism to explore despondency and dissociation resulting from trauma. Multiple characters struggle to maintain their *shutaisei* in the face of capitalist society. Women are objectified, violated and forced to wait on their male counterparts to rescue them. The wells represent an other type of space. These spaces are sites of resistance and refuge that offer the characters a reprieve from the harsh reality of city life. For Lieutenant Mamiya, his well provides him with an almost divine experience, but it costs him his *shutaisei*, and he is forced to live a half-life devoid of feeling. For Toru, the well shelters him from a society he finds repressive and provides a pocket of resistance from which he can fight against a contemporary Japan that demands conformity.

Conclusion

Space plays an active role in Murakami's fiction. Like Foucault, Murakami recognises that space is not a fixed entity but is subjected to social structures and networks of power. Murakami uses magical realism to create heterotopian pockets that his characters encounter as they embark on their quests. These characters are readily identifiable, and through their journeys, Murakami explores what happens when a person's *shutaisei* is compromised or lost.

These characters operate from the outskirts of society and dig out spaces of reprieve from the repressive cityscapes they find themselves in. Realising that the capitalist lifestyle is a hollow one, the characters go to extreme lengths to recover their core self and serve as a warning of the dangers of denying the self for the sake of social harmony. For these characters, access to the *achiragawa* is pivotal at it is only in the other world that they can find spaces of refuge and resistance to the capitalist ideology that dominates Japan and fills them with despair.

References

Borges, Jorge Luis. 1952. "The Analytical Language of John Wilkins." In The Total Library, edited by E. Weinberger, 229–232. London: Penguin.

Bowers, Maggie Ann. 2005. Magic(al) Realism: the New Critical Idiom. London & New York: Routledge Taylor & Francis Group.

Faris, Wendy B. 1995. "Scheherazade's Children: Magical Realism and Postmodern Fiction." *In Magical Realism: Theory, History, Community,* edited by Lois Parkinson Zamora and Wendy B. Faris. Durham: Duke University Press.

Foucault, Michel. 1966. *The Order of Things: An archaeology of the human sciences.* London & New York: Routledge Classics.

Foucault, Michel. 1986. "Of Other Spaces." *Diacritics* 16 (1):22–27.

Genc, Burcu. 2015. "Consumerism and the Possibility of an Authentic Self in Haruki Murakami's Hard-Boiled Wonderland and the End of the World." IAFOR *Journal of Literature & Librarianship* 4 (1):1–9. doi: org/10.22492/ijl.4.1.06.

Gonzaga, Elmo. 2002. "Anomie and Isolation: The Wind-Up Bird Chronicle, Ghost in the Shell, Serial Experiments Lain, and Japanese Consensus Society." *Humanities Diliman* 3 (1):39–68.

Huxley, Aldous. 1932. *Brave New World.* London: Chatto & Windus.

Lacan, Jacques. 1978. *The Four-Fundamental Concepts of Psychoanalysis.* Translated by Alan Sheridan. New York: Norton.

Murakami, Haruki. 1982. A *Wild Sheep Chase.* Translated by Alfred Birnbaum. 2003 ed. London: Vintage Books. Reprint, 2003.

Murakami, Haruki. 1985. *Hard-Boiled Wonderland and the End of the World.* Translated by Alfred Birnbaum. London: Vintage. Reprint, 1991.

Murakami, Haruki. 1988. *Dance Dance Dance.* Translated by Alfred Birnbaum. 2003 ed. London: Vintage Books. Reprint, 2003.

Murakami, Haruki. 1998. *The Wind-Up Bird Chronicle.* Translated by Jay Rubin. London: Vintage Books. Reprint, 2003.

Murakami, Haruki. 2021. *First Person Singular*. Translated by Philip Gabriel: Vintage.

Rees, Richard. 1961. *George Orwell: Fugitive from the Camp of Victory*. London: Secker & Warburg.

Rogan, Alcena Madeline Davis. 2009. "Utopian Studies." In *The Routledge Companion to Science Fiction*, edited by Mark Bould, Andrew M. Butler, Adam Roberts and Sherryl Vint, 308–316. Oxon: Routledge.

Slemon, Stephen. 1995. "Magic Realism as Postcolonial Discourse." In *Magical Realism: Theory, History, Community*, edited by Lois Parkinson Zamora and Wendy B. Faris. Durham: Duke University Press.

Strecher, Matthew C. 1999. "Magical Realism and the Search for Identity in the Fiction of Murakami Haruki." *Journal of Japanese Studies* 25 (2):263–298. doi: 10.2307/133313.

Vieira, Fatima. 2010. "The concept of utopia." In *The Cambridge Companion to Utopian Literature*, edited by Gregory Claeys, 3–27. Cambridge: Cambridge University Press.

Zamora, Lois Parkinson, and Wendy B. Farris, eds. 1995. *Magical Realism: Theory, History, Community*. Durham: Duke University Press.

Joseph Thomas Milburn

Haruki Murakami and Carl Gustav Jung: A Post-Jungian Perspective

Abstract: *This essay examines the connection between the writer, Haruki Murakami, and the psychoanalyst, Carl Gustav Jung. Prominent Jungian-influenced interpretations of the work of Murakami, particularly the essential findings of Matthew C. Strecher, will lead to an understanding of the other or metaphysical worlds in Murakami's fiction as fundamentally situated in this world. Secondly, a post-Jungian close-reading of Murakami's short story "Cream" will be carried out with reference to Roger Brooke's phenomenological development of an Existential Analytical Psychology; a key existential image of the story, a circle with infinite centres yet without circumference, will be amplified through such terms as the Self, Psyche, and Dasein. It is maintained that both Jung and Murakami present a metaphorical and poetic way of relating to the world. Finally, the intention is to put forward a post-Jungian perspective on the work of Murakami in order to prompt further philosophic, psychoanalytic, or otherwise conceptual engagement.*

Keywords: Haruki Murakami, Carl Gustav Jung, Post-Jungian, Roger Brooke, Phenomenology, Existential Analytical Psychology, *Cream*

1.   Introduction

Much secondary literature on the work of Haruki Murakami, particularly in the English language, refers to the Analytical Psychology of Carl Gustav Jung; this is notable given the generally low academic standing afforded to Jungian studies. I will first introduce such prominent Jungian interpretations of Murakami which variously consider the identity or Self of the individual, archetypal images, myth, and the unconscious. In particular, I will analyse Matthew C. Strecher's approach to the Other or metaphysical world in Murakami's fiction (Strecher, 1999; 2014; 2020); it is maintained that Strecher's understanding of the metaphysical may be clarified as fundamentally grounded in language and thus inextricably linked to *this world*. Subsequently, a post-Jungian close reading of Murakami's short story "Cream" (2021)[30] will be carried

---

30   Originally published in Japanese [クリーム, Kurīmu] in the literary magazine *Bungakukai* 文学界 (July 2018). First published in English in *The New Yorker* (21ˢᵗ January 2019) translated by Philip Gabriel and accessible at *https://www.newyorker.com/magazine/2019/01/28/*

out using Roger Brooke's phenomenological development of an Existential Analytical Psychology (Brooke, 2015). The close reading focuses on the existential image of "a circle that has many centres but no circumference" (Murakami 2021, 19); this will be discussed with reference to works of Jorge Luis Borges (Borges, 1945; 1964) which also deal with the image. It is argued that Murakami's fiction provides the material for personal conceptual engagement; the thought of Jung and Brooke is applied to "Cream" in order to work with such concepts as the Self, psyche, and Dasein. This *concept work* further establishes the connection between Jung and Murakami through an examination of metaphor and *poesis*. What results is a post-Jungian *perspective* on the work of Murakami: the subjectivism of Murakami's main characters reveals a central struggle with world-relation. Finally, this essay does not attempt to explain the meaning of Murakami's work through the biography of the writer or his sociological conditions; rather, Murakami's work is understood as highly philosophic as it provides specific *instances* of concepts that may be taken up by others for their own conceptual projects. I intend to work with Murakami's literary material *through* concepts which exceed and are irreducible to the literary material itself; in so doing, existential descriptions of the world are generated in response to the text. It is hoped that more extensive post-Jungian *approaches* to the work of Murakami will be taken up in the future.

2. Jungian Interpretations

Matthew C. Strecher's recent key work on Murakami (2014) is clearly influenced by Jungian thought.[31] He considers Murakami's central focus to be "the 'inner self' or 'core self' of the individual" (Strecher 2014, 13). Murakami characters explore their identity through contact with "the Other World" (Ibid., 15) or "metaphysical realm" (Ibid., 16)[32]. This metaphysical domain:

---

cream; now available in the collection *First Person Singular.* Murakami, Haruki (2021), *First Person Singular.* trans. Philip Gabriel. London: Harvill Secker. pp. 1–28.

31   Strecher's earlier work offers a more sociological and *post-modern* perspective. Identity remains central; the unconscious is approached through a Lacanian lens. Matthew C. Strecher (2002), *Dances with Sheep: The Quest for Identity in the Fiction of Murakami Haruki.* Ann Arbor: University of Michigan Center for Japanese Studies. See conclusion pp. 207–216. Interestingly, there have been recent attempts at a rapprochement between Lacanian and Jungian psychoanalysis. See *Thresholds and Pathways Between Jung and Lacan: On the Blazing Sublime* (2020), eds. Ann Casement, Phil Goss, and Dany Nobus. London: Routledge. Also, the Jung/Lacan Research Network
https://junglacan.wordpress.com/junglacan-dialogues/.

32   Strecher considers the notion of an inner narrative; Murakami himself has termed this the *monogatari* (16); maintaining or protecting such a narrative is an essential part of one's identity. Further, "all of our individual inner narratives are linked to and feed into one great

… shares numerous points in common with the unconscious as it was envisioned by both Freud and Jung, not merely as a repository for memories or a source of libido (à la Freud), but also as a sort of spirit world, a dwelling place for the souls of the dead, and a source of connection to a more collective sphere of human spiritual experience (Jung)." (Ibid., 24)[33]

It could be argued that locating the unconscious (as an entity), or unconscious content, as elsewhere in this way amounts to a kind of reification; however, Strecher suggests that Murakami's fiction participates in a shared cultural landscape which is, importantly, established through language (Ibid.). I would argue that Strecher's development of Murakami's two-storey house metaphor,[34] by extension his divide between the physical and metaphysical worlds as "this side" (*kochiragawa*) and "other there" (*achiragawa*) (Ibid., 73),[35] as well as his reference to a compensatory psychic energy system (Ibid., 103–105) distracts from this central insight; that is:

Language … grounds, expresses, and most importantly, constitutes both the physical and metaphysical worlds. The strategy of this manoeuvre is to deconstruct the privileging of 'physical' over 'metaphysical' (as, for instance, 'real' and 'unreal' …) to expose the fallacy of objective reality and argue that all realities are grounded in perception, language, experience, and culture. (Ibid., 24)

---

narrative, what I will call *the Narrative*, the story that has been written and continues to be written constantly, incessantly … in some ways it is like Carl Jung's 'collective unconscious'" (Strecher 2014, 19). According to Strecher, Murakami's fiction taps into the collective unconscious through its metaphysical elements; that is, through presenting an inner narrative that is somehow connected to the narratives we all share; importantly, this is not an *intrapsychic* domain but fundamentally interpersonal; the narratives, ideologies, and ideas of others impinge upon individual narratives/identity.

33   Strecher maintains that the metaphysical in earlier Murakami work is more similar to the Freudian conception, while the later work shifts towards the Jungian: "From *The Wind-Up Bird Chronicle* onward … the metaphysical world is thrown wide open, depicted as a kind of 'shared space' to which all characters appear to have access, wherein they meet, engage one another, and return to 'this side.' … it permits Murakami a considerably wider range of imaginative depiction for the "other world," for what was personal, individual memory is now a collective one—*the* Narrative—that grounds all humanity from the beginning of time. In Jungian terms this is called the 'collective unconscious'" (76).

34   Strecher includes an excerpt from an interview in which Murakami likens human existence to a two-storey house; there is a basement level underneath the usual basement (dreams, memories) which one only has access to through a "special door"; Murakami maintains that the novelist can consciously enter this space (as well as return to reality); this deeper space is understood by Murakami and Strecher to be one's "own soul" (21). Strecher adds to this image the "underground plumbing" in which the second-floor basement (core identity, narrative) connects to the collective unconscious/*the* Narrative (22–23). He argues that Murakami manages to bring something back to the surface from the imaginative depths.

35   *Kochiragawa* (the physical world, consciousness, the land of the living) is separated from *achiragawa* (metaphysical world, unconscious, land of the dead) by an entrance stone, gateway, or special door. Murakami characters may travel to/from the realms through certain passageways (wells, elevator shafts, subways, sewers, telephone lines, sub-terranean caverns).

Strecher's usage of the two-story house metaphor, for example, is comparable to the classical Jungian approach as it envisions the collective unconscious as existing underneath (perhaps, independently of) the personal or social consciousness;[36] "it is precisely this second-level basement wherein the drama of the Murakami novel is enacted, to where his characters must go in order to confront themselves and those who seek to appropriate their selves" (Ibid., 22). According to this interpretation, Murakami's fiction takes its characters [as well as its readers] to an Other, non-physical place which is deeply connected to their own inner minds.

I would argue that this interpretation can be re-envisioned or more clearly stated in line with Strecher's original premise; the metaphysical space is not *entirely* physical or non-physical;[37] further, the characters are connected to each other and the world. In other words, Murakami's work is not only understood as *unreal* or as situated inside the subject[38] but, equally, as representative of reality and its external foundation. As Strecher writes, "the uses for this metaphysical realm … are varied, but virtually all are tied to the idea of establishing, maintaining, or otherwise protecting individual identity—the internal narrative—*while at the same time establishing contact with others*" (Ibid., 25). Strecher draws parallels between the metaphysical realm of Murakami's fiction and the unconscious;[39] this latter understanding of the unconscious has an internal dimension, yet it also necessarily participates in linguistic and cultural (interpersonal) systems. The metaphysical is just as much *over there* as it is, inextricably, *over here.*[40]

---

36   In this sense, archetypal figures of the unconscious have an objective existence; they are ahistorical and transpersonal; they exist prior to and endure individual existence. The classical Freudian approach, on the other hand, is more concerned with the personal and social aspects of the unconscious; figures of the unconscious are generated in relation to one's historical and psychobiological (including psycho-sexual) existence.

37   In contract to the purely linguistic approach, Olaf Schiedges relates the binary opposition of Murakami's fictive worlds to the spatial theory of Juri Lotman; it is argued that Murakami's use of imagined space (both metaphysical and historical) is structurally connected to societal conditions and identity-formation; it would be productive to take this further through an analysis of the real-imagined spaces in Murakami's work; the central notion being *movement* between boundaries and the subsequent effects. See pp. 185–194 of this special issue.

38   Here, I mean the subjectivity of the character which the reader may or may not engage with; the fictional reality is concurrent or conceptually continuous with typical reality.

39   See notes 32 and 33.

40   The "Other World" is very much *this world.* When Strecher writes that "For Jung—and for Murakami—the inner psyche and the 'other world' share certain characteristics and might even be conflated into a single entity" (op cit., 75), I would say that he is moving away from an essential external and socio-culturally constituted dimension of the metaphysical. As I will argue, there is no need to demarcate the inner from the outer, especially

It must be questioned, however, why we are considering the metaphysical in Murakami's work. For instance, does the usage of Jungian terms (such as the collective unconscious or archetypal images) mean that we are attempting to psychoanalyse Murakami, his characters, or perhaps engage in a form of self-therapy? (Dil, 2010). After all, Jung was primarily a clinician. Or, more simply, are we trying to better understand or explain Murakami's fiction through psychological concepts? It seems to me that whilst the latter may be the case (as it is in Strecher's detailed works), there is also present the assertion that Murakami's work, and one's work with it, has high philosophic importance in addition to its literary function;[41] for instance, one may draw on or extend material found in the imaginative texts to make conceptual statements; these conceptual statements may be relevant to other academic discourses. Murakami's magical realism (Strecher, 1999) or articulation of the Fantastic (Suter, 2016), through his use of the metaphysical, provides a literary example of the dissolution between reality and unreality (the imaginative, the fictional, and so forth); myself, Strecher, and many other readers recognise that Murakami's stories provide the material for conceptual work on such issues related to consciousness and existence, as well as the ontological status of fiction and metaphor; importantly, Murakami's work is accessible and relevant to contemporary audiences. While Murakami is often disparaged as a writer of popular fiction or the dull global novel,[42] it could be said that it is this apparent depth (a depth which Jungian studies lends itself to)[43] that accounts for his popularity and for the increased interest from academics of various backgrounds and fields.

Strecher also emphasises the "mythological undertones" in Murakami's stories which seem to *resonate* with his global audience (Strecher 2014, 5); it is argued that his work somehow taps into the archetypal, collective layer of the

---

in regard to the *psyche*. *Psyche* is a central term in my reading of Murakami's work from the standpoint of existential analytical psychology.

41   For a more detailed account of my understanding of the philosophical relevance of fiction, see: Milburn, Joseph Thomas. 2022. "Concept Work: A Philosophic Approach to Literature," *Sofia Philosophical Review* Vol XIV, No. 2.

42   Further, see "The Dull New Global Novel" by Tim Parks (2010). https://www.ny books.com/daily/2010/02/09/the-dull-new-global-novel/. A more critical perspective, Karolina Watroba *World Literature and Literary Value: Is "Global" The New "Lowbrow?"* (2017). CUP.

43   In particular its theoretical and interdisciplinary forms. Susan Rowland, for instance, presents a Jungian literary criticism (as well as an important recasting of anima-theory which is, arguably, relevant to Murakami). Rowland, S. (1999), *C. G. Jung and Literary Theory: The Challenge from Fiction*, London: Macmilllan.

unconscious.[44] In particular, Strecher considers "passages to the World of the Dead" (Ibid., 82–84) in which "the world of the unconscious and the metaphysical land of the dead are finally inseparable" (Ibid., 88). More recently, Strecher has expanded on the mythic ritual and the *return* to the physical world (as *rebirth*) from the underworld manifest in Murakami's most recent novel *Killing Commendatore* (2018) (Strecher 2020).[45] He concludes that:

> … both myth and its inquiry remain alive and well in the fictional production of writers like Murakami, and it is, therefore, most fortunate that he has such a widespread global audience … it will also be useful, I think, to draw closer connections between the mythic presence and its obvious links to the psychological, philosophical, and spiritual; for if the idea[46] is truly an archetype, then the Underworld from which he emerges is not merely the land of the dead, but the very place from which our perception and understanding of the world around us gains meaning and sense, and thus becomes truly real. (Strecher 2020, 357–358)

My understanding of Strecher's position, then, is that one's existence in the world is grounded and gathers meaning through contact with the land of the dead, the metaphysical, or unconscious content. This space of shared archetypal images and mythos is encountered through language and has direct bearing upon one's actual or ordinary existence; that which is experienced imaginatively or conceptually in fantasy or fiction (such as in Murakami's) forms an essential part of one's[47] authentic reality with others.[48] Further, it

---

44   Further, "Yes, Murakami is Japanese, and he writes in Japanese. His cultural specificities are Japanese. They could hardly be otherwise. But the core story, or *monogatari*, as he likes to put it, in his soul is one that makes sense to us all. It begins as the story of one Japanese individual attempting to find his unique place in an increasingly globalized world. At the same time, like the rest of us, Murakami is the product of several millennia of "stories" that ground the entire human race, what Carl Jung called the "archetypes" of the collective unconscious. His "story" is connected to *our* stories, and that is why, whatever specificities he brings to it, that story still resonates in the souls of his readers. It simply "makes sense" to us." (Strecher 2016, 133). *Haruki Murakami: Challenging Authors* (2016). Eds. Matthew C. Strecher and Paul L. Thomas. Rotterdam: Sense.

45   One may successfully forge links (and contrasts) here with the post-Jungian James Hillman, of the archetypal or imaginal school. *The Dream and the Underworld* (1979), New York: Harper Perennial.

46   Strecher equates the character of the *Kishidancho*/the Commendatore, who describes himself as an idea (or *eidos*), to a Jungian archetype (350; 352; 355); in which he means an *archetypal image* as the archetype itself is irrepresentable. I would add also to this reading of *Killing Commendatore* the archetypal image of the *divine child* which manifests in an actual birth within the story.

47   *One* being the characters themselves within the story and, more generally, as an existential statement concerning individuals in the world (engaged audiences).

48   Strecher concludes that "all perceptions of reality are ultimately subjective" (op cit., 158) and yet, at the same time, argues for a universal Narrative or an *objective*, archetypal dimension of one's personal unconsciousness. To clarify this, we could say that artistic work

could be argued that Murakami's mythic symbolism is not unlike the amplificatory process found in Jungian therapy and studies; in Jungian theory, myths, like dreams, establish contact with and project collective experience; Murakami's fiction seems to function in a similar way.

Other Jungian interpreters of Murakami also forge links between his fiction, myth, and the collective unconscious. Martinez considers Murakami's novel *Kafka on the Shore* (2005) to be a reimagining of *Oedipus Rex*,[49] and writes, "If there is a contemporary writer who fulfils Jung's vision of the artist as a 'vehicle and moulder of the unconscious psychic life of mankind' (Jung, 1930/1950, para. 157),[50] it is the Japanese author, Haruki Murakami" (Martinez 2008, 56). It is argued that Murakami's work, through its mythic content, allows for cultural and psychological transformation; he has "plunged into the healing ... depths of the collective psyche" (Jung 1930/1950, para. 161), or Strecher's metaphysical realm, and has resurfaced with new imaginative possibilities; as stated above, such imaginative possibilities are understood as concurrently real interpersonal possibilities. Megumi Yama considers Murakami's relationship with the Jungian analyst Hayao Kawai[51] and maintains (again, like Strecher) that Murakami's personal stories (or modern myths) possess a universal relevance:

> By sinking deep into the unconscious, he [Murakami] goes beyond the personal and reaches the collective level. His works, written in such a way, are collective stories told through one individual ... Murakami does not write his personal story, but his work is considered to be comparable to Jung's attempt to tell his personal myth in its depth. When we read *Memories, Dreams, Reflections*[52] we feel that it is a collective story told by one person

---

such as Murakami's, and our reading of it, amounts to subjective expressions, statements, or *perceptions* of reality which may or may not have objective validity.

49   Of course, a central myth within Freudian psychoanalysis as well. Martinez's interpretation is that responsibility for unconscious content is collective (and imaginative); one may overcome Sophoclean guilt through empathy or love for others: "Murakami thus offers readers metaphorical experience of patricide and incest as a healing initiation through imagination" (63). Further, "Murakami sheds hope on the human condition by portraying taking responsibility for unconscious acts as a group task that, if conscientiously and lovingly undertaken, leads to life-generating transformation. Instead of living as a blinded, ostracized beggar, Kafka, the cursed son, becomes a life-embracing, initiated young man. Rendering the psyche as shared, Murakami's reimagining of the Oedipus drama may indeed be important—for the entire world" (64). Reference is also made to the work of James Hillman, see note 45.

50   For more of Jung's though on literature, see *The Spirit in Man, Art and Literature* (2003), Abingdon: Routledge (particularly part V on *Ulysses*) and *On Psychological and Visionary Art* (2015), Princeton: Princeton University Press, which considers Gérard de Nerval's *Aurélia*.

51   See further, *Haruki Murakami goes to meet Hayao Kawai* (2017), Einsiedeln: Daimon Verlag.

52   It should be noted that *Memories, Dreams, Reflections* perhaps mispresents Jung the academic or clinician as it was most likely mainly written by Aniela Jaffé and not the aged Jung himself.

> who managed to live his individuation process. Through his own creative process, Murakami is a modern-myth maker, one who dips down into the deepest layers of the unconscious, crosses the 'wall' barrier, and returns with stories that are not only personal but also universal. (Yama 2016, 93–94)

It must be said that readers of Murakami, especially those of us who enjoy and relate to his work, should be careful of establishing a Murakami myth in the sense that Jungians have been criticised as forming a Jung cult;[53] and here I simply state my own preference for reading Murakami's work as somewhat separate from Murakami the individual;[54] that is, for one's own conceptual engagement to be distinct from the author's statements about his work, his writing process, or biographical (particularly, psychobiographical) interpretation. What is clear, however, is the sentiment shared by many readers that Murakami's work utilises, articulates, or participates with unconscious content; this is seen to occur through the mythic, archetypal characters and situations that are presented in his fiction; this metaphysical engagement is felt to have a collective resonance which is perhaps partly substantiated by Murakami's global appeal.

Jay Rubin, one of the main translators of Murakami in English,[55] does indeed provide biographical information about the writer. For instance, Rubin writes that "He [Murakami] has been stubbornly consistent in denying that there are "symbols" in his writing" (Rubin 2012, 34). As Jung writes in "Psychology and Literature": What a poet has to say about his work is often far from being the most illuminating work on the subject. What is required of us, then, is nothing less than to defend the importance of the visionary experience against the poet himself" (Jung 1933, 161); while I am not arguing that Murakami is a visionary poet, I would say that his own admission that his work contains no greater meaning or depth may not be taken as the final word on the matter; equally, it is not the place of the academic to equate the writer's reluctance to a psychological complex; rather, once the text is shared, the reader's engagement with any symbolism, depth, or extended meaning has validity independently of the writer's engagement. Rubin also allows himself to make reference to the metaphysical in Murakami's fiction:

---

53   See *The Jung Cult: Origins of a Charismatic Movement* by Richard Noll (1994), Princeton: Princeton University Press.

54   For example, I would avoid the suggestion that Murakami is in the process of *individuating*. Of course, for most interpreters, the life of the author and the creation of the work are inseparable.

55   Alongside Alfred Birnbaum, Philip Gabriel, and Ted Goossen.

> Murakami may not have 'understood' everything in his first book [Hear the Wind Sing], but he knew he was rooting around in his psychic past among half-forgotten memories and half-understood images that would surface unpredictably from the 'other world' … Lack of rational understanding, forgetting, free association: these open the deep wells and dark passageways to the timeless other world that exists in parallel with this one, a world that Murakami would go on to explore with increasing confidence. (Rubin 2012, 33–34)

We see here again an understanding of the unconscious in Murakami's fiction which conflates the personal and other/collective; we see, also, the separation of the other world from *this world*; Rubin states further that other characters in Murakami stories often function as part of the main character's "psyche" (Ibid., 39). There is possible confusion regarding what exactly this interpretation of *psyche* means; by psyche, are interpreters of Murakami designating a part of a purely fictional world or a metaphysical world which is both fictional and actual? Does it, perhaps, refer to the subjectivity of the main character (or the writer himself)? I will argue, in the final section of this article, that *psyche* in Murakami's work (as well as in interpretations of it) is better understood through the phenomenological concept of *Dasein*[56] or world-relation; as being which is both internal and external.

Rebecca Suter does not refer to Jungian theory, but like Yama above comments on Murakami's creative process; Suter focuses on Murakami's protagonists frequently having an occupation related to artistic production; for instance, in *Killing Commendatore*, the main character works in portraiture and his paintings are key features of the novel. It is maintained that the narrator is a medium who acts "as a conduit between conscious and unconscious layers of the psyche, and between natural and supernatural levels of reality" (Suter 2020, 365); further, this is itself a metaphor "for the role of the literary author as a catalyst that enables people to connect with their inner self and with each other" (Ibid., 361); importantly, Suter connects this to the responsibility of the artist (in this case, Murakami) to bring into both his artistic work and, as a result, the consciousness of audiences, *hidden realities* (Ibid., 365). For Suter and Yama, Murakami works with unconscious content and brings it to consciousness, the surface, or *this world*. Suter adds a more social, interpersonal dimension to the interpretation as "the characters and realities that come into existence through portraits and novels do not stay contained in the realm of fiction—they enter 'our' reality and enact changes in it" (Ibid.,

---

56   Brooke employs *Dasein* in the Heideggerian sense throughout his work; I also refer to *Dasein* here in this more general usage; of course, philosophers such as Husserl, Sartre, and Levinas offer different avenues from which to attempt a rapprochement between *Dasein* and the *Self* of analytical psychology.

376). It can be seen that the *inner self* here is not only personal, in the sense of a subjectivised psyche, but is a Self or Psyche (a world) *with-others*; as a conceptual statement concerning Murakami's fiction, I maintain that the texts provide the material to explore notions relating to Self and Psyche or, through our upcoming examination of Roger Brooke's existential analytical psychology, *Dasein*. Finally, Suter recognises the similarities between her notion of the artist as a medium and that of a therapist but argues that the main characters of Murakami's work (which is extended to Murakami himself) act more as unconscious conduits or facilitators than agents of "rational analysis and interpretation" (Ibid., 371); further:

> For the narrator, the trigger for drawing things is a 'request' from the things themselves—be they human beings, material objects, or supernatural entities—and the process of drawing out hidden elements in them is an unconscious one that happens through the artist, bypassing, so to speak, his rational mind. The artist's role is then to record these stories by rearranging the pieces of the puzzle into a narrative, acting as a medium of communication between different levels of reality. (Ibid., 374)

It could be said, in contrast, that Jungian therapy does not in fact deny the irrational; the irrational or the unconscious is a central aspect of the individuation process (the development of individual consciousness); *acting as a medium of communication between different levels of reality* may very well be the main task of the analyst or individual engaged with Jungian thought; the notion of the artist establishing a narrative from irrational content is comparable to Yama's idea of the individual forming a personal myth out of one's participation with the collective level. Rather than Murakami himself completing this therapeutic process through his creative production, as we cannot speak for his psychology, I argue that Murakami's fiction provides the *material* for one's own conceptual engagement; instead of providing a literary example of individuation or the role of the writer, for instance, the literary material may be taken up for personal, philosophic, or artistic projects due to its unconscious or archetypal dimensions; or, to be more Jungian, it may be worked on and put to work for one's development of Self.[57] It is the engagement of readers themselves which potentializes contact with hidden realities or the actualisation of imaginative possibilities in the world.

---

57   Such personal activity may be deepened through connection with others and their projects, yet this is a secondary movement; the fact that the activity may or may not be relevant for others does not diminish its importance.

3.   Cream

Of course, another reason readers make a connection between Murakami and Jung is that Murakami explicitly refers to Jung in his texts. An interesting example is noted by Lica Hashimoto (2015), a translator of Murakami into Brazilian Portuguese. In *1Q84* (2011), a bodyguard named Tamaru mentions Jung's home, called 'The Tower,'[58] in Bollingen; he states that the following is carved into the entrance: whether it is cold or not, God is present (Hashimoto's translation); this sentence can also be found as the title of chapter 25 of book 3 (Murakami 2011, 188).[59] However, Tamaru is actually incorrect; the Latin phrase is carved above the door of Jung's house in Kusnacht and it reads: bidden or not, God is present.[60] Hashimoto considers whether to correct this in her translation of *1Q84* or to include a footnote; ultimately, Hashimoto decided to leave the intertextual reference as it was due to it perhaps being an intentional adaptation on Murakami's part related to the character's personal experience of growing-up in Hokkaido.[61] Aomame, one of the main characters in *1Q84*, also directly quotes Jung concerning the concept of the shadow in book 2 chapter 13, so we can infer that Murakami is familiar with

---

58   Jung built his house *(The Tower)* at Bollingen over many years; he built four main parts of the building which he felt, retrospectively, related to the alchemical quaternity; he also added a final, upper-storey which could be said to represent the ego-personality or Self. "It gave me a feeling as if I were being reborn in stone. It is thus a concretization of the individuation process … During the building work, of course, I never considered these matters … It might be said that I built it in a kind of dream. Only afterward did I see how all the parts fitted together and that a meaningful form had resulted: a symbol of psychic wholeness." *Memories, Dreams, Reflections* (Jung 1995, 223–237).

59   In the English translation: *Cold or not, God is present.*

60   In Latin: VOCATUS ATQUE NON VOCATUS DEUS ADERIT. This may also be translated as *Called or not …* which sounds similar to *Cold or not.* See: http://www.jungnewyork.com/photo_vocatus.shtml.

61   Despite historical inaccuracy, the phrase seems deeply important to Tamaru. "I'm not sure myself what it means. There's some kind of deep allusion there, something difficult to interpret. But consider this: in this house that Carl Jung built, piling up the stones with his own hands, at the very entrance, he found the need to chisel out, again with his own hands, these words. I don't know why, but I've been drawn to these words for a long time. I find them hard to understand, but the difficulty in understanding makes it all the more profound. I don't know much about God. I was raised in a Catholic orphanage and had some awful experiences there, so I don't have a good impression of God. And it was always cold there, even in the summer. It was either really cold or outrageously cold. One or the other. If there is a God, I can't say he treated me very well. Despite all this, those words of Jung's quietly sank deep into the folds of my soul. Sometimes I close my eyes and repeat them over and over, and they make me strangely calm. 'Cold or Not, God Is Present.'" Following this statement, Tamaru goes on to murder the man he is speaking to. Additionally, we will see similarities here with the main character's attitude towards the *metaphor* presented in "Cream."

the life and work of Jung.[62] Further, in Murakami's work, we find implicit references to Jung; this is apparent in the recent short story "Cream"[63] and, I would say, may be missed by some readers.

The narrator[64] in "Cream" is recounting a "strange incident" (Murakami 2021, 3) to a friend which took place when he was 18, in-between high school and university, waiting to retake his entrance exams after failing the first time. He receives an unexpected invitation to a piano recital from a girl a year younger who had the same piano teacher as a child; after he stopped taking lessons at 16, they had lost touch. The narrator decides to attend the recital so he takes a train and bus up to the top of a mountain in Kobe[65] where the recital is to take place. However, when he arrives, the recital hall is closed and it is clear that no recital will be held. He reasons later that, for some reason, he may have been duped by the young woman and questions why he has made the trip in the first place. He eventually finds a small park, sits on a bench, and feels a "strange kind of exhaustion, as though I'd been worn out for quite a while but hadn't noticed it" (Ibid., 11). He hears a man's voice projected in the distance by a loudspeaker; the voice gets louder and the narrator realises that it is a Christian message coming from the top of a car. The narrator seems prepared to receive a profound message:

> … the voice spoke precisely, without a trace of emotion, as if trying to convey something extremely important as objectively as possible. It occurred to me that maybe this was a personal message directed at me, and me alone. Someone was going to the trouble of telling me where I'd gone wrong, what it was that I'd overlooked …
>
> 'Everyone will die,' the voice said in a calm monotone. 'Every person will eventually pass away. No one can escape death or the judgment that comes afterward. After death, everyone will be severely judged for his sins.' (Ibid., 12)

---

62   Professor Jonathan Dil considers this, as well as the reference in *1Q84*, further in his article for the special issue, "Oh My *Kamisama*! God in the Fiction of Murakami Haruki"; for instance, Murakami actually visited Bollingen in 2008.

63   See note 30.

64   The main characters in Murakami fiction frequently have no name and use the Japanese pronouns *Boku* (more casual) and *Watashi* (more formal). Boku is used in "Cream"; however, the effect is somewhat lost in English as both pronouns translate as *I*. Rubin (2012, 37–38) discusses Murakami's use of *Boku*/*Watashi* in relation to the Japanese literary tradition of the *I-novel*. Also, the title of Murakami's collection, *First Person Singular* (Murakami uses *Watashi* in the titular short story), seems to add another layer of meaning here; Midori Tanaka Atkins discussed this further in her review, "*Killing Commendatore*; From *Boku* to *Watashi*, Healing on Canvas and in the Darkness of the Pit." See pp. 215–221 of this special issue.

65   Murakami's hometown.

The narrator waits for the mission car, "hoping to hear words spoken in a reassuring, resolute voice, no matter what they were" (Ibid., 13), but the car never appears. He feels as though he has "been abandoned by the world" (Ibid., 14). He starts to have trouble breathing and, in the present, comments to his friend that he suffered such bouts once or twice a year; yet he no longer experiences these issues: "I'd panic, as if I were being swept under by a rushing current and were about to drown, my body would freeze" (Ibid., 15). He closes his eyes, trying to regain composure and witnesses "strange patterns behind his eyelids" (ibid.);[66] when he finally opens his eyes, he sees an old man sitting on the bench opposite who must have been watching him in his discomfort. The old man says the following and provides the key metaphor of the story:

> 'A circle with many centres' …
>
> 'Circles, did you say' I reluctantly asked. He was older than me, and politeness dictated that I respond.
>
> 'There are several centres—no, sometimes an infinite number—and it's a circle with no circumference' … 'Are you able to picture that kind of circle in your mind?' (Ibid., 17)

The narrator tries but cannot successfully visualise the form. The eighteen-year-old and the old man continue talking about such a circle on the park benches:

> The old man spoke again. 'Listen, you've got to imagine it with your own power. Use all the wisdom you have and picture it. A circle that has many centres but no circumference. If you put such an intense effort that it's as if you were sweating blood—that's when it gradually becomes clear what the circle is.'
>
> 'It sounds difficult,' I said.
>
> 'Of course it is,' the old man said … 'There's nothing worth getting in this world that you can get easily.' … 'But, when you put in that much time and effort, if you do achieve that difficult thing it becomes the cream of your life' … 'The cream of the cream. It means the best of the best. The most important essence of life—that's the *crème de la crème*. Get it? The rest is just boring and worthless.' (Ibid., 19)

The old man advises that this is a "critical time" for the narrator "to think about difficult things" but he cannot "grasp the meaning of it" (Ibid., 20); he

---

66   I am reminded here of the geometric patterns (often mandala-like) one sometimes sees before sleep or while meditating; although, they may simply be migraine phosphenes.

considers how a circle with an infinite number of centres can exist. While he is thinking, the old man disappears and his breathing returns to normal: "the rushing current was gone" (Ibid., 22).

After the narrator finishes telling his friend about his strange experience, he admits that he did not reach any final understanding of the image: "it was permanently unsolved, like some ancient riddle" (Ibid., 23); the narrator concludes that, instead of finding a *point* to the events, he has reached a detached attitude towards them; it no longer hurts that he was, perhaps, tricked into travelling to the mountain recital: "it came to feel insignificant, not worth getting upset about. I felt as though it had nothing at all to do with the cream of life" (Ibid., 24). The old man's metaphor seems to have been internalised by the narrator, resulting in an attitude of acceptance towards that which he does not understand (such as fake invitations and circles with many centres):

> Things like this happen sometimes … Inexplicable, illogical events that
> nevertheless are deeply disturbing. I guess we need to not think about them, just close our
> eyes and get through them. As if we were passing under a huge wave. (Ibid.)

I would say that the narrator's attitude also has a bodily aspect, as it helps not only with psychological confusion but with his trouble breathing. Regardless, the narrator's conclusion moves away from relation to body and world as it locates the circle within the subjectivity of the individual:

> In my life, whenever an inexplicable, illogical, disturbing event takes place, …
> I always come back to that circle—the circle with many centres but no circumference—
> And, as I did when I was 18, on that arbour bench, I close my eyes and listen to the beating
> of my heart.
>
> Sometimes I feel that I can sort of grasp what that circle is, but a deeper understanding
> eludes me. This circle is, most likely, not a circle with a concrete, actual form but, rather
> one that exists only within our minds. (Ibid., 25)

The narrator seems unable to grasp the full meaning of the circle as he separates the body-world (the beating of the heart) from the purely internal image; his reasoning that it is without actual form is at odds with the following:

> When we truly love somebody, or feel deep compassion, or have an idealistic sense of
> how the world should be, or when we discover faith (or something close to faith)—that's
> when we understand the circle as a given and accept it in our hearts. (Ibid.)

Reading in translation, one wonders on the accuracy of hearts here, as opposed to 'mind' or 'consciousness.'[67] We see, then, in Murakami's short work, a depth which concerns existence, divinity, faith, and the illogical, amongst others; we will return to what I maintain, is a fundamental limitation in the narrator's conception:

> And even now, whenever something disturbing happens to me, I ponder again that special circle, and 'the boring and the worthless.' And the unique cream that might be there, deep inside me. (Ibid.)

As opposed to this introspective position, I will consider how the cream of life may be established within one's relation to the world; the unique cream and the special circle, then, may be understood as psyche or Self. The metaphor of the circle, however, is not of Murakami's creation; in fact, we may assume that Murakami intentionally made use of the metaphor for his own literary and conceptual purposes.[68] Finally, it should be noted before we begin that there is no need for any archetypal or mythic interpretation of the story in the Jungian sense; for example, concerning the figure of the old man, the ascension of the mountain, the call of the trickster or anima and so forth. Rather, I will employ insights from Roger Brooke's post-Jungian, phenomenological development of an Existential Analytic psychology with specific reference to notions of Self, psyche, and Dasein or world-relation.

Readers of Jung may immediately notice the similarity of Murakami's circle with the famous quotation which Jung attributes to St Bonaventure[69]: "God [the *Self*] is a circle whose centre is everywhere and circumference is nowhere" (Jung 1921/1971, 461). In fact, the saying has been attributed to thinkers, particularly alchemists, throughout history including Trismegistus, Giordano Bruno, Francois Rabelais, and Blaise Pascal. Jorge Luis Borges

---

67   The Danish translator of Murakami, Mette Holm, notes the following: "Another example of direct translation is from *Hādo-boirudo Wandārando* [Hard-Boiled Wonderland and the End of the World], where I chose to translate the word 'kokoro' directly as 'hjerte,' the Danish word for 'heart.' In the English translation, 'kokoro' is often translated as 'mind,' in German the translator uses 'Seele' [soul], but in French it was 'coeur' [heart]. Strecher also refers to kokoro as soul or core identity which is 'by no means permanently fixed' to the physical body, which is understood, in Murakami fiction, to be an empty vessel or container" (207).

68   However, Murakami denies any knowledge of the metaphor in an interview with Jonathan Dil. Murakami says that he thought of the circle as a kind of Zen *koan*. See Dil's article in this special issue, pp. 3–27.

69   Also attributed by Jung to Augustine. For instance, *C. G. Jung, Nietzche's Zarathustra: Notes of the Seminar Given in 1934–1939* (1988), 2:1048, ed. James L. Jarrett, 2 vols., Princeton: Princeton University Press; *Visions: Notes of the Seminar Given in 1930–1934* (1997), 306–3971 ed. Claire Douglas, Princeton: Princeton University Press.

considers the history of this metaphor in his essay "The Fearful Sphere of Pascal" (1964) in which the original interpretation of the circle as God has gradually changed into *nature* or *the universe*; for Pascal, this state of affairs is felt to be *fearful*[70] as the all-encompassing universe and its overwhelming physicality has replaced the divine as the centre of Being. Borges provides a more literary treatment of the circle or sphere whose centre is everywhere and whose circumference is nowhere in his short story, *The Aleph* (1945).

In *The Aleph*, the main character Borges (a fictional representation of the writer), visits a family member of the woman he loves, Beatriz, who passed away some time ago; the family member, Carlos Argentino, is lamenting that his house is to be bought and renovated by local businessmen; more than losing his family home, Argentino is aghast at the thought of losing the Aleph in the cellar, "one of the points in space that contains all other points" (Borges 1945, 6). Argentino initially found the Aleph when he fell down the cellar steps, so Borges recreates the position by lying on the floor and focusing on the nineteenth step in order to see it for himself. Surprisingly, Borges does in fact see the Aleph:

> On the back part of the step, toward the right, I saw a small iridescent sphere of almost unbearable brilliance … The Aleph's diameter was probably little more than an inch, but all space was there, actual and undiminished. Each thing was infinite things, since I distinctly saw it from every angle of the universe. I saw the teeming sea; I saw daybreak and nightfall; I saw the multitudes of America … I saw, close up, unending eyes watching themselves in me as in a mirror; I saw all the mirrors on earth and none of them reflected me; I saw the rotted dust and bones that had once deliciously been Beatriz Viterbo; I saw the circulation of my own dark blood … I saw the Aleph from every point and angle, and in the Aleph I saw the earth and in the earth the Aleph … I saw my own face and my own bowels; I saw your face; and I felt dizzy and wept, for my eyes had seen that secret and conjectured object whose name is common to all men but which no man has looked upon—the unimaginable universe. (Ibid., 9)

For Borges, it could be said, the circle whose centre is everywhere but whose circumference is nowhere, or the formless sphere of absolute space, is the universe or the world. This differs from the main character's conception in "Cream" as it is not limited to the parameters of an internal Self but includes an understanding of Self as world-relation; that is, as inextricably bound up with others and the multiplicity of the physical world.

How many readers recognise the alchemical allusion or have come across this metaphor before? In an interview with *the New Yorker* (2019), the interviewer seemed entirely unaware of its historical significance; it is merely

---

70   *effroyable*

referred to as an *impossible riddle* and a *puzzle*. I agree with Borges when he states, "It may be that universal history is the history of a handful of metaphors" (Borges 1964, 168). Murakami not only introduces the metaphor to his global audience, but also offers an alternative attitude towards it; rather than God or the universe, the circle with infinite centres and no circumference may be understood as a representation of the Self; the inner *cream* or essence of the individual relates to this wider intra-psychic unity. It could be maintained that Murakami follows the classical Jungian approach here. The metaphor has remained the same, yet attitudes towards it have changed; the *different intonations* may represent shifts in personal, historical conceptions of Being. For instance, the religious dimension in Murakami's story, even with the previous announcements from the Christian loudspeaker, may not be immediately apparent to contemporary readers. The conceptual transformation to universe or Self also reflects external possibilities; the new attitude or position allows for and is a prerequisite of both theoretical and bodily-enacted ways of being, conceptualising, and relating. Murakami's (and Jung's, according to traditional interpretation) diminishment of the circle to an individual Self, disconnected from the body, world, and others, in my view, requires comment; that is, a kind of conceptual therapy.

Arguably, a transference from God and the universe to an isolated Self represents a troubling conceptual turn.[71] Therefore, Murakami's short story provides the material for a general analysis of Self in the contemporary epoch as well as a potential rapprochement between literature, philosophy, and psychoanalysis through working with concepts relevant to the material. I propose to add a novel attitude to this metaphor, a post-Jungian extension, which has been established in response to Murakami's literary text and which may deepen subsequent conceptual work with it. The objective is not to psychoanalyse Murakami, or to subordinate the literary purpose of the text to the philosophic, but, primarily, to provide a personal treatment of the key metaphor in the story which may be put to work by others or standalone as a testament to the conceptual depths of Murakami's short text. Post-Jungian theory is not employed to explain the text; rather, it forms part of a creative activity which uses elements apparent in the literary text for its own purposes; in this sense, Murakami's work provides merely an *instance* of the metaphor and so does not bound it; conceptual work with such a metaphor allows for discussion which may or may not return to the text itself and which is nonetheless meaningful in its own right. I would argue, however, that the following

---

71   A schizoid retreat into inner worlds, perhaps.

post-Jungian perspective does allow for an insight into Murakami's central characters; in particular, their strong tendency towards subjectivism[72] and their ongoing struggle to escape such confinement in order to successfully relate to the world.

4.   A Post-Jungian Perspective

In *Jung and Phenomenology* (2015), Roger Brooke rearticulates analytical psychology in light of terminology and perspectives from existential phenomenology; in so doing, analytical psychology is better clarified or extended. Arguably, Brooke's key contribution to post-Jungian theory is the phenomenological insight that experience is existentially situated (Brooke 2015, 20); this point of view is shared by Jung and Heidegger. However, Jung frequently loses touch with this fundamental grounding. For example, he states that "the human psyche lives in indissoluble union with the body" (Jung 1937/42, 114) and yet, elsewhere, seems to put forward a subjectivist psychology. Brooke maintains that there are two Jung's; the poetic Jung who understood psychic activity as essentially metaphorical and imaginative; in contrast, there is the natural-scientist Jung who struggles to fit his psychological insight into the empirical mould. What will be discussed, then, and which will make use of or amplify the key image of "Cream," is a return to *the poetic* understood as a return to the world; analytical psychology will be *thought* (or hermeneutically *rethought*) poetically, with theoretical support from existential phenomenology, in order to bring Jung's therapeutic intentions to light and to generate new engagement with Murakami's work.

Brooke's understanding of *poetry* derives from the Greek *poesis*, to make:[73] "To make involves both the 'thing,' or raw material out of which poesis occurs, and the one who works that transformation" (Brooke 2015, 20). Therefore, there is a "mutually transformative relationship" between Jung and his work (Ibid.), or between Jungians and theirs; if the work of analytical psychology is approached as "the cultural therapeutic endeavour … to reawaken for modern humanity a sense of soul in the world of things" (Ibid., 21), then there is also the endeavour to reawaken the world of things in man's sense of soul or Self. This is what is intended by the term *poetic* in relation to Jung's thought. To think *poetically* is to think *imaginatively*, just as the metallurgy and transformation of the *prima materia* of the alchemists was ultimately a psychological, creative activity. Poesis, as a psychological attitude,

---

72   And here I mean the privileging of the inner over the outer which also presupposes a substance dualism.

73   Further, *to compose* and *to bring into Being*

can be said to have an imaginative, perhaps fictive quality; certainly, it is metaphorical. As we have seen in "Cream" with the circle, "through metaphor reality becomes intensely alive, yet at the same time remains strangely elusive" (Ibid. 8). The "metaphorical character of psychological life" (Ibid., 50) is expressed aptly as "a confusion that clarifies, a detour that puts one more directly on the road" (Murray 1975, 287); one's symptoms (or one's images), then, may provoke the cure.

Metaphors are both imaginative and grounded in the reality of the world. To forget the latter is to misunderstand poesis, and Brooke argues, to misinterpret Jung's essential psychological claims. It is frequently the case that in Jung's thought, and in Murakami's work, "the dichotomy of subject and world, knower and known" is prevalent (Brooke 2015, 21); the Cartesian subject-objective divide manifests in psychological statements which disregard the legitimacy of socially embodied human experience. In Murakami scholarship, for instance, we see this attitude in claims that Murakami explores *other* worlds; additionally, in the view that supporting characters in Murakami novels are a part of or express the main character's consciousness (or unconscious).[74] The post-Jungian task, according to Brooke, is to recognise such assumptions and to engage Jungian thought with the world; in so doing, academics, clinicians, creative writers, and readers, who are influenced by Jung, may also reconnect (and put analytical psychology to work) with a larger conception of the world; further, *material* or *texts* influenced by or conducive to Jungian thought may also be reconnected in this way. The value in analytical psychology is found in its underlying metaphorical attitude; the capacity to form/receive metaphors (to think poetically) is the existential capacity to imagine links between one's subjective perspective or situation and the field of external relations.

However, an issue with Jung's theory is its unnecessary empirical bias. *By rearticulating Jung's work in phenomenological terms,* Brooke attempts to offer an alternative perspective from the Cartesian split, from the "natural-scientific version of reality," and to re-establish the world "as the authentic home of psychological, imaginal life" (Ibid., 24). To provide a brief summary of Jung's position: firstly, there are present archetypal images which give expression to transpersonal, potential human behaviours or experiences; such images are culturally and historically dependent, malleable, and various; the underlying

---

74   As we have discussed, academics frequently use the term *psyche* to refer to the main character (his total consciousness) as well as the fictive world he or she inhabits; relations with secondary characters who are themselves functions of the main character's *psyche* limits any conception of psyche to the subjective level.

similarity of the images is apparent as they occur in relation to the collective experiences or situations of the world, as manifest in dreams, art, fantasies, and delusions. The archetypes cannot themselves be explicated, understood, or expressed apart from their affects and approximation in such motifs or *stereotypes* (Samuels 1986) as the shadow, anima/animus, wise old man, trickster, divine child and so forth. Further, archetypal images, and thus general psychic life and functioning, are "relational" (Brooke 2015, 31): for instance, through polarity, conflict, and resolution. Jung's various theoretical constructs, including ego-relation and the unconscious, are envisioned as taking place within a total psychic whole or *psyche*. For Brooke, the psyche does not refer to some subjective aspect of the individual as a singular, *inner mind*, but is inextricably bound to the body and to incarnate life with others in the world. He maintains the following:

> The term psyche is an intuitive attempt on Jung's part to refer to the essential structure of human existence. Interpreted in terms of the life-world, psyche as understood by Jung approaches Heidegger's explication of Dasein, and interpreted in terms of Dasein it achieves ontological and structural clarity. (Ibid., 25)

Additionally, the relational processes of psychic functioning seem to exhibit "an ordering tendency" (Ibid., 31) or telos: "this tendency to create order and harmony within the psyche is often revealed symbolically" (Ibid.); psychic integration or development is contingent upon the generation of symbols; that is, the creation of images and metaphors (I would add, concepts) grounded in the matrix of collective potentials, local conditions, and individual appropriations; the tendency, or creative function, is termed the Self.

It is argued that Jung's thought points towards the perspective that psyche, body, Self, and the world are essentially inseparable. This connects to Heidegger's notion of *Dasein*; "an entity for which … its Being is itself an issue, has ontologically, a circular structure" (Heidegger 1962, 195); any enquiring into one's psyche, or world, in this view, is inevitably circular or self-reflexive. The tautological nature of psychological understanding is emblematic of the psychic quality of existence and its (poetic) interrelation. If the psyche is understood without relation to others and world, then it may constitute a form of psychologism in which there is "no ontologically separate other to whom one is existentially indebted" (Brooke 2015, 79);[75] the effect of this is that the other has significance only as that which facilitates inner

---

75   Such criticism was put forward by Martin Buber. See *Eclipse of God* (1953), London: Gollancz.

psychological development for the individual; this seems to be the case with much analytical psychology today as well as, arguably, in much interpretation of Murakami; secondary characters may be understood merely as figures existing or created for the protagonist's/individual's development;[76] as Samuels states: "the apparently real figures with which the ego may be in contact are usually seen by him (Jung) as external manifestations of inner process" (Samuels 1985, 115). A post-Jungian perspective, in contrast, attempts to recover the connection with others and world; individuation or psychological development requires real relation with other existentially situated individuals; in terms of Murakami research, this may mean a move away from interpretations which focus on the subjective experience of the individual.

> The psyche as the means of observation and the world as observed cannot be that clearly distinguished, for they form a structural unity which precedes differentiation into this or that entity. (Brooke 2015, 81)

Brooke suggests, then, that Jung's notion of psychic reality is better understood (or uncovered) through Heidegger's term Dasein or world-relation, which more clearly articulates the self-reflexive nature of existence; further, Dasein is directed towards being with the other as being-there through the mode of care.[77] Therefore, analytical psychology differs from other forms of psychoanalysis as it recognises that the psyche, as the world (or life-world), as the setting and totality of experience, is not internal or subjectivized. Rather, "we are in the psyche" (Cahen, 1983, 82).

> I do not have a psyche, but am present in the world in a variety of ways, waking, dreaming, fantasising, but always in a characteristically human, that is physical, way.

> To be in the world psychically … leads us naturally to speak of psychic space, and of psyche itself as a space. Heidegger, too, speaks of man as a clearing. (Jung 1947/54 92; 95)

---

76   The autonomy and independence of the *other* is disregarded.

77   *Care*, concern, and solicitude could be productively applied in greater depth to the Murakami's work. "… Heidegger defines 'care' as the Being of Dasein. It is a name for the structural whole of existence in all its modes and for the broadest and most basic possibilities of discovery and disclosure of self and world. Most poignantly experienced in the phenomenon of anxiety—which is not fear of anything at hand but awareness of my being-in-the-world as such—'care' describes the sundry ways I get involved in the issue of my birth, life, and death, whether by my projects, inclinations, insights, or illusions. 'Care' is the all-inclusive name for my concern for other people, preoccupations with things, and awareness of my proper Being. It expresses the movement of my life out of a past, into a future, through the present" (Ed. note, 223). Heidegger, Martin. 1993. rev. and expanded ed. *Basic Writings: From Being and Time (19270 to The Task of Thinking* (1964). Edited by David Farrell Krell. New York: HarperCollins.

The psyche, then, is not spatialised as interiority (as an inner world), but is that space of human activity, gathering and disclosure: a gathering which is psychically experienced, embodied, and metaphorical. The Self, the elusive term, is that which gathers, or notices and makes sense of one's gathered matrix of relations; this gathering discloses others as well as ourselves. The Self is essentially related to world and psyche, but it is not the psyche exactly; if the psyche, as Dasein, is the total world and place of meaningful relations, then the Self is that which an individual may gather or take up from that world as one's own:

> the self comprises infinitely more than a mere ego. It is as much one's self, and all other selves, as the ego. Individuation (the coming-into-being of the self) does not shut one out from the world, but gathers the world to oneself. (Ibid., 226)

To summarise, psyche is that world which is "constituted through and disclosive of human existence" (Brooke 2015, 83). Therefore, "both psyche and Dasein are necessarily caught within the hermeneutic circle of self-understanding" (Ibid., 89); any answer to questions concerning psyche leaves a trace or image of the question itself. This connects to Heidegger's notion of Being's unconcealment which has ontological priority to logical thinking.[78] Psyche and Dasein are connected to Jung's notion of the Self which, as we noted above, is also described as the psychic totality of the individual:

> … the self as centre and totality, and as the psychological form of the most original author of one's life, is indistinguishable from the God-image, or even God in so far as God is experienced at all … the Self can be understood as both the source and goal of human life. (Ibid., 31)

It could be argued that the circle in "Cream," from a poetic or metaphorical perspective, is an archetypal image of the Self; I argue, further, that it metaphorically discloses or unconceals an aspect of Being-in-the-world. It could also be maintained that it is a God-image, particularly if we consider the religious themes of the story. However, I interpret God here to denote an Other or transpersonal aspect of psychological experience;[79] it may be stated that

---

78   'Unconcealment' relates to Heidegger's idiosyncratic notion of *truth*, translated from the ancient Greek *alêtheia*. Unconcealment opens up or gathers the world as a *clearing* (*lichtung*) and allows entities (the truth of entities) to show or present themselves; entities and their worlds may also be encountered (in the sense of this uncovering). In terms of Murakami, what does his work disclose or uncover about the world? See further, Wrathall, Mark A., 2010. *Heidegger and Unconcealment: Truth, Language, and History.* Cambridge: Cambridge University Press.

79   Importantly, not an *other world* but an otherness in or of this world.

the religious function of individuals is the need to relate in some way to this experience of the pre-personal, that is, non-personal (non-I) or, perhaps, supra-personal; whether this requires a sacrifice of the personal to an impersonal, greater reality or objective aspect of existence, exceeds the scope of this essay. The key point is that the development of one's psychology is inextricably linked to relations with the unknown, with others, and the world at large.

Brooke writes, "consciousness emerges by means of the realisation and integration of images in the life of the individual … [which] point to a reality beyond the immediacy of the image itself" (Ibid., 33); I argue that such symbolic activity is potentialized in Murakami's creative work; the image of the circle, for instance, may be taken up by readers (metaphorically) as material for their own symbolic and imaginative work, as Murakami himself has done so, as I am doing now, and as you may do so as readers of this article. Such work is fundamentally *linguistic*.

Whether or not this work is successful is beside the point; centrally, and I would say this is the philosophical value of Murakami and writers like him, is that his stories elicit a symbolic or conceptual response; the images present in Murakami's work, beloved around the world, clearly have potential transformative power.[80] In other words, Murakami could be said to produce, intentionally or not, modern archetypal situations; the young narrator in "Cream" is at a disorientating, liminal point of his life; instead of becoming lost in the desert, undertaking a heroic journey or so forth, he is waiting on a park bench for a piano concert and talking to a strange old man; consequently, an archetypal image presents itself which potentializes the transformation of the personality and a new life of the individual (or new ego-relation to the unconscious and the world). Of course, Jung is primarily concerned with *real* events that may occur to the individual, or personal fantasy that is generated; however, it may be said that the characters and worlds we encounter in fiction are no less cognitively real or meaningful than our ordinary conscious lives; in which case, the life of the individual includes the fictional lives we encounter. What is present in both experiences is intentional consciousness, imaginative involvement, and the possibility of creative work which is essentially related to one's physical or *everyday* functioning in the world.

---

80   Transformative power for both the writer (Murakami), the characters in the novels, and the reader; there is no clear cognitive distinction between images/concepts encountered in fiction or ordinary reality; our lives are far from being *non-fictional*.

To clarify, Brookes maintains that Jung is misunderstood if his psychological terms, such as psyche or the Self are interiorised; "the suggestion that Jung encapsulates human existence within a psyche separate from the world begs questions about the nature of the psyche and its relation to the world" (Ibid., 38). As considered earlier, the metaphysical questions in Murakami, in particular "Cream," are worked through *over-here* in existentially situated experience in contrast to an *over-there* reality. It is argued that these key terms:

> … need to be recovered as descriptions of relationships with the world, for that is the inescapable place of experience and setting within which the drama and meaning of human life unfolds. (Ibid., 62)

Murakami is essentially connected to Jung through such terms as psyche and Self which exist as central openings within and into his literary material. The Cartesian divide evidenced in academic approaches to Murakami's work (as well as uncovered from the work itself) misses the psychological importance and potential of metaphor; "a metaphor opens up the world and at the same time situates the imagination" (Ibid., 66); the imagination existentially situates the individual in relation to the world. For instance, an individual may appropriate or differentiate (individuation, authenticity) from their localised context; rejection, integration, or other usage of archetypal images is not viewed as the endeavour to constitute an isolated individual; rather, work with such images is always relational; that is, it takes place within an embodied, social, and historical setting. The main character in "Cream," and equally in most of Murakami's other works, could be said to be largely inauthentic in this sense as the necessary appropriation, or contact with archetypal images and metaphors, lacks a relational grounding; therefore, Murakami characters are individuals but not individuated. At the deepest level of psychological experience, the narrator in "Cream" does not relate to others and is alienated from the (life-)world. Does Murakami's global appeal owe itself, in some part, to a global readership who are struggling to relate to each other and the world? Or is it due to a readership who do not recognise such a state of affairs as a struggle, pre-occupied with their own images and situations, gathering from their external experience only that which reflects back on themselves and their inner worlds? The fact that Murakami's work presents characters who are disconnected from a reality outside of themselves, coupled with its immense popularity, may indicate a general psychological quality of our contemporary epoch.[81] [82]

Finally, to return to the Self. Brooke refers to Jung's definition, added in 1960 to his *Psychological Types* (1921/1971): "The self designates the whole range of psychic phenomena in man. It expresses the unity of the personality as a whole" (Jung 1921/1971, 460). For Jung, it seems, the Self, rather than the ordering tendency of psychic processes, can be terminologically clarified as the psychic totality, or *psyche-Dasein*.

> The inference would seem to be that every individual, by virtue of having, or being, a psyche, is potentially the Self. It is only a question of 'realizing' it. But the realization, if ever achieved, is the work of a life-time. (Ibid., 460n)[83]

Such a realization is perhaps Jung's cream of life or magnum opus, as the alchemists say. Our concept work comes to a head; the Self is the process of realising psyche, an ongoing relation to the non-personal. Brooke refers to Jung's use of the saying of St. Bonaventure (one which we are familiar with), and he adds the following from Jung, quoted by Serrano:

> So far, I have found no stable or definitive centre in the unconscious and I don't believe that such a centre exists. I believe that the thing I call the Self is an ideal centre … [a] dream of totality. (Serrano, 1968, p. 50)[84]

Therefore, Jung himself is working with the circle from "Cream," unable to entirely figure out that strange image. I maintain that such a circle refers to the non-personal aspect of psychological experience; an undefined circumference of which we all may be centres, looking for that ideal centre—the

---

81   This seems to be changing with Murakami's most recent novel, *Killing Commendatore*, in which the main character reunites with his estranged wife and becomes a father; again, one could interpret this as a reflection of the main character's subjective psychology in terms of an archetypal image of the *divine child* or of a personal rebirth; or one could interpret it as the attempt to establish connections with others.

82   Additionally, the main character in *Dance, Dance, Dance* (1988/1994) may be said to successfully relate to the *real* world by the end of the novel.

83   This is noted by the editors of Jung's *Collected Works*.

84   It must be noted that Miguel Serrano was a prominent supporter of Nazism. His friendship with Jung (as well as with the Nobel-prize winner Herman Hesse), then, is historically interesting and challenging; post-Jungians need to recognise and address areas of Jung's thought which were severely lacking; for instance, Jung is quoted as saying this in the same paragraph: "… the Hindus are notoriously weak in rational exposition. They think for the most part in parables or images. They are not interesting in appealing to reason. That, of course, is a basic condition of the Orient as a whole" (Serrano, 1968, p. 50). Jung clearly respects and has an extensive knowledge of Hindu philosophy, employing such terms as the *Atman* and *Purusha*, but could be said to have appropriated Eastern thought to his own psychological theory.

heart of the world, to be metaphorical.[85] As Borges maintains, "… universal history is the history of a handful of metaphors" (Borges 1964, 168) and the image of the circle in "Cream" certainly participates in this historical-metaphorical-linguistic and existential process; here we have added a novel perspective; Self, not as God or Universe or even World, but as individual world-relation and world-gathering; indeed, the capacity to relate and compose.[86] Self and psyche are terms which appear in Murakami's work as well as in the secondary literature; I have attempted to put forward a post-Jungian perspective or deepening of these terms which may be of use to others engaged in their own concept work. Further, it may be the case that Murakami characters are beginning to recognise and work with this existential situation. The core of psychic processes, reaching a total understanding of one's place in the world, is certainly a fantasy, and necessarily so.

Murakami presents us with material that may act as a springboard (or diving-board) for further imaginative and conceptual activity; his work has helped us to consider the existential centre. Any so-called *Murakami-world* is surely this world:

> … the self as centre, whether experienced existentially or only intuited as ('theoretical') possibility, does not refer to a reified entity within the psyche (however defined) but to the capacity of the self as a totality to structure psychic life around a centre … All too often, … that centre is understood in the humanistic sense, as a Self within the person,[87] but to do that is to muddle ego and self, and ultimately to deify the person. Rather, the centre of the Self is that to which I am related most deeply[88] and to which I try to return in times of ethical questioning, of crisis, of silence. (Brooke 2015, 98)

The narrator of "Cream" returns to the circle in just this way when he encounters "inexplicable, illogical, disturbing" events (Murakami 2021, 25): "It is a centre that is most intimately mine, yet it is not 'in me' unless I imagine it there" (Brooke 2015, 98), in which case the Murakamian conception of Self can be extended as a metaphorical gathering of the world. As Heidegger states, "the ownmost of Dasein consists in its existence" (Heidegger 1962, 68) in which existence is transcending towards Being-in-the world and others within the unconcealment of Being. Reading Murakami's work allows us to continue exploring such fictions of totality.

---

85   Of course, it is a task without resolution.
86   In the sense of *poesis*.
87   As Murakami writes in "Cream": This circle is, most likely, not a circle with a concrete, actual form but, rather one that exists only within our minds" (Murakami 2021, 25).
88   A key point: the centre of one's world is not necessarily oneself.

5.   Conclusion

Not all literary works offer the rich metaphorical material of Murakami's fiction; further, Murakami's work is understood as highly philosophic as it allows readers to explore such concepts as the unconscious (Strecher 2014; 2020), the Other, the role of myth (Yama 2016), the role of the artist (Suter, 2020), the Self and so forth. This philosophic value in Murakami is understood as an extension of the literary function rather than a superimposition; it offers an alternative, conceptual avenue into and from the works. Both Jung and Murakami present a metaphorical and poetic way of relating to the world; importantly, metaphors are existentially situated; that is, they require a foundation in this world; therefore, it is hoped that future approaches to Murakami's work consider this aspect alongside the more subjective position. In other words, I propose that Murakami's fiction takes place within a psyche which is always in relation to the world instead of an interiorised psychic space or inner mind.

Metaphors vital ways of living in and making sense of this world. As Brooke writes, "… for Jung all statements about the human being and his or her world are metaphorical" (Brooke 2015, 18). This sentiment is also expressed in Murakami's work; for instance, implicitly in the image of the circle in "Cream," and explicitly through the words of certain characters such as the librarian Oshima in Kafka on the Shore (2005):

> I'm repeating myself, but everything in life is metaphor. People don't usually kill their father and sleep with their mother, right? In other words, we accept irony through a device called metaphor. And through that we grow and become deeper human beings. (Murakami 2005, 185)

The titles of each part of *Killing Commendatore* (2018), 'The Idea Made Visible' and 'The Shifting Metaphor,' also suggest that Murakami recognises the metaphorical quality of his works. The work of Haruki Murakami certainly has a metaphorical depth; that is, it presents archetypal or mythic images which resonate with a global audience (Martinez, 2008; Yama, 2016). This allows for various and productive concept work for philosophic, artistic, and therapeutic purposes.

I maintain that metaphors and concepts are not only necessarily linguistic, but socio-historical; further, the philosophic activity of working with and towards concepts from metaphor, as I have done so in this essay, differs from reader-response theory in the sense that the metaphors are extracted from, rather than embedded in, the text; one's response or interpretation is not limited to a specific text; primarily, the reader *responds to a concept*; the reader is potentially a philosopher whose experience of the text forms part of a larger creative, conceptual project; therefore, the literary work, if approached in this way, amounts to an instance or component of a concept.

Whilst conceptual responses to a text are meaningful on an individual basis and remain meaningful regardless of their subsequent communication, the act of sharing one's response also participates in the socio-historical process; as a conceptual network, the individual is dispossessed or renounces ownership of the concept; the concept engages or disengages with other concepts and components to the effect that different combinations (different nodal connections, perhaps) may be generated; thus, novel extensions, engagements, and experiences are potentialized (and may be *repossessed*). One's concept work is meaningful on an individual and collective (networked) level; this is another intonation of the concept, *poesis*. For instance, I have worked with the concepts of psyche and Self, moving towards Dasein and world-relation; Murakami's texts do not own such concepts; and of course, neither do I; any ownership can only be understood as a momentary act of appropriation or participation within a linguistic, socio-historical process from one's local conditions to the extent of one's conceptual competency; the only real *telos* is to keep the experience (in this case, the communication of one's engagement with the literary work) or conversation going, as it were, and to put forward something interesting. One might add that there are no correct, incorrect, or complete interpretations of Murakami's work, only engagements which are more interesting, relatable, or popular (to continue the analogy, as denser network clusters).

Jung and post-Jungian thought allows us to explore the internal dimension of Murakami's work; further, Murakami's work allows us to explore the internal dimension itself; we are hermeneutically searching for the existential descriptions which are felt to be the most appropriate (or interesting) to our personal and contemporary situations. Finally, this essay is the first part of a larger project on Murakami which envisions more sustained post-Jungian or philosophic approaches to his work. For example, Brooke's thought or phenomenology generally may be applied more extensively; *Dasein* can be more rigorously examined in relation to Murakami; what exactly is the *Murakamian* Dasein? Are Murakami characters authentic? Has Murakami remained authentic to his own creative project?[89] *Unconcealment* can also be explored

---

89   Especially considering his commercial success and the huge, collaborative editing and translation project which gets his work to market. See further, Karashima, David. 2020. *Who We're Reading When We're Reading Murakami.* New York: Soft Skull.

further; what understanding of the world is disclosed through its *presencing* in his fiction approached as a space of imaginative possibility? Additionally, one could explore other existential metaphors in Murakami and consider how readers respond to them; what concepts are generated by this response? Readers and academics recognise that there is an element of the unconscious at play in Murakami's work whether this is understood as linguistic, mythic, or metaphysical; we are all interested in Murakami because he articulates and helps us to articulate this depth; that is why, I would say, there are frequent connections with Carl Gustav Jung. My existential description of the fiction of Haruki Murakami is as follows: the main characters struggle with moving beyond the subjective confinement of an inner mind or world; it may be the case that Murakami's literary worlds, as extended by the concepts of psyche, Self, and Dasein from analytical psychology and phenomenology, express the existential situation of living with others in a world which has an essential metaphorical quality and which exceeds oneself; the characters in Murakami's work, as evidenced by the conclusion to *Killing Commendatore* (2018),[90] may be beginning to relate more authentically to this world. I am hopeful that new questions and new disclosures concerning world-relation in the work of Murakami will be considered further through the conceptual network.

References

Borges, Jorge Luis. 1945. *The Aleph*. Translated by Norman Thomas Di Giovanni in collaboration with the author. https://web.mit.edu/allan mc/www/borgesaleph.pdf.

Borges, Jorge Luis. 1964. *Labyrinths*. Edited by Donald A. Yates and James E. Irby. New York: New Directions.

Brooke, Roger. 2015. Rev. ed. *Jung and Phenomenology*. London: Routledge. First Published 1991.

Cahen, Roland. 1983. "Do worry, it's psychic!" *Analytische Psychologie* 14, no. 2: 134–146.

Dil, Jonathan. 2010. "Writing as self-therapy: competing therapeutic paradigms in Murakami Haruki's Rat trilogy." *Japan Forum*, 22 (1–2): 43–64.

Hashimoto, Lica. 2015. "Translating Haruki Murakami's '1Q84' in Brazil: Transferring Culture, Transferring Alterity." *Japanese Language and Literature* 49, no. 1: 179–200.

---

90   See notes 81 and 82.

Heidegger, Martin. 1962. *Being and Time.* Translated by John Macquarrie and Edward Robinson. Oxford: Basil Blackwell.

Jung, Carl Gustav. 1921/1971. *Psychological Types.* Translated by R. F. C. Hull, C.W.6. London: Routledge.

Jung, Carl Gustav. 1930/1950. "Psychology and Literature." Translated by R. F. C. Hull, C.W.15: 133–62.

Jung, Carl Gustav. 1933. *Modern Man in Search of a Soul.* Translated by W. S. Dell and Cary F. Baynes. New York: Harvest.

Jung, C. (1937/42). "Psychological factors determining human behaviour." Translated by R. F. C. Hull, C.W.8: 114–25.

Jung, C. (1947/54). "On the nature of the psyche." Translated by R. F. C. Hull, C.W.8: 159–234.

Martinez, Inez. 2008. "Haruki Murakami's reimagining of Sophocles' Oedipus." In *Psyche and the Arts: Jungian Approaches to Music, Architecture, Literature, Painting and Film.* London: Routledge.

Murakami, Haruki. 2005. *Kafka on the Shore.* Translated by Philip Gabriel. London: Harvill Secker.

Murakami, Haruki. 2011. *1Q84.* Translated by Jay Rubin and Philip Gabriel. London: Harvill Secker.

Murakami, Haruki. 2018., *Killing Commendatore.* Translated by Philip Gabriel. London: Harvill Secker.

Murakami, Haruki. 2021. *First Person Singular.* Translated by Philip Gabriel. London: Harvill Secker. pp. 1–28.

Murray, Edward L. 1975. "The phenomenon of the metaphor." *Duquesne Studies in Phenomenological Psychology* 2, 281–300.

Rubin, Jay. 2012. *Haruki Murakami and the Music of Words.* London: Vintage. First published 2002 Harvill Secker.

Samuels, Andrew. 1985. *Jung and the Post-Jungians.* London: Routledge and Kegan Paul.

Samuels, Andrew, Bani Shorter, and Fred Plaut, eds. 1986. *A Critical Dictionary of Jungian Analysis.* London: Routledge and Kegan Paul.

Serrano, Miguel. 1968. *C. G. Jung and Herman Hesse: a Record of Two Friendships.* Translated by Frank MacShane. New York: Schocken Books.

Strecher, Matthew Carl. 1999. "Magical Realism and the Search for Identity in the Fiction of Murakami Haruki." *Journal of Japanese Studies* 25, no. 2: 263–298.

Strecher, Matthew Carl. 2014. *The Forbidden Worlds of Haruki Murakami.* Minneapolis: University of Minnesota Press.

Strecher, Matthew Carl. 2020. "Out of the (B)earth canal: the mythic journey in Murakami Haruki." *Japan Forum*, 32 (3): 338–360.

Suter, Rebecca. 2016. "Critical Engagement through Fantasy in Hard-Boiled Wonderland and the End of the World." In *Haruki Murakami: Challenging Authors*, Leiden, Brill.

Suter, Rebecca. 2020. "The artist as a medium and the artwork as metaphor in Murakami Haruki's fiction." *Japan Forum*, 32 (3): 361–378.

Treisman, Deborah. 2019, Jan 21. "Haruki Murakami on asking the right questions." *The New Yorker*. January 21. https://www.newyorker.com/books/this-week-in-fiction/haruki-murakami-01-28-19.

Yama, Megumi. 2016. "Haruki Murakami: Modern-Myth Maker beyond Culture." *Jung Journal*, 10 (1): 87–95.

Chikako Nihei

Time for Spaghetti in Haruki Murakami's Fiction: What Cooking Time Means in a Consumerist Society[91]

Translated by **Andrew Houwen**

Abstract *Today, a successful life is often thought to mean a busy one: being busy means finding and enjoying leisure time and material consumption by earning income from employment. The aim of this article is to consider why, at a time when such a busy lifestyle is taken for granted, Haruki Murakami has become so famous around the world for not depicting busy protagonists. It reflects on the origins of society's normalisation of being busy and sheds light on the peculiarity of the way the 'boku' protagonists pass their time. By doing so, it will reveal Murakami's perspective on capitalist society.*

Keywords: Murakami Haruki, cooking, spaghetti, time, capitalism, consumerism, salaryman

1. Haruki Murakami's International Popularity

Being busy, especially spending time working, is an ideal for many people today. Those who manage their time resourcefully and can use it effectively without damaging their health are judged to be superior. This is clearly evident in the fact that bookstores are full of self-help books on topics such as 'managing time to achieve success.' These do not change the busy lifestyle itself but instead outline methods for managing time well while maintaining such a lifestyle. Being busy is not a bad thing. The problem is being unable to deal with the work or tasks one is given. Yano remarks that, today, a "successful society" is thought to be one in which people are pressed for time and increasingly lack it. Their spare time is spent on material consumption. However, purchasing products and services and consuming goods also take time; our time is "driven by the consumption of goods." Furthermore, our busy

---

91   The original paper is, Nihei, Chikako. 2018. "Murakami Haruki no supageti no jikan: Shihonshugi shakai ni oite ryōri ni jikan o kakerukoto [Time for spaghetti in Haruki Murakami's fiction: What cooking time means in a consumerist society]." *Time Studies* 9: 9–22.

lifestyles are generated by the cycle of continuing to work to earn money for material consumption (Yano 1995, 33).

We tend to want to believe that the future will be better than the past and that time progresses forwards in one direction; technological advances have boosted productivity and lessened workers' hardships; and thanks to capitalism working hours have significantly decreased. However, in reality, while technology has developed and productivity has doubled, working hours have been extended and even more productivity has been sought from workers (Schor 1995, 10; Saitō 2006; Tanaka 2006). The belief that a lot of material things and increased material consumption represent progress in our lives, and the idea that the more we work the more our lives develop, have become totally dominant. To what extent the desire to improve one's lifestyle by working longer is a choice that is permitted to the individual, however, is open to question. The more increased productivity is sought, the more workers are constrained by mechanised time and lose their freedom. The reader empathises with the time-thieves in Michael Ende's *Momo* because there are so few individuals who can use their time freely (Yano 1995, 3).

The number of people living in cities now represents more than half of the total global population. Busy days have become the established sign of urban life and the difference between its lifestyle and culture is not large. In a society in which such a busy lifestyle has become ubiquitous around the world, there is an author who attracts readers by depicting protagonists who are not busy. That author is Haruki Murakami. The popularity of Murakami's works in Japan has been widely acknowledged, but their widespread popularity overseas arguably exceeds it. They have now been translated into more than fifty languages and every year he is discussed in the media as a nominee for the Nobel Prize in Literature; whenever it is announced that a new work is to be published, there is an auction for the translation rights; and at overseas universities, students of Japanese or comparative literature take courses on Murakami. The number of overseas researchers also continues to grow, monographs and articles are published every year, and conferences dedicated to Murakami are held both in Japan and abroad.

Murakami's popularity overseas is qualitatively different from previous works of Japanese literature. If we focus on Anglophone translations of Japanese literature, the works that arouse an Orientalist "nostalgic image of a lost past" in readers, such as those of Yasunari Kawabata, Yukio Mishima, or Jun'ichirō Tanizaki, have been most frequently translated (Venuti 1998, 72). These are read in order to imagine Japan as a distant, exotic country rather than with a sense of common ground. Murakami's works began to be translated in English-speaking countries from the 1990s onwards in particular, but the Orientalist, feminine image of Japan has remained and often appears in the widespread use of photographs of Asian women on the covers of the English versions. However, Murakami's works, which are full of characters who love American novels, jazz, eating donuts and drinking beer, swept away this previous image of Japanese literature.

The international popularity of Murakami's works has become researchers' focus of attention. Researchers have put forward various propositions concerning the reasons for this popularity, but they primarily observed the absence of a clear national identity in Murakami's works. These lean towards American culture and have few so-called Japanese cultural elements, so that they could just as easily be set in modern cities such as New York, London, Beijing, or Hong Kong. This is said to be connected to the acquisition of their international readership (Shibata et al. 2009). On the other hand, the familiar *boku* ("I") protagonists' unique characteristics, especially their love of independence, have also been proposed as a reason for this popularity. Many of Murakami's protagonists are single people in their 20s or 30s or married people without children; they work on their own as writers, for example, rarely for large companies. It is said that many readers are attracted to their tendency not to feel that time alone is lonely and to create and enjoy their own kind of lifestyle (McInerney 1992).

Once time has become a currency, it is said that it does not become something to "pass" but rather something to "spend" (Schor 1995, v). "Spending" refers to mechanised time for the purpose of economic growth, while "passing" refers to an individual's use of time based on their free will. People "spending" time every day on work do not appear in Murakami's works; there are only people who "pass" their time. One of the factors that strengthens the impression of characters "passing" their time is the length of time taken up by the *boku* protagonists' cooking and housework. Without ever being pressured by others or feeling a sense of obligation, they enjoy their cooking and housework. Murakami's perspective on the experience of Japan's post-war economic development is reflected in the *boku* protagonists' ways of passing the time. He remarks:

> After the end of the Second World War, people worked very hard to rebuild the country and did not mind making sacrifices. It was thought that work led to wealth and wealth led to happiness. They were perhaps naïve, and people really continued to hold this belief for a long time. It was because we believed this that my parents' generation and the people of my generation came to work so hard. Then at the time of the "bubble economy" in the

1980s, we finally achieved material comfort. We had become wealthy. But still without being able to find happiness. (Murakami 2012, 160)

When Murakami began writing novels in the late 1970s, Japan's economy was speeding up from the post-war period into the bubble economy. It was at just this time that working hard was the ideal and was deemed to be 'civilised.' People enjoyed material wealth. However, as Murakami says, material wealth did not lead to happiness. The fact that the *boku* protagonists, who do not seek happiness in material consumption and enjoy their own individual way of living, acquired such a large readership indicates a gap that society's material wealth cannot fill. Nonetheless, people's tendency to believe that material wealth leads to happiness and to spend most of their time on working excessively hard continues to this day.

This article will consider what modern people's use of their time says about the aims of society and will examine the particular ways in which the *boku* protagonists of Murakami's works pass their time. The protagonists do not simply reject work; instead, we can observe Murakami's intention to sound a warning about situations in which individuals' lives can be exploited at all levels by paid work and to allow readers to think about their own lives in this regard.

2.   The Young Man Cooking Spaghetti

Murakami made his debut as a novelist in 1979 at the age of 29. His début novel, *Hear the Wind Sing,* was awarded the Gunzō New Writers' Prize and was subsequently selected for literary prizes in Japan and overseas. He saw the economic development of post-war Japan's baby-boomer generation; experienced the new spiritual disillusion that appeared in a society that had achieved material wealth; and, as a student at Waseda University, witnessed the student movement of the late 1960s that sought to address this problem by destroying the 'system.' Traces of the student movement appear in Murakami's early works in particular; what these depicted, however, was not young people's despair at the failures of the past, which often appeared in the works of baby-boomer writers of the time, but rather young people dealing with the difficulties of the past by trying to move forward. The *boku* do not loudly express dissatisfaction. They do not think that the individual is opposed to society; they are aware that the individual has to live by depending on its benefits. They coolly observe society, are aware of its power, and express their views when necessary. There is no great opposition to or revolution against the 'system.' Instead, the individual avoids being constrained by authority, creates their own rules, and maintains their own views without being misled by information. This is expressed in the strength of the *boku* protagonists' free will. Readers' admiration for the *boku* indicates how difficult it is for us in this society to create our own views without being misled by social norms or the media, though it might seem an easy thing to do.

The *boku* live orderly lives. Usually they wake up every morning at a particular time, prepare food, take care of their housework, and if they have time, do some moderate exercise by swimming in a pool; at night, they do not drink heavily but go to bed. This appears to reflect Murakami's own regular habits of waking up at five o'clock every morning and running ten kilometres before breakfast. The *boku* are not especially wealthy. They do not have a high income, nor are they in positions of political power. They do not drive expensive cars or live in expensive apartments. They are lucky to have enough economic means not to experience hardship, but they seem to live a more or less humble life cooking for themselves.

Moreover, while most of Murakami's works are set in Tokyo, the way the *boku* pass the time seems unusual to city dwellers. Signature behaviours for salarymen such as commuting every day on crowded trains, going to noisy *izakaya* and karaoke bars, and shopping on busy streets or visiting regional tourist hotspots at the weekend are absent in the *boku* protagonists' lives. There are no mobile phones, televisions, or Internet connections in their homes, nor do they seek to satisfy material desires by buying things. Although their lives seem unremarkable due to their humble nature, these lives are actually unrealistic for many people today and difficult to put into practice. Without being ordered around by anyone, the *boku* get up at regular times, make healthy food, and carefully iron and clean. Their special kind of seriousness and sincerity is admired with a sort of respect by readers around the world.

The *boku* protagonists' disciplined lifestyles are shown in their obsession with housework. They apply twelve steps in their ironing (*The Wind-Up Bird Chronicle*), use six cloths to wax the floor of a mountain lodge (*A Wild Sheep Chase*), mop the floor every day, clean the windows every three days, and hang their futon out to dry once a week (*Norwegian Wood*) (Uchida 2012, 12). They clean and wash, even when they are married: they do not leave housework to their wives. Their obsession with cooking is especially noticeable. Below is a scene in the novel *Dance, Dance, Dance*. The bachelor protagonist is preparing dinner:

> Roughly chop two cloves of garlic and fry with olive oil. Tip the frying pan a little so the oil is evenly distributed and fry for a while on a low heat. After that, add whole red chillis, then fry them with the garlic. Take out the garlic and chillis before they become bitter. The timing for taking them out is quite tricky. Then slice and add ham and fry until crispy. Add boiled spaghetti and stir thoroughly with a handful of chopped parsley. Serve with a fresh mozzarella and tomato salad. (Murakami 1997a, 242)

Below are the small dishes "to go with alcohol" that the *boku* makes at his apartment for his friend Gotanda in the same novel:

> I made a side-dish of spring onions and *ume*, adding bonito flakes on top; made *wakame* and seaweed dressed in vinegar; mixed thinly sliced fish-cake with grated *daikon* and pickled wasabi; and fried potatoes in olive oil, garlic, and a small amount of salami. I made a quick pickled dish with finely chopped cucumber. There was some cooked *hijiki* and tofu left over. I used plenty of ginger for seasoning. "Amazing," Gotanda said, with a sigh, "you're a real pro!" (Murakami 1998, 165).

Whether it is food prepared for himself or for someone else, we can see the care with which the *boku* makes food. The *boku* protagonists' cooking satisfies both their friends and romantic partners, enriches their conversations, and helps build their relationships. The *boku* charm both their male friends and the women he invites over with his skillful cooking, which then contributes to the development of their relationships.

What is remarkable in the *boku* protagonists' cooking scenes is their detailed description, as if they were recipes. This is not uncommon in Murakami's works: sometimes they run to seemingly unnecessary lengths on the page. An example of this is the description of making a sandwich in *Hard-Boiled Wonderland and the End of the World*:

> That sandwich easily cleared my usual standard. The bread was fresh and soft, and cut with a clean knife. It's something that tends to be overlooked, but to make a good sandwich it's essential to have a good knife. No matter how good the ingredients are, if the knife is bad the sandwich can't taste good. The mustard was top-notch, the lettuce was crunchy, the mayonnaise was handmade or as good as. I hadn't eaten such a good sandwich for a long time. (Murakami 2007, 81)

This is a scene in which a "fat woman in pink clothes" impresses the *boku* with a fresh sandwich. The protagonist will later be helped in the exploration of the darkness of underground Tokyo by this woman whom he has just encountered, but the scene plays an important role in making the *boku* aware of her careful approach to her work through the way she makes a sandwich. Murakami's protagonists tend to understand their companions through the sincerity of their attitude to food. They trust those who take eating seriously.

Unfortunately, the above description of the sandwich was cut in the English translation. In the English versions of Murakami's works, it is not uncommon to cut out parts that are thought to be unnecessary for the development of the novels, but here we can observe the view of the English translator (and editor) that a lengthy depiction of food typical of Murakami's works is redundant.

Many cooking and food-related scenes appear in Murakami's works, but especially common dishes, as in the quotation above, are spaghetti and sandwiches. The scene in which spaghetti is being cooked at the start of *The Wind-Up Bird Chronicle* is impressive. As the unemployed *boku* is boiling some spaghetti for himself, an unfamiliar woman's voice speaks to him on the phone. The woman asks him to talk with her for ten minutes so that they can get to know one another:

> "Just ten minutes is fine, so I just need a moment of your time. Then we can get to know each other better," the woman said. Her voice was low, gentle, and elusive.
> "Get to know each other better?"
> "Our feelings."
> . . . .
> "Sorry, but I'm boiling some spaghetti. Could you call back later?"
> "Spaghetti?" the woman said in a voice that seemed startled. "You're boiling spaghetti at 10:30 in the morning?"
> "That's none of your business. What I eat and when I eat it's up to me," I said, slightly grumpily. (Murakami 1997b, 12)

When the *boku* asks her to wait for him to finish cooking, she gets the message and hangs up. Soon afterwards, the *boku* gets another phone call from the woman. Try as he might, he cannot recognise the voice of the woman who knows him so well. After that, he is amazed at the sexually charged story she begins to tell him and hangs up on her. Soon after this, his wife suddenly disappears. He does not understand her disappearance, as he thought their relationship was fairly strong. While the search for his wife proceeds, he realises that the woman who called him at the start of the novel was his wife. He cannot recognise the voice of the woman who thinks he recognises her and rejects her suggestion of them getting to know each other better in favour of cooking his spaghetti. He tries to reflect on his own mistake and on his relationship with his wife. This process of self-reflection leads to the search for his wife and the novel develops from there.

In this way, the opening spaghetti scene plays an important role in setting up the further development of the *boku* protagonist's adventure. His personality is shown here in the way he regards cooking and eating as something valuable. As stated above, his tendency to enjoy his time in his own way without paying attention to others' expectations is connected to how he creates an impression on the reader of a strong-willed, individual *boku*. However, in *The Wind-Up Bird Chronicle*, this can at times cause him to be misunderstood by others and result in the breakdown of relationships.

The protagonists in Murakami's works are as obsessed with sandwiches as they are with spaghetti. As the quotation above suggests, they have a keen eye for detail regarding sandwich ingredients and the way to use kitchen utensils. It is not uncommon for the phone to ring while spaghetti is cooking in Murakami's works. For the *boku* obsessed with boiling exquisite spaghetti, the last thing he wants is to have his cooking interrupted by a phone call. Later in *The Wind-Up Bird Chronicle*, he is about to enjoy a sandwich he has just made when he is interrupted by another phone call:

> As I was making lunch, the phone rang again.
> Standing in the kitchen, I sliced the bread, spread butter and mustard on it, and inserted some tomato and sliced cheese. Then I placed it on the chopping board and was about to cut it in half. (Murakami 1997b, 70)

In this straightforward depiction, beginning with the slicing of the bread, we can observe the attempt to draw out to the full the deliciousness of this simple dish. Not only the sandwiches the characters make for themselves, but also those they make for others play an important role in Murakami's works.

As shown above, spaghetti and sandwiches frequently appear in Murakami's works. They play a specific role in the works' development, but I would like to mention something else about the significance of the *boku* protagonists' love of cooking. It is common for the protagonists to cook during the day. This means being at home during the day. As mentioned earlier, in Murakami's works, they rarely work for a company and are often unemployed. They have little to constrain them and can freely decide how to use their time. Even if they are married, not having children is a factor in ensuring they have this time. They choose when to cook and when to eat. This is something that most men in Japan do not experience on weekdays. The peculiarity of the protagonists' environment is further emphasised by the frequent appearance of spaghetti and sandwiches, dishes which taste best when they have just been cooked. In this way, the *boku* protagonists' lives are infused with the delight of being able to taste freshly boiled spaghetti and freshly made sandwiches.

The absence of salarymen in Murakami's works reflects his own life. Postponing his graduation from university, he started a jazz bar in Tokyo with his wife, whom he married while he was a student. After graduating, he did not work for a company, choosing instead to become a professional writer. In the wake of the 1995 subway sarin attack, he listened to the accounts of victims and Aum Shinrikyō members; when he published the interview collections *Underground* and *At the Appointed Place*, Murakami touched on the kind of life he had avoided; that is, of people who belong to the "system" and commute every day to the city centre. Reflecting on the experience of the interviews, Murakami says:

> The victims were ordinary people who got onto subway trains in the morning to commute and work hard. Listening to these people struck me to the core, even though they belonged to the society I had consciously avoided and distanced myself from. Conformity, overwork … I have always disliked this kind of life. (Murakami 2012, 170)

The victims Murakami mentions were hardworking, "ordinary people." They could not choose how to use their time and spent the majority of their day working for their companies. Most of these "ordinary people" were not the Kasumigaseki types that Asahara wanted to *phoba*, or eliminate from Japanese society, but rather people who worked hard and were exploited by that system. They were, as Murakami shows, certainly not the kind of people who were allowed to cook lunch at home on weekdays. Compared with these "ordinary people," the seemingly simple lives of the *boku* protagonists appear luxurious.

3.   The Gender Division of Labour and Gender Norms

Japan's economic development accelerated in post-war society. This was supported by a gender division of labour. It was thought that the system whereby men worked at companies and women took care of the home and brought up the next generation of corporate warriors was the most effective one in supporting the nation's economic development. Women were asked to learn the necessary knowledge and skills to be wives and mothers; men had to work for a company to achieve financial independence and to be considered a man by working for a company, achieving financial independence, and having and financially supporting a family. Together with the appearance of the post-war concept of the "corporate warrior," this led to those who worked for companies (or "salarymen") being thought of as "normal citizens" (Dasgupta 2017). Even today, when women's participation in further education and the workforce has increased, the tendency to emphasise women's happiness as coming through marriage and for men to act as the main breadwinner is still deeply rooted in society (Yamada 2010).

This gender division of labour has also made a significant contribution to the formation of masculinity and femininity. The idea that learning the necessary knowledge and skills to be wives and mothers was a necessary element in being a woman was widespread in the mid-1970s, when the post-war baby-boomer generation reached the age at which it was common to marry (Taga 2009, 13). This was also the time when Japan's GNP had become the second-largest in the world. Both women and men had to fulfil the expectations of their particular roles; women's and men's identities were established, so that 'masculinity' and 'femininity' became normalised and reproduced as something beyond question. The origins of these concepts were forgotten. In this way, the financially powerful man, the woman who skilfully took care of housework and childcare, and their children became established as the contemporary ideal of the 'modern family.'

Regarding the establishment of gender norms in everyday life, Anne Allison's (1991) study of *bentō* culture is especially noteworthy. She pays attention to *bentō* culture at Japanese nursery schools and considers the extent to which food in everyday life is affected by social ideologies. According to Allison, a mother first becomes aware of being one through the duty of making *bentō* due to nursery schools' requirement for children to bring *bentō* with them to school. By eating their mothers' *bentō*, the children are recognised as the children of their mothers. Here we can clearly observe the deeply rooted way of thinking in Japanese society that the realisation of a happy family is one in which the mother makes the family's food. Allison's aim is not simply to criticise Japanese society, but rather to demonstrate how society's invisible power is manifested in everyday actions such as how food is eaten, how this is made into unquestioned 'common sense,' and how domestic responsibilities are justified. In Allison's study we come to understand how, just as the goals of the nation's economic development serve as the background for the 'common sense' in Japan that women do the housework and men support the family financially by being the main breadwinner, everyday habits are unconditionally justified by the realisation of society's aims.

Some thirty years have passed since Allison's study, but the idea of the happy family as one supported by the mother's cooking is still deeply rooted and continues to this day. In the 2000s, while the media drew attention to so-called *sōshoku danshi* ('herbivorous men' or 'beta males') househusbands among others, women's load has not been lightened. Despite the food education boom following the passing of the Ministry of Agriculture, Forestry and Fisheries' Basic Food Education Law in 2005, the emphasis on mothers' responsibility for managing food in households continues as before.

Murakami's *boku* are almost never the main breadwinners and cannot be thought of as following food-related social norms. Regarding the role of food and gender, there is an interesting difference between Murakami's works and previous novels related to food. Historically, the idea that women were responsible for non-professional cooking and men for professional cooking at restaurants permeated Japanese society. The impurity women were believed to have did not allow them to participate in cooking at the élite level (Aoyama 2008, 173). This is also a common tendency in many countries and regions outside Japan (Lupton 1998, 11). Because of this tradition, professional cooking has many associations with masculinity, which has been emphasised in the luxurious meat dishes and so-called "strange foods" including the organs of various animals eaten on foreign adventures in the works of food writers such as Kazuo Dan and Takeshi Kaikō (Aoyama 2003). By comparison, the *boku* protagonists' cooking in Murakami's novels is less pretentious. Their food is, if anything, not *hare* (non-everyday food), but rather the *ke* (everyday) cooking for which women have until now been responsible. The masculinity of the *boku* does not appear in this way, nor do they cook to conform to others' expected standards.

Furthermore, although the depiction of women in Murakami's works tends to be criticised for their lack of subjectivity because of their passive roles and their habit of suddenly disappearing, so-called 'housewives' almost never appear in them. The women the *boku* encounter do not conform to the 'ideals' sought by society, such as wives who leave the cooking to men and women who form romantic relationships with the *boku* in which they seek freedom from domestic duties. On the contrary, the characters who perform gender roles, in the case of women, often cannot escape their predicament and meet a tragic fate, while in the case of men, the *boku* are often confronted with men who scheme and use their power to further their ambitions. Murakami's works give the reader an impression that refusing received gender norms is 'right.'

4.   The Value of Housework as "Working Time"

Allison clearly indicates that the social norm of a mother doing housework is deeply rooted, but that the time taken up doing housework does not have a high social value. Society connects the value of daily activities with paid work. The history of how the gender division of labour has made a large contribution to economic development has been discussed above. When a high level of economic development has succeeded and material wealth has been achieved, society welcomes the beginning of the social advancement of women. It has come to value 'working time' outside housework. Whether the work has a high or low value depends on how strongly it is connected with its market value. The concept of work is split into work that pays and work that does not, which forms the basis for the lack of social value placed on the latter (Ochiai 2002, 34–35; Pollan 2009).

The way of thinking that connects time spent outside the home with the improvement of women's social rights has encouraged the mechanisation of housework. During the twentieth century, a variety of new products and services were introduced across the country to support housewives, including home electrical products such as washing machines, vacuum cleaners, and rice cookers; factory foods, such as instant and processed food products; and services such as family restaurants and convenience stores. Instead of supporting economic development by being housewives, they have been given a new role as consumers in a consumerist society; mothers who keep up to date with the latest information and technology are described as *kashikoi* ("smart") (Iwamura 2010, 161–69; Yamaguchi 1996, 93).

The American food researcher Michael Pollan criticises the view in American society that the time spent by women in the kitchen is unproductive and that uncritically welcomes the shift to outsourcing cooking as a tool for the "emancipation" of women. He claims that, in contemporary American society, more of people's time is taken up watching television programmes about food than on cooking at home, and that such food programmes introduce recipes that make use of various kinds of artificial food products including canned food, frozen food, and artificial additives while viewers are urged to purchase products made by the food companies that sponsor such programmes. Because of this, he is concerned that the meaning of "cooking" has changed to heating artificial and frozen foods in saucepans and microwaves and adding dressing to washed vegetables (Pollan 2009). His analysis indicates that the ethical goal of the social advancement of women's rights has been achieved through the uncritical acceptance of outsourcing cooking. It also suggests that viewers find it difficult to notice how the sponsoring of media content is sustained by corporate sponsors whose aims are not necessarily to improve people's lives but rather to urge them to purchase their products.

Regarding food programmes and outsourcing cooking, Japan's situation is similar. Through the food programme boom beginning in the 1980s, a wide range of television programmes including animations, soaps, and variety shows broadcast food-related content; their popularity has continued to increase. Especially in programmes nowadays, there is little deeper analysis of the changes in contemporary food culture; most consist of information urging viewers to use more artificial food products and spend more money on going out to restaurants. Due to the shift to outsourcing cooking, the frequency of eating at home has decreased and the amount of time spent cooking has also dramatically decreased (Suisanchō 2012). Survey results suggest that there are an increasing number of both men and women who make use of recipes introduced to them by television programmes or the Internet compared with those who are taught how to cook by their families (Murata et al. 2016).

In a society in which participation in paid work outside the home is connected with women's rights, time taken up by cooking is hardly valued at all. People today are judged according to how efficiently they can cook in a small amount of time and how they can pass their time more productively outside the kitchen. This also appears in popular books on cooking. In the 'cooking' section of a bookstore, books with the keywords 'quick,' 'easy,' 'for busy people,' and 'for working mothers' are arranged, and many of the recipes, as Michael Pollan has indicated above, rely on canned and frozen food products and artificial additives.

Factory foods are not absent in Murakami's works. The *boku* protagonists sometimes buy fast food donuts and coffee, and sometimes canned or pre-packaged food suffices. On special occasions, they go to a restaurant. However, what is unique about the *boku* protagonists' cooking is that they are completely focused on cooking for the sake of eating, without being influenced by media information. While various social standards are created in everyday life that are often ultimately connected with economic profitability, the *boku* protagonists only cook for the sake of eating.

5.   Material Consumption and Free Choice

As stated above, the image of the 'modern family' was formed with the aim of developing the economy after the Second World War. People's lives were connected in every aspect with a capitalist society. Populations gathered in urban areas and work and leisure time were split in two, with a cycle created of weekdays devoted to earning income and weekends to material consumption in leisure industries. This has given rise to a structure that is inseparable from market forces in both the public and the private sphere (Ichii 2006, 68). However, material wealth does not result in more free time; time is taken up by the use of large quantities of consumer goods and the negative consequences of this are linked to a loss of sleeping time (Yano 1995, 87).

Nonetheless, people continue to believe in the generation of material wealth and continue to work. What generates the concepts of wealth and happiness is information. Murakami sounds a warning about individuals' susceptibility to ways of spreading information in contemporary society. Below are Murakami's words in an interview:

> Whatever is meant by the "system," in most cases, it does not allow individuals to make their own decisions … This kind of closed-minded thinking, when you think about it, is really frightening. Especially in today's Internet society overflowing with information, it is becoming hard to understand even what you are being compelled to do. Even the things you intend to do spontaneously are in fact probably unconsciously driven by information. (Murakami 2010, 34–35)

Murakami's protagonists are also conscious of the fact that the expectations of a large capitalist society lie hidden in all the choices made in their everyday lives. This is evident in the words of this character in *Dance, Dance, Dance*:

> The things we need are artificially produced. Nothing's naturally created. They're made up. Things no-one needs are given the illusion of being necessary. It's easy, you know. You just need to produce information. For a place to live, it's Minato ward. For cars, it's a BMW. For watches, it's a Rolex. (Murakami 1998, 173)

Information produces people's desires. You are not made aware of the possibility that the product you think you have chosen of your own free will has been chosen for you. Eating is a similar everyday choice. Below are the words of a female protagonist in *1Q84* who is conscious of this:

> Whether it's from a menu or something else, we feel as if we are choosing by ourselves, but maybe we're not choosing anything. Maybe it's all been decided in advance and just seems to be a choice. Maybe free will is just an illusion. (Murakami 2009, 344)

It is difficult to realise that, whether it is in a family restaurant or a supermarket, we think we are blessed with a wealth of choices but do not in fact choose: we are made to choose from a limited number of options. The food product and food service industries tend to be dominated by a small number of large corporations: for example, it is known that 60% of the supply of food products in the US are made by ten large manufacturing corporations, while four large supermarket chains are responsible for more than 50% of the sales of general food products in Europe (Guptill et al. 2017, 126–27). Murakami tries to make his readers aware through the casual conversations of the characters that when an individual thinks that they are choosing something of their own free will, it is perhaps just an option that has been chosen for them.

Murakami's thoughts on the industrialisation of food also appear in *After Dark*. One of the characters, a young man called Takahashi, orders a chicken salad and toast late at night at the family restaurant Denny's. Even though the waiter acknowledges his request for the toast to be so crispy that it is "almost burnt black," the toast that is brought to him has been toasted the same amount as for other customers. Looking at this unsatisfactory piece of toast, Takahashi says:

> No matter how often I remind them, there's no sign that the toast has been made as I asked them to. I don't get it. With Japanese people's diligence, a high-tech culture, and with the market share Denny's seeks to achieve, it shouldn't be so difficult to make a piece of toast crispy. Right? So why isn't it possible, then? What's the value of a civilisation that can't produce a single piece of toast as ordered? (Murakami 2006, 20)

With a heavy dose of sarcasm, Murakami depicts the inefficiency of the contemporary system in which, in the pursuit of profitability and efficiency of food provision, no service that goes against the manual is possible. Because of the heavy reliance on the manuals in such family restaurants whose aim is to provide fast, cheap, and delicious food for busy modern-day people, there is no flexibility, and toasting the bread for longer is impossible. However, because customers believe they save time and use time effectively, it is difficult for them to notice the inconvenience of chains. Perhaps, in fact, they might want to buy some bread at a convenience store and toast it until it is crispy enough at home, which might be faster than going to a chain restaurant.

When criticising the system, Murakami values the point of view of the individual. Rather than taking up the perspective of politicians or economists, he lets the ordinary individual think about such issues. He does so to demonstrate the extent to which the system's influence over the lives of individuals can be observed, and how easily it can be seen when the individual becomes conscious of it. However, as mentioned above in Murakami's words, noticing the "closed-minded thinking" caused by information is not easy when living in an information society. There needs to be a trigger for noticing forced ways of seeing something. Regarding his work as a novelist, Murakami explains that "a novelist is someone whose work involves observing a lot and only judging a little" (Murakami 2011, 20). By "observing a lot," he gives readers the opportunity to think about reality from multiple perspectives and allow them to notice things from a point of view of which they would not normally be aware; by "only judging a little," he tries to allow them to develop the ability to think and decide for themselves. Regarding cooking and food, Murakami's proposition of "observing a lot" also becomes a trigger for readers to question the "common sense" of everyday life.

6.   Conclusion

This article has considered how the independent-mindedness of Murakami's protagonists, which has been an important factor in his ability to acquire global popularity, appears through their use of time and choices about food. It is possible to observe characters throughout Murakami's works who try to resist the pressure placed on the individual in a capitalist society, but this is more clearly shown in the *boku* protagonists' way of passing their time. They do not "spend" their time for the sake of society, trying instead to "pass" their time for the sake of their individual preference, but this is a kind of battle for them. While living in a system which they cannot escape, they find a way of adapting to it on their own terms without being exploited by its power (as expressed in the 'dance' of *Dance, Dance, Dance*). In particular, by understanding how the use of time at home has been used by the development of a capitalist society, the uniqueness of the *boku* protagonists who value cooking and eating food stands out. In depicting the *boku* in this way, Murakami proposes a way of living in which time is passed rather than spent.

Nevertheless, it should not be forgotten that there is something unreal about the easy-going lives of the *boku* that appear throughout Murakami's works. One of the elements in creating this sense of unreality is the absence of poverty in them. The *boku* lead humble lives, but in many cases they are financially supported in some way; there are only protagonists who, while not living in luxury, have enough savings to live without problems. It is clear that their ability to "pass" their time in their own ways is supported by financial security. At a time of concern about economic problems after the economic bubble burst, including the lost decade turning into thirty years, inequality continuing to spread, and the increase in child poverty and the number of working poor, it would be extremely difficult, especially for city dwellers, to put into practice a Murakami-style life of having free time and not getting up at dawn to work. Furthermore, in a world in which urban populations continue to increase in many countries, Japan's problems are not unique. Why is it, then, that Murakami continues to attract readers from both inside and outside Japan? It is because there are many readers who identify with the *boku* who try to live as individuals while living in a society in which having a busy life is demanded. Murakami's works continue to demonstrate how it is necessary for the individual to think and decide for themselves in order to live without being exploited by society's power. The *boku* protagonists' daily activities, such as cooking and housework, show how we can easily put this into practice.

References

Guptill, Amy, Denise A. Copelton, and Betsy Lucal. 2017. *Shoku no shakaigaku: Paradokusu kara kangaeru* [The sociology of food: Thinking from paradoxes]. Translated by Shigeru Itō. Tokyo: NTT.

Ichii, Yoshifusa. 2006. "Sengo Nihon no shakai tōgō to 'rejaa': Rejaa seisaku kara jiyū jikan seisaku e no tenkan to sono ito [Social integration and 'leisure' in post-war Japan: The shift from leisure policies to free-time policies and their intentions]." *Ritsumeikan sangyō shakai ronshū* 42 (3): 67–86.

Iwamura, Yōko. 2010. *Oya no kao ga mite mitai* [I want to try and see my parents' faces]. Tokyo: Chūō kōron.

Murakami, Haruki. 1997a. *Dansu dansu dansu* [Dance, dance, dance], vol. 1. Tokyo: Kōdansha.

Murakami, Haruki. 1997b. *Nejimakidori kuronikuru* [The wind-up bird chronicle]. Tokyo: Kōdansha.

Murakami, Haruki. 1998. *Dansu dansu dansu* [Dance, dance, dance], vol. 2. Tokyo: Kōdansha.

Murakami, Haruki. 2006. *Afutaa daaku* [After dark]. Tokyo: Kōdansha.

Murakami, Haruki. 2007. *Sekai no owari to haado boirudo wandaarando* [Hard-boiled wonderland and the end of the world]. Tokyo: Shinchōsha.

Murakami, Haruki. 2009. *1Q84*, vol. 1. Tokyo: Shinchōsha.

Murakami, Haruki. 2010. "Murakami Haruki rongu intabyū [A long interview with Haruki Murakami]." *Kangaeru hito* 33: 20–100.

Murakami, Haruki. 2011. *Zatsubun shū* [Miscellaneous works]. Tokyo: Shinchō bunko.

Murakami, Haruki. 2012. *Yume o miru tame ni mainichi boku wa mezameru no desu: Murakami Haruki intabyū shū* [I wake up every day to dream: Interviews with Haruku Murakami]. Tokyo: Bunjun bunko.

Murata, Hiroko, Miki Masaki, and Junji Hagiwara. 2016. "Chōsa kara mieru Nihonjin no shokutaku [Japanese people's dinner tables seen from surveys]." *Hōsō kenkyū to chōsa* 10 (October): 54–83.

Ochiai, Mieko. 2002. *Nijūisseiki kazoku e* [Towards the twenty-first-century family], 2nd ed. Tokyo: Yūhikaku.

Saitō, Osamu. 2006. "Nōmin no jikan kara kaisha no jikan e: Nihon ni okeru rōdō to seikatsu no rekishiteki hen'yō [From farmers' time to company time: Historical changes to work and life in Japan]." *Shakai seisaku gakkai shi* 15: 3–18.

Schor, Juliet. 1995. *Hatarakisugi no Amerika jin* [Overworking Americans], 2nd ed. Translated by Kōichi Morioka. Tokyo: Mado.

Shibata, Motoyuki, Shōzō Fujii, Inuhiko Yomota, and Mitsuyoshi Numata, eds. 2009. *Sekai wa Murakami Haruki o dō yomu ka* [How does the world read Murakami?]. Tokyo: Bungei shunjū.

Suisanchō. 2012. *Shokuryō shōhi no zentaiteki keikō* [General trends in food consumption]. Tokyo: Suisanchō.

Taga, Futoshi. 2009. "Otoko rashisa no gendaishi: Dankai no sedai o chūshin ni" [A contemporary history of masculinity: The baby-boomer generation]. *Kyōiku kagaku seminarii* 40: 11–25.

Tanaka, Yōko. 2006. *Chō jikan rōdō no rekishi genzai mirai, hatarakisugi: Rōdō seikatsu jikan no shakai seisaku* [The past, present, and future of working long hours: Social policies on working hours]. Tokyo: Hōritsu bunka.

Uchida, Tatsuru. 2012. *Uchida Tatsuru intabyū: Ima, Murakami Haruki o yomu beki riyū* [Tatsuru Uchida interview: Reasons to read Haruki Murakami now]. Tokyo: Ketoru.

Yamada, Masahiro. 2010. *"Konkatsu" genshō no shakaigaku: Nihon no haigūsha sentaku no ima* [The sociology of "marriage-hunting": Choosing Japanese spouses today]. Tokyo: Tōyō keizai shinpōsha.

Yamaguchi, Masatomo. 1996. *Daidokoro sengoshi: Iro to yoku* [A post-war history of the Kitchen: Eros and desire]. Edited by Ueno Chikako. Tokyo: Shōgakkan.

Yano, Masakazu. 1995. *Seikatsu jikan no shakaigaku: Shakai no jikan kojin no jikan* [The sociology of people's time: Society's time, the individual's time]. Tokyo: Tokyo daigaku shuppankai.

PART II:
REFLECTIONS

Matthew C. Strecher

Seeking the Living Among the Dead:
The Other World of Murakami Haruki[92]

Abstract: *This essay outlines some thirty years' work examining and explicating the nature and structure of the "other world" in the fiction of Murakami Haruki. The essay traces the development of this other world from its early inception as a personal repository of the Murakami protagonist's memories of the dead to its development into a quasi-Underworld, as a shared unconscious space, and finally, as a metaphor for the imagination itself. Throughout, the essay describes the other world as a means of establishing or maintaining connections amongst persons separated by space and time, or for re-establishing contact between characters' conscious and unconscious selves, exposing tension between "inner" and "outer" worlds, but also suggesting the need for balance between them.*

Keywords: Murakami Haruki, other world, psychology, mythology, imagination, metaphysical, time, space

Introduction: The Birth of the Dual-World Structure

My approach to Murakami Haruki's (b. 1949) literary output has, from the beginning, been focused on the contrast and tension between the physical and metaphysical worlds in his work, how they are depicted, how they function, what they mean. *Dances With Sheep: The Quest for Identity in the Fiction of Murakami Haruki* (2002; University of Michigan Press) examines things that emanated out of the metaphysical realm into the physical, as well as discussing their aesthetic, social, political, historical, and linguistic significance. Twelve years later, *The Forbidden Worlds of Haruki Murakami* (2014; University of Minnesota Press) tackled the nature and structure of the metaphysical realm itself, connecting it more explicitly to the constitutive function of language and representation, that is, how language, perception, and the imagination have the power to construct new realities. Throughout both of these texts, the dualistic nature of the Murakami literary structure informed the basis of my analyses.

---

92   Japanese names in this essay are given in Japanese order, surname followed by given name.

The dual-world structure of Murakami's literary landscape has been evident almost since his début novella *Kaze no uta o kike* (1979; Hear the Wind Sing), but it has developed significantly in the forty-three years since that time. Initially, one suspects, the author himself may not have known what this dual structure would look like; *Hear the Wind Sing* is a generally realistic novella, stronger in its simplistic style than its plot, and only the tongue-in-cheek references to the fictional novelist "Derek Hartfield," whom the narrator seems to admire, give us glimpses into the peculiarity of that world. Near the end of the novella, one of Hartfield's novels contains a scene in which a youth throws himself into a fathomless well on Mars, seeking death. But he does not die; after falling for an immeasurable length of time, he finds his way into a sub-Martian tunnel system, wherein he wanders, experiencing neither fatigue nor hunger. When he emerges, more than 1.5 billion years have passed (Murakami 1990c, 1:96–97).

The timeless nature of this underground system suggests that the youth left behind not merely the surface of Mars, but its physical constraints of space and time. That tunnel system represents, if not an "other world," then at least an "other consciousness," one governed by metaphysical rules. Here the literary landscape employed by Murakami is not divided into "physical and metaphysical," but rather into "narrative and subnarrative," wherein the protagonist lives in the narrative world, representing reality, and the subnarrative lies in the books he reads by Derek Hartfield. It is, nevertheless, Murakami's initial effort at making a distinction between modes of consciousness.

That distinction becomes much stronger in his second and third works, *1973-nen no pinbōru* and *Hitsuji o meguru bōken* (1980; Pinball, 1973 and 1982; A Wild Sheep Chase, respectively), which form a trilogy with the début novella. In the former, the protagonist lives in a relatively realistic depiction of Tokyo, pining for his deceased college girlfriend, Naoko. Late in the novel, in search of a pinball machine he played in his youth called "the Spaceship," which reminds him of his time with Naoko, he makes a journey out of the city proper to find the object of his quest in a lonely cold-storage warehouse that once contained dead chickens. The taxi ride he takes to this place is interesting; looking out the window, he is confronted by a darkness so complete that it looks "as if someone had plastered it on like butter with heavy paint" (Murakami 1990a, 1:230), and it makes him think he has reached "the end of the world" (Murakami 1990a, 1:232). In a sense he is right: the threshold of the cold-storage warehouse is, in fact, the entryway to the Underworld, where he finds not only "the Spaceship," but the voice and soul of Naoko.

Murakami's third novel, *A Wild Sheep Chase*, is also a quest story, and also contains dual quest objects: on the surface, the narrator seeks a magical sheep capable of granting immense powers to those it inhabits; beneath the surface of the text he seeks out his best friend, Nezumi ("Rat"), whom he has not seen since the end of *Hear the Wind Sing*. His quest is simpler than expected in that Rat and the sheep are in the same location, but the journey he must make is more arduous. Beginning in Tokyo as usual, he makes his way by degrees to a most out-of-the-way part of Hokkaido, the northernmost of Japan's four main islands, passing through different stages of "rural" as he goes. The final stage involves a difficult and unnerving trek around a mountain pass that gives the clear impression of passing from the world of the living into that of the dead:

> As the caretaker had said, there was definitely something ominous about the place. I had a vague sensation of its ill will in my body, and soon that indistinct bad feeling was setting off alarms in my head. It was like crossing a river, and suddenly stepping into a much colder bit of water. (Murakami 1990b, 2:293)

Once past this place, however, the narrator feels quite at home, and completes his journey to a mountain villa owned by Rat. There, he finally meets and bids farewell to his friend, who admits, however, that he has been dead since the previous week.

In these three opening works by Murakami the "other world" quite obviously represents the land of the dead, and yet we cannot help noticing that death is far from final; rather, the dead maintain not only presence but consciousness in that place.

Bringing the Mountain to Mohammed

Virtually all of Murakami's fiction has played on this idea of an "other world" lurking always at the edge of our peripheral vision. In some works, however, the characters of the story do not enter into that world, but rather interact with things that come out of it.

Consider, for instance, Murakami's bestselling novel to date, *Noruwei no mori* (1987; Norwegian Wood), which the author himself has called a "realistic" novel (Murakami 2010, 22). That text centers on a young woman, again called Naoko, and her struggle to come to grips with the death of her soul mate, Kizuki. The story is narrated, however, by a young man named Watanabe Tōru, who loves Naoko and wants to save her from her suicidal tendencies. As Murakami suggests, the "other world" is not clearly evident in most of this text, but it is nonetheless a constant presence. After Naoko has gone to live in a sanatorium in the hills near Kyoto to seek treatment for her depression, Watanabe Tōru makes a journey to visit her, and once again we have a moment that reminds us of that frightening mountain pass in *A Wild Sheep Chase*:

> The wind that came through the window of the bus suddenly became cold, its dampness painful on my skin. We ran along the river in that cedar wood for a long time, and just when I was starting to think the world had been buried in an endless expanse of cedar woods, we came out of it. (Murakami 1991, 6:135)

If this is not enough, we have the comments of Naoko herself, who hears the voice of Kizuki calling to her from the "other world," inviting her to join him, telling Tōru: "'I'd swear I can feel Kizuki reaching his hand out of the darkness to me. "Hey, Naoko, we can't be apart," he says. I never know what to do when I'm told such things'" (Murakami 1991, 6:206). While this might be attributed to Naoko's severely neurotic state, previous and later Murakami works suggest that the "other world," whether here representing the land of the dead or merely her own damaged unconscious, is a central presence in this work.[93]

The Other World as Shared Space
If the "other world" functioned as a land of the dead for the first decade or more of Murakami's writing career, it did not necessarily continue solely in this role. In the mid-1990s, at a moment many critics have called Murakami's "turning point" (*tenkan*),[94] the author produced what may be his most important novel to date, *Nejimakidori kuronikuru* (1994–96; The Wind-Up Bird Chronicle), a complex narrative in which the novel's present is layered over remembrances of horrific war atrocities during the Second World War in Asia. On its surface, however, *The Wind-Up Bird Chronicle* is yet another quest tale in which the protagonist, Okada Tōru, seeks to discover the whereabouts of his wife Kumiko, who has disappeared. By novel's end we know that Kumiko lies imprisoned in a labyrinthine metaphysical hotel, and it is into this space that Okada Tōru must journey to rescue her. His journey is more challenging than those of previous protagonists in the author's work: Okada Tōru must climb down into the bottom of a deep, dry well and sit in total

---

93   While brevity precludes discussing it at any length, readers of *Kokkyō no minami, taiyō no nishi* (1992; South of the Border, West of the Sun) will find a similar phenomenon occurring, except that in this case the protagonist, Hajime, is visited from the "other world" by his childhood love Shimamoto, who attempts at one point to draw Hajime to her own place. This novel may also be read as a "realistic" novel, but I am more inclined to Saitō Eiji's (1993) description of the work as a "modern-day ghost story" (*gendai no gōsuto sutōrii*).
94   See in this regard Kuroko Kazuo (2007) and Yoshida Haruo (1997).

darkness, emptying his mind until the walls of the well absorb him (presumably only his mind, leaving his body behind). From thence he must navigate the labyrinth and find Kumiko's room.

What really makes *The Wind-Up Bird Chronicle* interesting, however, is how this newly conceived metaphysical space works. No longer a land for the dead, it is now a collectively shared space in which the disembodied minds—perhaps "souls" is the correct term—of the living may meet and interact. In several scenes, for instance, Okada Tōru dreams of making love to one of the female characters in the novel, Kanō Creta, yet he hears her speaking in his wife's voice. Some chapters later, to Tōru's surprise, Kanō Creta refers to the dream they shared. Late in the novel, Tōru encounters the wicked brother of Kumiko, Wataya Noboru, who is responsible for her imprisonment, in her hotel room, and he beats Noboru about the head with a baseball bat; at that same moment in the physical world, Noboru collapses from a brain hemorrhage and sinks into a coma. We may thus conclude not only that the metaphysical space is shared amongst all characters, but that what happens there casts its effects into the physical realm as well.

The Other World as Wormhole

In other instances, we see the metaphysical realm act as a conduit by which characters may escape the confines of physical space and time. In *Umibe no Kafuka* (2002; Kafka on the Shore), for instance, the eponymous Tamura Kafka runs away from his home in Tokyo, seeking to escape his father's ominous prophecy that Kafka will kill his father and then locate and have sexual relations with his long-lost mother and older sister. After awakening from a mysterious trance behind a Shintō shrine in Takamatsu City on the island of Shikoku covered in fresh blood, Kafka reasonably concludes that he has killed his father by remote control; somehow his soul has traversed the hundreds of kilometers between Takamatsu and Tokyo and done, in astral (unconscious) form, precisely what his physical (conscious) self has sought to avoid. Having come this far, recognizing that his father's prophecy is inescapable, Kafka later takes active steps to fulfill the rest of it: he selects a woman who could be his mother and has sexual relations with her (thus effectively casting her into the role of his mother), and later, he uses a vivid dreamscape forcibly to penetrate a young woman whom he has cast into the role of his missing sister.[95]

---

95   A much more sinister instance of this is suggested in *Shikisai o motanai Tazaki Tsukuru to, kare no junrei no toshi* (2013; Colorless Tsukuru Tazaki and His Years of Pilgrimage).

But the wormhole of the metaphysical realm, as in *The Wind-Up Bird Chronicle*, also links up distinct historical moments. Early in the novel Kafka meets a beautiful, fifty-something woman named "Miss Saeki" who is about the right age to be his mother. Miss Saeki lost her lover and soul mate to a tragic incident in the 1960s, and as Kafka takes steps to fulfill the final part of his father's prophecy with her (i.e., sexual intercourse), he appears to take the place of Miss Saeki's dead soul mate. Following their brief sexual union, Miss Saeki dies in the physical world, but Kafka later journeys to the heart of the labyrinth—now taking the form of an expansive forest—and discovers her there. He makes his farewells, achieves roughly the same degree of closure as the narrator does with Rat in *A Wild Sheep Chase*, and returns to the physical realm just in time before the gateway between worlds closes.

The function of the metaphysical realm as conduit is even more pronounced in later Murakami works. In *1Q84* (2009–2010; 1Q84), for instance, two characters who are fated to join together and create a child, yet cannot locate one another, are brought together by an act of creation and one of destruction: Kawana Tengo, the male protagonist, lies prone and paralyzed while a young woman mounts his rampant penis and causes him to ejaculate; miles away, an assassin named Aomame Masami pierces the brainstem of the girl's father, known as the Leader, with an ice pick-like weapon, killing him. At this moment, we are led to believe, Tengo and Aomame are joined and conceive a child. A similar event occurs in Murakami's most recent novel to date, *Kishidanchō-goroshi* (2017; Killing Commendatore), in which the narrator has a vivid dream of making love to his estranged wife, Yuzu; at roughly the same time, Yuzu (in an entirely different location) conceives a child.

Functions and Purposes for the Other World

The above descriptions should make amply clear that the metaphysical "other world" in Murakami Haruki's fiction is not limited to a single guise or method, but takes multitudinous forms and roles in the wider breadth of his literary repertoire. We have seen the "other world" as a realm for the dead, as a repository for memories, as a collective shared space in which the living may interact in astral form, and as a pathway by which the snares of physical time and space may be transcended, with both good and evil results.

The central role of the metaphysical "other world" can hardly be overstated in Murakami fiction, but what does it finally mean to us as readers? Equally important, what does it mean to the characters within this author's fiction?

One broad conclusion we may draw is that the dual worlds here mirror a duality in the self. Numerous commentators, myself included, have noticed, for instance, that the characters of Rat and the narrator in the first three novels, despite being inseparable friends, are virtual opposites of one another; Rat is angry, boisterous, and active, while the narrator is shy, silent, and passive. Are they two sides of the same coin? In *The Wind-Up Bird Chronicle*, too, one has the uncanny sense that Okada Tōru and Wataya Noboru are one person, the good and the evil, especially when Kanō Creta says that "Wataya Noboru belongs to a world that is the exact opposite to yours. … In a world where you are rejected, Mr. Wataya is accepted" (Murakami 1994–96, 2:256–257). This suggests most strongly that while one of them lives in the physical world, the other must occupy the metaphysical. Perhaps the real issue here is one of dominance; who occupies which world? As with Rat and the narrator, we have a dichotomy between the character who speaks and acts, and the one who remains passive and silent.

That same question of dominance seems to drive *Kafka On the Shore* as well. The Oedipal prophecy given to Kafka by his father actually expresses a *desire* to be killed, and when Kafka flees Tokyo, his father (who now takes the form of Johnny Walker, the scotch whisky icon) recruits another to kill him instead. Is it not reasonable to suspect that Kafka's father seeks death in order to move himself to the "other world," that is, to the metaphysical side? The purposes of such a move are unclear, but perhaps it would be to make use of the liberation from the spatial and temporal constraints that bind the physical world, as noted above. Having once entered the metaphysical realm as conduit, one may travel any distance, any direction, and to any point in time.

This may be what happens in *Shikisai o motanai Tazaki Tsukuru to, kare no junrei no toshi* (2013; Colorless Tsukuru Tazaki and His Years of Pilgrimage), as well. In that novel the title character is forced to accept the possibility that, unbeknownst to himself, he *might* have raped and murdered a woman he loved in the metaphysical space. No real evidence of this is offered within the narrative; we have only the narrator's admission to himself that "even if it was no more than a dream, he could not help feeling that he was in some way responsible … *something* in himself, without his ever knowing about it, had gone off to Hamamatsu and strangled her lovely, swan-like neck" (Murakami 2013, 317). A similar moment of fear strikes the narrator of *Killing Commendatore* when he recalls a one-night stand he had in Tōhoku while traveling after his wife kicked him out, and recalls the woman asking him to strangle her during sex:

> She had said that I could "just pretend," but maybe that hadn't been enough. Maybe it hadn't ended with "just pretending." And the reason why it didn't end with "just pretending" was inside me. (Murakami 2017, 1:443)

That "reason … inside me" would then be identifiable as the narrator's inner, evil self. Not all attempts to escape the bonds of the physical are quite so sinister. Returning briefly to the story of "colorless Tazaki Tsukuru," we note a close friend of his during university, a young philosophy student named Haida who claims to be able to separate his mind from his body at will. This is not a matter of switching places with an internal doppelgänger, but rather of entering a state—fully conscious—of pure thought. Haida describes this as the ultimate kind of liberation:

> "To think freely about things is also to separate ourselves from the flesh we are stuffed into. To escape from that limiting cage that is our flesh, to break free of our chains and take flight into pure reason. In reason lies the natural life. That's what lies at the core of freedom of thought." (Murakami 2013, 66)

Haida appears to be an example of one who can make use of the metaphysical realm without surrendering himself to the dark and dangerous impulses of his "inner demons." However, a peculiar and unexplained knife scar on his neck leaves open the possibility that Haida, like Rat before him, is not actually alive, and thus is no longer subject to the constraints of the physical world in any case.

Conclusions: What It All Means

Murakami Haruki's metaphysical "other world" serves a variety of functions, as we have seen. It puts the narrators into contact with things and people (but mostly people) from their pasts as a means of reconsidering the present, understanding how that present came about. The "other world" also serves as a home for the dualistic "inner self," the doppelgänger each of us carries inside, what Jungian psychoanalysis might call the "shadow," which balances our everyday self, and in Murakami's fictional world, sometimes attempts to trade places with the typically "nice guy" narrator who lives out the narrative.

There is no way of knowing precisely what Murakami means to show his readers through this dualistic structure, but we can say with some certainty that his narratives suggest the importance of balance between the forces of good and evil, light and darkness, consciousness and unconsciousness, aggression and passivity, peace and violence, in the true Platonic (to say nothing of Taoist) fashion. We can also suggest that these balancing forces permeate the world and everything in it, and that such worlds, in miniature form, exist also within our minds, whose structure mirrors that of these narratives.

Finally, and perhaps most importantly, his works suggest that the dead continue to exist, within our memories or within the metaphysical space that is also occupied by our memories. Murakami never steps right out to declare his belief in the "other world," and in fact, his stories do not speak of this so much as they show it to us. Yet the narratives we have discussed here do clearly offer a vision of a world that contains a larger interior than exterior, one invisible to us and accessible only through the mind and the imagination. And perhaps this is all that Murakami means to say: that the imagination—and the stories contained within it—is bigger than anything we perceive with our five senses in the physical world. My own work over these past thirty years has sought to show that "imagination" is synonymous with the metaphysical "other world," and that memories, the imaginary, the unconscious, the land of the dead, and even Plato's famous Realm of Forms, are all one and the same thing. Perhaps this is why Murakami's depictions of the metaphysical realm take so many different forms.

References

Kuroko Kazuo. 2007. *"Sōshitsu" no monogatari kara "tenkan" no monogatari e [From stories of "loss" to stories of "change"]*. Tokyo: Benseisha.

Murakami Haruki. 2017. *Kishidanchō-goroshi* [Killing Commendatore]. 2 vols. Tokyo: Shinchōsha.

—. 2013. *Shikisai o motanai Tazaki Tsukuru to, kare no junrei no toshi* [Colorless Tazaki Tsukuru and his years of pilgrimage]. Tokyo: Bungei Shunjū.

—. 2009–10. *1Q84* [1Q84]. 3 vols. Tokyo: Shinchōsha.

—. 2002. Umibe no Kafuka [Kafka On the Shore]. 2 vols. Tokyo: Shinchōsha.

—. 1994–96. *Nejimakidori kuronikuru* [The Wind-Up Bird Chronicle]. 3 vols. Tokyo: Shinchōsha.

—. 1992. *Kokkyō no minami, taiyō no nishi* [South of the Border, West of the Sun]. Tokyo: Kōdansha.

—. 1991. *Noruwei no mori* [Norwegian Wood]. In Murakami Haruki Zansakuhin 1979–1989 [Complete works of Murakami Haruki, 1979–1989]. 8 vols. Tokyo: Kōdansha. Volume 6.

—. 1990a. *1979-nen no pinbōru* [Pinball, 1973]. In Murakami Haruki Zansakuhin 1979–1989 [Complete works of Murakami Haruki, 1979–1989]. 8 vols. Tokyo: Kōdansha. Volume 1.

———. 1990b. *Hitsuji o meguru bōken* [A Wild Sheep Chase]. In Murakami Haruki Zansakuhin 1979–1989 [Complete works of Murakami Haruki, 1979–1989]. 8 vols. Tokyo: Kōdansha. Volume 2.

———. 1990c. *Kaze no uta o kike* [Hear the Wind Sing]. In Murakami Haruki Zansakuhin 1979–1989 [Complete works of Murakami Haruki, 1979–1989]. 8 vols. Tokyo: Kōdansha. Volume 1.

Saitō Eiji. 1993. "Gendai no gōsuto sutōrii" [A contemporary ghost story]. In *Shinchō* 90:2 (February).

Strecher, Matthew C. 2014. *The Forbidden Worlds of Haruki Murakami*. Minneapolis: University of Minnesota Press.

Strecher, Matthew C. 2002. *Dances With Sheep: The Quest for Identity in the Fiction of Murakami Haruki*. Ann Arbor: University of Michigan Press, Center for Japanese Studies.

Yoshida Haruo. 1997. *Murakami Haruki, tenkan suru* [Murakami Haruki, about face]. Tokyo: Sairyūsha.

Olaf Schiedges

A spatial approach to the fictional world of Murakami Haruki[96]

Abstract: *In my analysis of literary works by Murakami Haruki, I pay special attention to the spatial dimension of his texts. Through the spatial order specific to each of his literary worlds, Murakami initiates socio-critical counter-discourses and thought-provoking impulses. Following the 'spatial turn' in literary studies, space is no longer perceived as a mere backdrop to character and plot, but as an integral component in the construction of fictional worlds. In analyzing the significance of space in Murakamis's texts, this study draws on Jurij Lotman's model of binary spatial oppositions, but also refers to other key thinkers of the spatial turn, notably Michel Foucault, Michel de Certeau and Marc Augé. This theoretical focus opens up insightful perspectives on the fictional worlds of Murakami Haruki in four of his works: A Wild Sheep Chase [1989], Norwegian Wood [1989], Hard-Boiled Wonderland and the End of the World [1991], and After Dark [2007].*

Keywords: literary space, spatial turn, non-places, heterotopia, semiosphere, intertextuality

In my research on Murakami's novels, I have turned to the analysis of space by utilizing spatial phenomena as instruments for studying and understanding the Japanese author's narrative texts. I have demonstrated that the analysis of spatial elements in literary texts encompasses a variety of textual elements and structures. The analysis of space can make other, non-spatial elements in his texts more visible. At the same time, of course, spatial aspects cannot be analyzed without considering non-spatial aspects.

First, I assumed that the events in Murakami's narratives not only take place in a particular time, but in a particular place, too. What becomes evident from this perspective is that space is more than a backdrop to his narratives. Space plays rather an active part in the plot, functioning as a vehicle for Murakami to express his view on the individual's struggle to cope with the realities of contemporary Japanese society. Spatial relations in Murakami's texts

---

96   Published as PhD thesis: Schiedges, O. 2016. *Die Raumordnung in ausgewählten Romanen des japanischen Schriftstellers Murakami Haruki* [The spatial order in selected novels by the Japanese writer Murakami Haruki]. Würzburg: Ergon, (365 pages).

185

correspond to the narrative events and are closely related to the protagonist's loss of and search for his own identity.

As Mieke Bal has emphasized in her book *Narratology: Introduction to the Theory of Narrative* (2009), events in narrative texts always happen 'somewhere' (Bal 2009:219). I am strongly convinced this statement should always be kept in mind while reading Murakami's texts. In my analysis of the following novels I have shown that spatial elements play an active role: *Hitsuji o meguru bōken* (1982, *A Wild Sheep Chase* [1989]), *Sekai no owari to hādoboirudo wandārando* (1985, *Hard-Boiled Wonderland and the End of the World* [1991]), *Noruwei no mori* (1987, *Norwegian Wood* [1989]) and *Afutā Dāku* (2004, *After Dark* [2007]).

Since this paper is intended as an overview of my research, I cannot present a detailed summary of all my results. Instead, I will try to give a brief impression of the variety of aspects in Murakami's texts that appear in a slightly different light from a spatial perspective. First, I will give some indication of the theoretical background to my research. This is important, because it was long taken for granted that space, like time, is a substantial component of human reality; little attention being paid to the significance of space in narrative texts. Before the 1980s, spatial elements were mostly ignored in favor of analyses of narrative time. Since the late 1980s, however, a paradigm shift has emerged in cultural, social and literary studies, known as the 'spatial turn.' This turn conceives of geographic space as a cultural quantity. An important theoretical foundation of this new spatial thinking has been provided by Henri Lefebvre. In *The Production of Space* (1991) he introduced a concept of space as both a precondition and result of social structures. This led to a reassessment of space as being of relational character and not merely understood as an unchangeable, fixed container.

The post-1980s emergence of spatial theory generated a growing interest in already existing prior studies of thinkers of space. Michel Foucault, who stated in *Of Other Spaces* (1967) that our epoch will be above all an epoch of space, provided an influential model that helps us to identify counter-spaces in narrative texts. His 'other spaces,' which he calls heterotopias, can be used to describe discursive spaces that are incompatible with or contradictory to the majority of social space. They often reveal a subversive character by reflecting conditions of society, which they expose or criticize. In his book *The Practice of Everyday Life* (1984), Michel de Certeau contributed to an understanding of the difference between 'space' and 'place,' by analyzing the individual's way of moving through 'urban space.' In his *Anthropology of Supermodernity* (1995), Marc Augé has introduced a concept of so-called 'non-places' which—he claims—are representative places of contemporary society, but not of sufficient cultural or historical significance for the modern individual to consider them as places to identify with.

The most important fundamental instrument of spatial analysis for my reading of Murakami's texts is Jurij Lotman's structuralist model of literary space. In his book *The Structure of the Artistic Text* (1977) Lotman claims that narratives produce spatial models which function as analogies of spatial constructions of the world, thus helping us to comprehend reality. The structure of narrative texts can be described by topological and semantic binary oppositions. The semantic topology is then realized in topographical relations such as town=safety/forest=danger. These oppositions are always separated by a boundary (physical or metaphorical) which divides the text into two mutually non-intersecting subspaces. This boundary is mostly impenetrable, and characters are usually fixed to their designated space so they cannot violate the given order of the narrative. But at least one character must be able to move across the boundary and merge into the oppositional subspace. It is through this movement that the narrative dynamics of the text are constructed (Lotman 1977: 229).

In Murakami's texts we can clearly recognize the topological double-structure that Lotman describes in his structuralist model. Murakami himself has referred to this structure of his narratives in an interview with Shibata Motoyuki (Murakami/Shibata 1989). The structural world of his texts, the author stated, is always determined by a binary order which contains 'this world' (*kochira no sekai*) and a so-called 'other world' (*achira no sekai*). This double structure is a fundamental element of Murakami's narratives, even of his more or less realistic novels, as he himself has pointed out (Murakami/Shibata 1989: 18). In addition, we can observe that relevant semantic features in Murakami's texts are always associated with distinct spatial areas. Let me now briefly illustrate Lotman's spatial approach to narratives by using Murakami's works. I will then touch on other textual structures to show how fruitful a spatial approach to Murakami's novels can be.

For example, a spatial reading of *A Wild Sheep Chase* draws attention to a clear topological and semantic division of the fictional world. First, Murakami presents to the reader a rather ahistorical and culturally superficial space of urban Tokyo, where students hardly show any interest when Mishima's suicide is reported on television. Here in the urban space, the nameless narrator *Boku* (Jap. first person pronoun mainly used by males) does not try to interact with his social environment until he is forced to leave the city to search for a mysterious sheep that has the power to manipulate people. Opposite to the urban space of Tokyo, Murakami presents the historically rich landscape of Hokkaido. Leaving the Japanese capital, the narrator gets more and more involved with Japan's historical past, specifically with two rather dark aspects of Japanese history, which Murakami introduces to the reader. One is the settlement of the northern island, Hokkaido (also called *shin sekai*—new world); the other is the colonial activity of the Japanese empire during World War II in Manchuria. Both these dark aspects are—using Edward Said's (1973) terminology—aimed at the establishment of an 'imaginative geography.'

The title of *Hard-boiled Wonderland and the End of the World* already hints at the double structure of the book. Two parallel stories are narrated in alternating chapters here. One is set in the Japanese capital in the near future (Hard-boiled Wonderland), depicted as an alienating city where citizens' lives are determined by technological progress, competition, and consumerism. This version of Tokyo appears as a 'contact zone' (Pratt 1991) where east meets west. The other narrative is set in the subconscious of the protagonist's brain, in which a mad scientist has implemented the vision of a dystopian town called 'the end of the world.' This town is lacking progress and competition while, in exchange for eternal life, the inhabitants are forced to give up their souls. Surrounded by a huge wall, it is reminiscent of a post-apocalyptic village missing any features of Western origin.

In *Norwegian Wood*, we can also notice a distinctive spatial structure that has a binary character. Again, it consists of the urban space of Tokyo, where universities are shaken by protests by the student movement. Here, Watanabe, the protagonist, tries to adapt to campus life while falling in love with two girls: his former school friend, Naoko; and Midori, whom he meets at university. Far away from the city space, Murakami provides an opposite space in the shape of a remote sanatorium for mental patients. Called *Amiryō*, it is located in the mountains near the old capital of Kyoto. Naoko decides to retreat to this place, because she feels the pressures of growing up to be unbearable. The sanatorium is an idyllic place, where patients maintain contact with nature and find relief from the stresses of life in the outside world. It appears as a place of cure and—in Foucault's words—as a heterotopia of deviation, where patients can find refuge from the urban realities of Japan's capital. But *Amiryō* also reminds the reader of a very similar place in Thomas Mann's novel *The Magic Mountain* (1924), which Murakami is imitating in various ways. The sanatorium setting is not the only similarity between Mann's and Murakami's novels. Moreover, literary space plays an important role in the creation of intertextual relations in both works. The spatial structure of *Norwegian Wood* reflects the intertextual connection across literary boundaries.

Literary space itself, so it seems, constitutes intertextuality. When Watanabe visits Naoko, he even takes an edition of Mann's *The Magic Mountain* with him to read. This is not Murakami's only reference to Mann's book. Taking a spatial perspective, the beginning of *Norwegian Wood* being set in Hamburg, Germany also appears as a reference to Mann's book. The famous German novel describes the experiences of Hans Castorp, a young man who travels from the northern German city to a sanatorium for pulmonary patients in the mountains of Davos in Switzerland. Keeping in mind that the title of Murakami's novel is taken from a song written by The Beatles, that famous British music group whose career started on stage in the very same northern German city, it is no longer a coincidence that in the beginning of the book Watanabe's flight has to arrive in the city of Hamburg.

The novel's binary structure, though, is not limited to topographical elements of the narrative. Rather, it includes the female characters the narrator falls in love with, too. Midori is working for a publishing company and writes descriptions of locations for maps. She is able to read cartographic descriptions of the city, and moreover is very talkative and does not hesitate to ask questions in her university courses. And, despite difficult circumstances she can maintain control over her life. In contrast, Naoko, when taking a walk with the narrator, has problems finding her way through the city space, sometimes losing her sense of orientation. She also complaints about difficulties in finding the right words to express her feelings to others. Her state of mind reminds us of what de Certeau wrote about the pedestrian's practice of walking through the city to get access to urban space. The act of walking, he writes, is to the urban system what the speech act is to language, or the statements uttered. For de Certeau, walking becomes a space of enunciation (de Certeau 1984: 91–110).

Next, I would like to draw attention to another aspect that would not be so striking without taking space into account. This concerns the spatial dimension of the text itself. Murakami's bestseller has often been called a romance novel; indeed, this is indicated on the advertising strip (*obi*) with which books are wrapped in Japan. Here—as well as in the novel's epilogue, written by the author himself—it is explained that Murakami wanted to write a 'one hundred percent love story.' We can assume that Murakami's statement had a certain influence on the reception of the book. Interestingly, readers of the German edition are advised about the literary genre of the narrative through a corresponding subtitle (*Eine Liebesgeschichte*) that has been added to the cover of the book. Therefore, in Germany, too, the book has been received as a romance novel. One function of advertising strips or epilogues is to influence readers' expectations of a book and to contribute to its' success. On another, rather textual level, however, subtitles, epilogues and advertisement strips belong to the group of so-called 'paratexts' that Gérard Genette names 'seuils' (thresholds). As a threshold, the paratext takes on a spatial position in the text. It becomes a transitional space that allows the reader to enter or exit the novel's actual narrative. Narrative texts do indeed have spatial character. Lotman points out that a literary text is to be understood as an area that is surrounded by a frame or a boundary which separates the text from everything that is not text. Uwe Wirth (2009) also understands paratexts as texts that form a transitional zone. Via the paratext, Wirth concludes, the reader is supposed to transition from the real world into the fictional world of the text (Wirth 2009:167).

Seemingly in contrast with those analyzed so far, *After Dark* is a very short Murakami novel which lacks a clearly recognizable binary structure. Instead, in narrating the experiences of numerous people during one night in the center of Tokyo, *After Dark* contains a variety of Augé's non-spaces, through which characters pass as anonymous individuals. These non-spaces are transitory places such as love hotels, artificial fast-food restaurants, convenience stores and office spaces; all of which are so heavily monitored that, after entering them, people are under constant surveillance. *Alphaville*, Murakami's love hotel in the novel, is the perfect example of such a non-space, as I will show below.

What also sets *After Dark* apart from prior Murakami works is the point of view it takes. The narrative is told from the perspective of an anonymous camera eye. This could lead us to the conclusion that Murakami's book is an example of a narrative style that incorporates a cinematic aesthetic, a style Irina Rajewski (2003) refers to as intermedial (between novel and cinema). Using the third person plural, Murakami also includes the reader who is thereby transformed into a spectator of the events. The narrative begins with the camera zooming in on the city landscape. It then turns to Mari, a young student who spends the night at fast-food restaurants in the center of Tokyo. She does not go home, because her sister Eri—a so-called TV talent—is trapped in deep sleep, and has not left their room for weeks. During the night, Mari meets people like Takahashi, a friend of her sister and Kaoru, who is a former wrestler now working as a manager of a love hotel called *Alphaville*. The camera then follows Shirakawa, an office worker, who earlier that evening abused a Chinese prostitute at this love hotel. Because Mari speaks Chinese, Kaoru asks her to help talking to the woman. The narration continues; but parallel chapters repeatedly return to the sleeping Eri, in whose room the

TV set turns on, to show a strange man wearing a mask watching her. At the end of the book, Mari finally returns to her sister, and lies down in bed next to her. The ending being set at home with the two sisters could be understood as a positive hint for some hope for the future, since most characters in Murakami's narratives do not inhabit any places that could be called 'home.' Indeed, in Murakami's texts, this is the effect a high-capitalist city like Tokyo is seen to have on the life of its inhabitants. They either completely retreat from urban space, as does Eri; or they are forced to stay in transitional spaces, as do Mari and the other characters moving like nomads from one 'non-place' to another. Consequently, *After Dark* does not contain any utopian space, because the utopian literary genre describes imaginary places wherein humans try to realize ideal states of perfection. Murakami's non-places, on the other hand, are real places that do not provide any possibility for the individual to reach such a state of happiness.

However, in *After Dark*, it is one specific place that reveals Murakami's real topic in this work. This becomes clear when we take a closer look at the significance of the love hotel named *Alphaville*. The origin of the hotel's name is explained by Mari. She tells Kaoru, the manager, that *Alphaville* was originally a film directed by French director, Jean-Luc Godard in 1965. In the film, *Alphaville* is a place in the future where people are not allowed to have feelings, their lives being watched by a supercomputer that controls the city. Murakami's reference fits perfectly, since the love hotel as well as the future city in the French film are cold, unpleasant places that are under constant surveillance. But it is not only visitors entering the premises of the love hotel who are monitored by security cameras. Takahashi, Mari's friend, is the only person in *After Dark* who is aware that—like the people in Godard's film—he is a prisoner of a system that constantly watches people in the urban space while abolishing their individuality. We can conclude that, through its concern with the subject of surveillance, *After Dark* is more than an example of intermedial storytelling, but a work of fiction with a socio-critical approach. As in *Norwegian Wood*, the significance of spatial structures becomes an important element that supports our understanding of Murakami's narrative.

Finally, I would like to set aside this analysis of Murakami's narratives by turning to the author himself, and his position within the Japanese literary landscape. Again, Lotman's theoretical framework proves helpful. In his book *The Universe of the Mind* (1991), Lotman describes the space of culture by using the spatial metaphor of the 'semiosphere,' which can be understood as a spatial construct comprising a core and a periphery, always enclosed by a boundary (Lotman 1991: 121–214). A semiosphere can be a real topology, such as the city of Tokyo; or a metaphorical space of rather abstract character. Nevertheless, it consists of spatial relations, because Lotman distinguishes between internal and external spaces of the semiosphere. In the periphery, we can recognize communication and exchange with other semiospheres. But while the periphery is therefore the space wherein the creation of new information is realized, the core is the space for established norms that are fully accepted. If we turn to Murakami's position in Japan, it becomes clear that he is an author who can be localized in the periphery of the Japanese literary landscape. Through his use of language and his references to Western literature, he has constantly distanced himself from the core of the Japanese semiosphere, occupied as it has been by the literary establishment of the *bundan* and the literary genre of the Japanese I-novel. Instead, Murakami has deliberately placed himself in a peripheral position in the realm of the Japanese semiosphere. This has enabled him on the one hand to escape the *bundan's* literary criticism; while on the other to use his peripheral position—Lotman would call it a place on the boundary between different cultures and languages—to be part of a constant process of literary and linguistic exchange between Japanese and Western (especially American) fiction. In Lotman's sense, therefore, we can call Murakami a writer who shifts across cultural boundaries. This helps us understand why Murakami has been interested in translating American fiction from the beginning of his writing career. Like his protagonists, who always move away from the Japanese capital, he has distanced himself from the center of the Japanese literary scene, spending many years overseas. But unlike his protagonists—who mostly end up without a place of their own—since the late 1990s, Murakami has been able to relocate himself as a Japanese writer, by extensively writing about contemporary issues of Japanese society.

I hope that my thoughts on Murakami help increase critical attention to spatial aspects in his fictional worlds. These are worlds that becomes even more fascinating when interpreted in spatial terms. As the historian Karl Schlögel writes in his book *Im Raume lesen wir die Zeit* (2003), once you have taken a spatial perspective on the world, and truly tasted it; you cannot ever give it up again (Schlögel 2003: 15).

References

Augé, M. 1995. Non-Places. *Introduction to an Anthropology of Supermodernity.* (Howe, J. Trans.) London, New York: Verso.

Bal, M. 2009. *Narratology: Introduction to the Theory of Narrative.* Toronto: Toronto University Press.

De Certeau, M. 1984. *The Practice of Everyday Life*. (Rendall, S., Trans.) Berkeley: University of California Press.

Foucault, M. 1986. Of Other Spaces. (Miskowiec, J., Trans.) *Heterotopias, Diacritics*, 16, 22–27.

Genette, G. 1997. *Paratexts. Thesholds of Interpretation*. (Lewin, J. E., Trans.) Cambridge: Cambridge University Press.

Lefebvre, H. 1991. *The Production of Space*. (Nicholson-Smith, D. Trans.) Cambridge: Blackwell.

Lotman, J. 1977. *The Structure of the Artistic Text*. (Roland, V., Trans.) Ann Arbor: University of Michigan.

Lotman, J. 1991. *The Universe of the Mind. A Semiotic Theory of Culture*. (Shukman, A., Trans.) Bloomington, Indianapolis: Indiana University Press.

Murakami H. 1982. *Hitsuji o meguru bōken*. Tokyo: Kōdansha.

Murakami H. 1985. *Sekai no owari to hādoboirudo wandārando*. Tokyo: Kōdansha.

Murakami H. 1987. *Noruwei no mori*. Tokyo: Kōdansha.

Murakami H. 2004. *Afutādāku*. Tokyo: Kōdansha.

Murakami H.; Shibata M. 1989. *Murakami rongu intabyū. Yagi san yūbin mitai ni meiroka shita sekai no naka de* [Long interview with Murakami. In the maze-like world of goat mail]. In: *Yuriika sōtokushū. Murakami Haruki no sekai*. No. 21–8, 8–38.

Pratt, M. L. 1991. Arts of the Contact Zone. *Profession*, 33–44.

Rajewsky, I. 2003. *Intermediales Erzählen in der italienischen Literatur der Postmoderne*. [Intermedial narratives in Italian postmodern literature] Tübingen: Narr.

Said, E. W. 1978. *Orientalism*. New York: Pantheon.

Schlögel, K. 2003. *Im Raume lesen wir die Zeit. Über Zivilisationsgeschichte und Geopolitik*. München, Wien: Hanser. [*In space we read time. On the history of civilization and geopolitics*. (Jackson, G. Trans.) New York: Bard Graduate Center].

Wirth, U. 2009. Paratext und Text als Übergangszone. [Paratext and text as transient zone] In: Hallet, W; Neumann, B. eds.: *Raum und Bewegung in der Literatur. Der Spatial Turn und die Literaturwissenschaften*. [Space and movement in literature. The spatial turn and literary studies]. Bielefeld: Transcript, 167–177.

Karen Connie M. Abalos-Orendain

Layered Frameworks:
Thoughts on Japanese-ness and the Cosmopolitanism of Haruki Murakami

Abstract: *This work joins the discourse on whether or not Murakami is a "pure" Japanese writer. However, it attempts to analyze the problem using a philosophical lens instead of a literary one. Using the concept of basso ostinato as articulated by Maruyama Masao and further emphasized by the thoughts of Kato Shuichi, this article attempts to pose a new way of looking at this question.*

Keywords: Haruki Murakami, cosmopolitanism, basso ostinato, Maruyama Masao, Kato Shuichi

Introduction

There have been numerous works discussing the phenomenon of Haruki Murakami (Hansen, 2020; Wakatsuki, 2017). Since he is a popular writer—known globally through his translated works (Akashi, 2014)—Murakami joins an exclusive league of authors whose popularity may have overshadowed their potential contributions to literature, that is, the curse of the best-selling list puts into contention the possible depth of their literary "genius" (Wakatsuki, 2017). Stephen King, Anne Rice, Isabel Allende may be a few examples.

In his native Japan, Murakami has been generally viewed as a popular writer as opposed to being a serious one (Hansen, 2020). In this work, I attempt to contribute to the discussion by focusing on the tension between Murakami's liberal use of Western cultural references contra his reflections on Japanese society. I believe that this spurs the debate, i.e. his free use of continental references muddies the discussion of whether he is indeed a "pure" Japanese writer. This work does not delve into the complexities of that purity or *junbungaku*[97] nor does it engage in literary criticism. Rather I analyze the Murakami framework or philosophy: how his utilization of pop

---

97   純文学 translates to pure literature as opposed to popular literature. This means that pure literature is considered as serious and more literary (highbrow) as opposed to pop culture (low brow) (Strecher, 1998).

& high culture references grounds his deeper reflections of self and his own society. I believe that this layering methodology is similar to Maruyama Masao's concept of *basso ostinato* (Heisig, 2011, 927–928) and is reminiscent of Kato Shuichi's thoughts on Japanese literature and culture as well (Shuichi, 1979, 5). I try to explain that in this very process, which may appear as cosmopolitan, we may find the Japanese-ness that literary analysts seek in Murakami's works.

The first part of the paper examines some of the recurring themes in Murakami's work that pertain to this cosmopolitanism. I then analyze these themes using Maruyama Masao's *basso ostinato* and Kato Shuichi's thoughts on Japanese literature and culture. Lastly, I conclude with an explanation as to why the debate on pure literature and his cosmopolitanism is reductionist.

On Cultural References and Popularity

There is a certain symmetry to the idea that Haruki Murakami, whose writings are peppered with pop and high culture references,[98] has become a global, cultural phenomenon himself (Wakatsuki, 2017). His global, commercial success is both a bane and boon. Murakami scholars have said that his popularity has actually prevented him from getting heftier literary accolades, including the elusive Akutagawa Prize as well as the Nobel Prize for Literature (Ibid.).

His humor, cultural references, and writing style have indeed transcended cultural barriers.[99] For now, permit me to loosely use the term *philosophy* to refer to these elements. While a literature expert might say that there these are literary tools, my focus in this work is on his outlook—his perspective towards the world. Hence, the word philosophy or framework seem apt, but I do not mean to say that there is a dogma that may be easily identified here. Instead, there are certain motifs in Murakami's style of writing that allude to his *weltanschauung* or worldview. This phenomenological approach carries over to Murakami's attitude towards the literary world. There is an edifying expectation towards Japanese literary writers: that their works should continue the rich tradition of *junbungaku* or pure literature.[100] The author has

---

98   Some examples of Murakami's work where he references Western music and movies: (*First Person Singular*, 2020, 50–125), (*1Q84*, 2011, 111, 507, etc.), (*The Wind-Up Bird Chronicle*, 2003, 5, 278, 499, etc.), (*The Elephant Vanishes*, 2003, 116–117, 139).

99   "In person, Murakami is charming and thoughtful, attentive to the nuances of the English language and gifted with a trans-cultural sense of humor" (Kelts, 2009).

100   "His style was instead seen as a threat to the rich tradition of jun-bungaku (pure literature) and it was in this environment that Miyoshi Masao, for example, called Murakami's (along with Yoshimoto Banana's and other new writers') works 'disposables'" (Hansen, 2020).

shown his disregard for such expectations.[101] Murakami deliberately rejects the methods and traditions of *junbungaku* (Murakami and McInerny, 1992; Murakami, 2010; Strecher, 2014). His (indeed very untraditional) celebrity, now a global phenomenon, is one result of the storytelling method Murakami has developed to replace this traditional model (Strecher, 2018).

This anti-traditional model is precisely why his Japanese-ness is put into question.[102] Even though almost all of his stories are set in Japan and all his main protagonists are Japanese, audiences across the globe easily seem to identify with the ennui that his heroes face. I argue that his cultural references—both high and pop—ground these existential questions. Every time Murakami talks about the Beatles or jazz, he is able to set a mood that makes it easier for his readers to connect to his heroines and heroes. In addition, Murakami does not simply refer to musical pieces and book titles for the sake of showing his vast knowledge of culture.[103] It seems as if he uses these as tools to draw in the reader and it helps to show that our worlds (i.e. the character and the reader) are the same. Thus, the otherworldly setting does not alienate the reader because the Beatles are playing in the background.[104]

Murakami also uses classical music to usher shifts in mood and even place. For example, in *1Q84*, he uses Janáček's Sinfonietta to somehow transport his heroine, Aomame, to that "other" world (Murakami, 2011, 3–9). In *The Wind-Up Bird Chronicle*, Rossini's The Thieving Magpie was not simply the perfect music to listen to while cooking pasta, it was also setting the mood that strange events are about to transpire (Murakami, 2003, 5–7). He uses music to not only set the tone but to change the tone, it helps the reader realize that they have entered a different sphere. Without these

---

101   "I was a black sheep in the Japanese literary world," Murakami recalls—partly because his books, with their absence of any sense of being rooted in Japan, and their multitudes of American cultural references, were seen as "too American-like" … But anyway, by and by I got my own style. Not Japanese or American style—my style" (Murakami, 2018).

102   "unlike his peers, Murakami could not be accepted as a 'Japanese' writer because he failed the test of 'Japaneseness' by refusing to establish a clear sense of opposition between 'Japan' and 'everything else.' Clearly, as Ichikawa's reflections suggest, literary authenticity in the Japanese tradition requires, a priori, a sense of 'Japaneseness' on the part of the writer" (Wakatsuki, 2017).

103   "Music is an indispensable part of my life … When I'm writing I usually have some Baroque music on low in the background—chamber music by Bach, Telemann, and the like" (Murakami, n.d.).

104   "But I can't always see the borderline between the unreal world and the realistic world. So, in many cases, they're mixed up. In Japan, I think that other world is very close to our real life, and if we decide to go to the other side it's not so difficult. I get the impression that in the Western world it isn't so easy to go to the other side; you have to go through some trials to get to the other world. But, in Japan, if you want to go there, you go there" (Murakami, 2019).

grounding tools, it may be difficult for some readers to follow that Murakami's characters have fallen down the rabbit hole.

His references show a cosmopolitanism and worldliness that are not traditional for the Japanese sensibility. This is part of the reason why his critics in Japan argue that his works are too American (Wakatsuki, 2017). I counter that one cannot refer to pop culture without appearing American. However, his interests are culturally varied so the argument for his cosmopolitanism has more foundation compared to his Americanism. His penchant for classical music, for example, belie these Americanism claims. He, himself, talks about this tension present in his writings, we well as in his approach towards his popularity.

> I think transcultural exchange is the most important thing right now," he adds, resting his hands lightly on the table between us. "I know that because I lived in many countries. When I was in America in the early '90s, Japan was rich, and everyone talked about it. But we didn't have a cultural face. And I thought: Somebody should do something. I have to do something for Japanese culture. It's my duty. I've been getting more popular in Europe and America, so I am in a position to be able to talk to people directly, and exchange opinions. That's a great opportunity. Only a few people can do it. And I'm one of them. (Kelts, 2009)

To talk of duty as a representative of Japan shows that he is rightly aware of his position as a cultural icon. Since he is a consumer of culture himself—as an avid fan of various genres of music—he must be well aware of the power and potential of this position. But, has he undermined his own stature as a Japanese writer because of his cosmopolitan views and interests? This is an interesting question to ask in the face of these accusations but is outside the scope of this paper. It is almost as if the universality of his narratives, as evidenced by his cultural references as well as the familiar themes of ennui his characters suffer from, are the reasons why he is not considered as espousing a pure Japanese spirit.

On Purity and Layering Frameworks

Kato Shuichi's classic work entitled *A History of Japanese Literature* is the encyclopedia of Japanese literature, covering all forms and genres. His impressive work ensured his status as a cultural critic (Kato Shuichi on Everything—one of Japan's Last Renaissance Men 2020). For the purposes of this essay, I refer the reader to his description of Japan's literature, culture, and aesthetic values:

> It has never been simply the case of one particular form and style being influential in one period only to be succeeded by a new form in the next. In Japan, the new did not replace the old, but was added to it. (Shuichi, 1979, 4)

I view Shuichi's apt description as "layering" frameworks.[105] By this, I mean, that as Japan is exposed to new waves of thought or foreign forms of art, they add some parts of it to what they currently have or accept it and tweak it to suit their own tastes and utility. This process of intertwining and enmeshing until the old becomes novel—results in something that is still familiar—but, for all intents and purposes, is already different. As Shuichi says, "the old is never lost, there is a considerable unity and continuity in Japanese literary history. At the same time, since new is always being added to old, with each new age literary forms and aesthetic values become more diverse and multifaceted." (Shuichi, 1979, 5). This comment by one of their foremost literature and cultural intellectual is at odds with the purity claim of traditional sects and groups.

Shuichi further claims that while China has to contend with conflicts when the old faces the new, this is not the case in Japan: "the expectation was not that the old should be replaced by the new, but that the two should co-exist" (Shuichi, 1979, 5). This peaceful co-existence is in keeping with the way Japan embraced modernity and their attitude towards technology. Shuichi stresses that this is apparent even in modern Japanese society where "there is a love for all things new" even while it remains "extremely conservative." At this point, I wish to share that Shuichi is not alone in these views. It is also shared by political philosopher and public intellectual Maruyama Masao.

In his essay, *In Search of a Ground* (1984), Maruyama explores the problems inherent in looking for a foundationalist Japanese worldview.[106] He underscores that there is a tendency to commit two major mistakes in the pursuit of understanding Japanese thought. The first mistake is to look at Japan's intellectual history only as an amalgamation of "distorted foreign ideas." That is, to think of Japan as merely importing innovations and novel ways of thought, then claiming it as their own. The second mistake is when people "search for a 'homegrown' Japanese way of thinking, independent of what is considered 'foreign thought'" (Heisig 2011, 923). Maruyama, like Shuichi, questions the adherence to a pure concept of Japanese-ness. Since both methodologies are questionable, how then are we supposed to approach the study of Japanese thought or how do we assess someone like Murakami?

---

105   In a forthcoming journal article, I discussed the same idea, using Kato Shuichi's concepts on this matter and Maruyama Masao's *basso ostinato* to describe Japan's culture.

106   His two translated works such as *Thought and Behavior in Modern Japanese Politics* (1963) and *Studies in the Intellectual History of Tokugawa Japan* (1974) have more or less reiterated and reexamined this theme and problems in various ways.

Maruyama agrees with Shuichi in saying that once foreign ideas infiltrate Japanese shores, "they underwent certain changes and even sweeping 'correction'" (2011, 924). He posits that Japan does not merely consume whatever is new and foreign. These elements become something that the Japanese can comprehend and then it is redesigned, reworked to adhere to their circumstances as well as their aesthetic and moral framework.

A good example is Japan's concept of democracy. In Maruyama's essay entitled *Thought and Behavior Patterns of Japan's Wartime Leaders*, which is found in the translated collection, of essays *Thought and Behavior in Modern Japanese Politics*, he explains in detail how the Japanese notion of democracy might be "an inverted form of democracy." (1969, 113) In another essay, *Nationalism in Japan: its Theoretical Background and Prospects*, he reiterates this point by saying that "So long as democracy remains for Japan a lofty theory, an edifying doctrine, it will continue to be an indigestible import." (Ibid., 152) Maruyama uses this idea to argue for the problems inherent in Japanese modernity and political attitude, indicating that the Japanese do not truly understand, let alone practice, "true" democracy. The development of an autonomous and rational Japanese modern citizen is necessary for democracy to flourish but this was not the case in Japan due to outside pressures and internal conflict.

If one looks from this historical perspective and then analyzes closely, one can discern a pattern emerging. At first, Maruyama used the term "stratum" to refer to what he argues as the persistence of Japanese-ness despite outside influences. This geological metaphor of stratification captures not only the addition of foreign influences but more importantly, it alludes to the continuity and fundamentality of this developmental pattern. The *old stratum* conveys a sense of grounding, even as layers of thoughts and influence are placed on top of it. However, this very foundationalism is something that Maruyama wrestled with. Thus, he turned towards music to find a different word, which is better suited for what he had in mind to describe Japanese-ness. He preferred the term, *basso ostinato*. "Basso ostinato—in English, "ground bass"—refers to the obstinate repetition of a low sound … It is a specific sound but not *necessarily* the main melody" (2011, 927–928).

Maruyama's use of a musical metaphor shows how he is also struggling with succinctness and clarity: To encapsulate the development of Japanese thought with a single word is impossible but one must start somewhere.[107]

107　"Maruyama argues that despite Japan's reliance on foreign inspiration for its political and historical values, what has been imported has always been modified to fit aversion to transcendence, speculative theory, and absolute moral principles grounded beyond the existing social order." (Heisig, 2011, 922)

The term *basso ostinato* will at least provide a jumping-off point. It was able to capture his thought process on this matter because, as he explains, "I had found, it seemed, the image I was looking for to express the 'essentially Japanese' as a kind of obstinately repeated pattern of thinking and feeling." (2011, 928) Despite the methodological problems he encountered with these reflections on Japanese intellectual thought, he was able "to show there is a recurrently repeated tone *within* the patterns of change themselves, that is, in the *way* in which the changes take place." He then states that this "alacrity with which people adapt to changes in the outside world has become a part of 'tradition.'" (2011, 928) If this is how tradition becomes cemented as a ground for the identity and essence of a nation or a people, then this is not simply a matter of purity of the cultural artifacts themselves that should be the focus, instead, it is how these are produced, consumed, appreciated, rejected, and dissected that becomes that tradition.

Maruyama adds that "The idea was that, in spite of numerous historical changes, there is a 'Japanese spirit' that has remained unaltered since ancient times, and that Japan's historical development amounted to no more than different manifestations of this Japanese 'essence' (2011, 929)." Based on my reading of *In Search of a Ground*, Maruyama seems hesitant to use the term 'essence'; hence, his use of *basso ostinato* instead. The musical term was able to somehow capture the consistency and persistence of that elusive Japanese-ness without dogmatically saying that there is one.

Conclusion

Based on the discussions abovementioned, what we call homogeneity and purity is not as simple as the critics claim. This may also be applied to the discourse on Haruki Murakami's Japanese-ness.

In this article, I showed how Murakami uses transcultural references to ground the reader even as he lets them peek into otherworldly realms. It is an oversimplification to say that he is too Western because of his love for jazz, for example. It is fairer to use the term cosmopolitan where his interests are concerned. His cosmopolitanism then may be viewed in two senses: the first is his obvious transcultural appeal to readers from all over the world and the second pertains to his cosmopolitan views, which may be seen in his consumption of culture both high and low. It would be interesting to study later how these relate to one another.

When we closely examine some of the recurring themes in Murakami's work that pertain to this cosmopolitanism, there is a literary purpose or utility which is an author's license to use as he sees fit. These motifs, which are a part of his writing method or a process, may be loosely seen as his framework for viewing the world or, more accurately, a way for him to present his world through his writings.

Kato Shuichi's thoughts on Japanese literature and culture already sets how this discussion is not as simple as it seems since Japanese thought has always been enmeshed and intertwined with foreign ideas. He even goes as far as to say that what is Japanese is actually a result of these combinations and interactions. Using Maruyama Masao's term *basso ostinato*, gives us a more nuanced concept to work with, that is, even as this so-called "Japanese essence" interacts with outside influences, an obstinate sound persists and remains throughout this process. If we apply this concept to Murakami's works, what we should look for then is that tenacity, that persistence of tone, which might pertain to his Japanese-ness. If this is indeed the case, while his readers enjoy his cultural references, his critics should attempt to see past them if they wish to answer the question of his Japanese-ness.

References

Akashi, James Hadley & Motoko. 2014. *Translation and celebrity: The translation strategies of Haruki Murakami and their implications for the visibility paradigm.* Vol. 23. Perspectives Studies in Translation Theory and Practice.

Gitte Marianne Hansen, Michael Tsang. 2020. "40 years with Murakami Haruki." *Japan Forum* 32 (3): 311–315.

Heisig, James W., Kasulis, Thomas P. and Maraldo, John C. eds. 2011. *Japanese philosophy: A sourcebook.* Honolulu: University of Hawaii Press.

Kelts, Roland. 2009. "haruki murakami interviewed." *3:AM Magazine*, March 28.

Maruyama, Masao. 1969. *Thought and behavior in Modern Japanese Politics.* Expanded Edition. Translated by A Fraser, D. Titus, R. Dore, P. Varley, A. Tiedemann, B. Ruch, D. Sisson, F. Baldwin, G.C. Hurst I. Morris. London: Oxford University Press.

Murakami, Haruki. 2011. *1Q84.* Translated by Jay Rubin and Philip Gabriel. New York: Alfred A. Knopf.

—. 2020. *First Person Singular.* Translated by Philip Gabriel. New York: Knopf, Borzoi Books.

—. 2003. *The Elephant Vanishes.* Translated by Alfred Birnbaum & Jay Rubin. London: Vintage.

—. 2003. *The Wind-Up Bird Chronicle.* Translated by Jay Rubin. London: Vintage Books.

Murakami, Haruki, interview by Oliver Burkeman. 2018. *Haruki Murakami: 'You have to go through the darkness before you get to the light'* (October 11).

Murakami, Haruki, interview by Deborah Treisman. 2019. "The Underground Worlds of Haruki Murakami." *https://www.newyorker.com/culture/the-new-yorker-interview/the-underground-worlds-of-haruki-murakami*. The New Yorker, (February 10).

Murakami, Haruki. n.d. "Questions for Murakami about Kafka on the Shore." *https://www.harukimurakami.com/resource_category/q_and_a/questions-for-haruki-murakami-about-kafka-on-the-shore*.

Shuichi, Kato. 1979. *A History of Japanese Literature: The First Thousand Years.* London: The Macmillan Press Ltd.

Shuichi, Kato, interview by Marc Peter Keane and Jeffrey Irish. 2020. *Kato Shuichi on Everything—one of Japan's Last Renaissance Men* (May 18).

Strecher, Matthew C. 1998. "Beyond 'Pure' Literature: Mimesis, Formula, and the Postmodern in the Fiction of Murakami Haruki." *The Journal of Asian Studies* 57 (2): 354–78.

Strecher, Matthew C. 2018. "The celebrity of Haruki Murakami and the 'empty' narrative: a new model for the age of global literature." *Celebrity Studies* 255–263.

Wakatsuki, Tomoki. 2017. "Haruki Murakami as a cosmopolitan phenomenon: from 'ordinary' to 'celebrity'." *Celebrity Studies* 9 (2): 248–254.

Jonathan Dil

*Haruki Murakami and the Search for Self-Therapy: Stories from the
Second Basement* (SOAS Studies in Modern and Contemporary
Japan). London: Bloomsbury Academic, 2022. ISBN-10:
1350270547; ISBN-13: 978-1350270541 (hardback), 272 pp.

Haruki Murakami (or Murakami Haruki in the Japanese order) has said that
he started writing fiction as a means of self-therapy. What he has not talked
about as much is what he needed self-therapy for. Haruki Murakami and the
Search for Self-Therapy: Stories from the Second Basement, published in
2022 by Bloomsbury Academic as part of the SOAS Studies in Modern and
Contemporary Japan series, is a book which takes Murakami's claim above
seriously, seeking to understand both why he began to write fiction, and how
he transformed his therapeutic motive to write into literary fiction capable of
capturing the hearts of millions. The book offers detailed readings of each of
Murakami's fourteen novels to date and explains the role of several important
influences in shaping these works, including the literature of F. Scott Fitzgerald, Raymond Chandler, and Raymond Carver; the philosophy of Friedrich
Nietzsche; and the psychoanalytic thought of Carl Jung. While Murakami is
more open about the literary and philosophical influences above than he is
about the psychoanalytical one, a strong case is made in the book for the deep
influence of Jung on Murakami's novels.

The introduction of the book starts with the question of why Murakami
needed self-therapy to begin with and offers two biographical answers: Murakami's falling out with his parents (particularly his father), and the suicide
of a former girlfriend. Utilizing interviews and secondary sources, this part of
the book offers new information and fresh perspectives on the beginnings of
Murakami's therapeutic fiction. The introduction then looks at the question
of how Murakami writes, explaining that his method is not to seek for the
catharsis which comes through confession, but rather relies on the mysteries
of the unconscious—what Murakami has described as a second basement
hidden with the human mind. While Murakami started writing fiction as a
means of self-therapy, he does not, strictly speaking, write biographical fiction. Instead, he values spontaneity in his writing process above all else, and
he claims to not really understand where his stories come from. Reading Murakami's fiction as an evolving therapeutic project is thus not a straightforward exercise and requires a thoughtful engagement with questions about the

relationship between an author, their unconscious, and their work. The introduction seeks to engage with these questions and to provide a broad framework for understanding how Murakami's fiction might be read in relation to his traumas.

Moving into the five chapters of the book, we see a focus on four therapeutic threads which are woven through Murakami's novels, and which are useful for understanding the main strands of his therapeutic project. The first thread, which is particularly prominent in Murakami's early fiction, describes the journeys of protagonists from melancholia to mourning. Informed by Freud's writings on the topic, Chapters One and Two of the book look at the melancholia of these early protagonists and how they seek, through the interventions of the unconscious, a return to the healthier process of mourning. This aspect of Murakami's fiction can be connected to the death of his former girlfriend discussed in the introduction.

A second therapeutic thread examined explores the nature of intergenerational trauma and how Murakami's fiction seeks to heal it through symbolic acts of self-sacrifice. This therapeutic thread first shows up in Murakami's third novel, *A Wild Sheep Chase* (Hitsuji o meguru bōken; 1982) and reaches its apex in his eighth novel, *The Wind-Up Bird Chronicle* (Nejimaki-dori kuronikuru; 1994–1995), though it continues to show up in later novels too, such as *Killing Commendatore* (Kishidanchō-goroshi; 2017). This therapeutic thread can be related to Murakami's relationship with his father, a World War II veteran who clearly carried trauma from his wartime experience.

The third therapeutic thread borrows ideas from attachment theory and looks at the ways Murakami's avoidant protagonists seek to overcome their distance from others and find love. This is a theme found throughout Murakami's oeuvre, but major breakthroughs are seen in *1Q84* (2009–2010) and *Killing Commendatore*. This therapeutic thread is arguably also related to Murakami's complicated relationship with his parents.

The fourth therapeutic thread described is that of Jungian individuation as a response to nihilism. Again, this is a thread found in each of Murakami's fourteen novels to date, but it finds a particularly strong presentation in Murakami's most recent novel, *Killing Commendatore*. Borrowing ideas from Peter Homans, *Haruki Murakami and the Search for Self-Therapy* argues that individuation is a process that grows out of mourning and is an attempt to take self-therapy beyond the overcoming of personal traumas and into the realm of personal and even spiritual growth and development. The conclusion of the book returns to this question of what the aim of self-therapy might be and whether Murakami might be said to have found salvation through writing.

Beyond these broad strokes, what *Haruki Murakami and the Search for Self-Therapy* offers are close readings of each of Murakami's fourteen novels, and the book offers rewards and insights for even the most dedicated Murakami reader. Who is the librarian the protagonist meets in the "End of the World" sections of *Hard-Boiled Wonderland and the End of the World* (Sekai no owari to hādo-boirudo wandāranda; 1985)? Why does the protagonist in *Dance Dance Dance* (Dansu Dansu Dansu; 1988) need to sleep with Mei (May) and then June on his road to recovery, and who is the final, unidentified sixth skeleton? What is the significance of the colors in the names of each of Tazaki Tsukuru's friends in *Colorless Tsukuru Tazaki and His Year of Pilgrimage* (Shikisai o motanai Tazaki Tsukuru to, kare no junrei no toshi; 2013)? Who is the Commendatore who appears in *Killing Commendatore* and why must he be murdered? Reading Murakami's fiction through a therapeutic lens suggests answers to all these questions and more and adds to the voices of those who value Murakami as a serious author deserving of close critical attention.

Masaki Mori

Haruki Murakami and His Early Work: The Loneliness of the Long-Distance Running Artist, Lexington Books, 2021: ISBN 978-1-7936-3597-6, 115 p.

This book is a result of my research interest in Murakami and his works over two decades. When I first read *Hardboiled Wonderland and the End of the World*, I found him distinct from his contemporary Japanese writers in the sense that his fiction could be appreciated on the world stage outside of his native soil. That has come true probably far beyond his own expectation. I have made a number of publications on his writings since. Unlike most other cases, however, I began with analyzing some of his early short stories as well as his other activities related to his writing for a few reasons. His novels, especially multivolume ones, are undoubtedly important among his oeuvres, but to exclusively focus on a few of them might miss some essential aspects of what he is as a novelist. Rather than embarking on such an undertaking, therefore, I felt it necessary to examine his short stories, because they rival his acclaimed novels in terms of complexity and textual depth. They also succinctly point to the problems he has entertained from the beginning. This does not mean that I ignore his novels. In the current book, I refer to them for comparison to support my argument, while intending them for my potential future research. At the same time, his fiction-writing can be holistically understood only in the context of his other interests, such as music, running, translation, and the self-awareness of his position in the world of literature.

The seven chapters are arranged to this end, with the first three ones addressing those activities or interests in relation to his writing profession. Chapter 1, "Murakami's Self-Conscious Ambivalence as a Japanese Writer," discusses the question of his cultural identity. While his works and his personal lifestyle abounds in Western cultural references or consumer products and avoids mentioning their Japanese counterparts extensively, Murakami considers it a duty of a Japanese novelist to represent his native country abroad, actively engaged in public occasions like interviews, speeches, and award ceremonies. Chapter 2, "Beyond National Canonicity: Murakami and the Japanese Literary Canon," approaches the same aspect from another perspective. In his introduction to a new English translation of Akutagawa Ryunosuke's short stories by one of his principal translators, he poses the question of criteria for the canonization of a modern Japanese novelist as a *national* one. By examining the introduction, one can infer that, while showing certain interest in, and understanding of Japanese literature, Murakami would rather forgo such canonical encapsulation of *national* prestige in preference for a broader arena of challenge and recognition. Chapter 3, "Translation as a Beneficial Diversion for Murakami's Fiction Writing," points out the importance of translation for Murakami's fiction-writing. The number of books he has translated from English, mainly in modern/contemporary American literature, into Japanese is substantial and growing, rivaling that of books of his own creation. Far from hampering his novelistic pursuit, he greatly benefits as a writer in multiple ways from the act of translating stories by the authors he admires for their writing skills, narrating styles, or unique imagination. I also suggest that his translating act can be metaphorically compared to a mid-distance running as part of another passion of his, running, as he likens the writing of a novel to a marathon and that of short stories to short-distance dashes.

Those activities are not only closely tied to Murakami's writing of novels but also enhances it. Even listening to music, including jazz, rock and classical music, contributes to his fiction-writing because he learns the stylistic rhythm of writing a text from the appreciation of music. On the basis of this understanding, the next three chapters analyze short stories representative of his early writing career, titled respectively "'The Second Bakery Attack': The Induced Burial of Young Aspirations," "'The Elephant Vanishes': What Efficiency Produces," and "'TV People': The Slick Assault by Electronic Media." Typical of Murakami's fiction, each of these short stories discussed seems absurd on the surface reading. A close investigation, however, reveals a deep-rooted distrust of the contemporary sociopolitical system that he has problematized since his young days. What lies under the guise of nonsensical, even humorous stories is an unwavering critique of postindustrial society that seeks its capitalistic end with no regard for the plight of humanity. From a detached standpoint, the unnamed narrator in each story exposes, without comprehending what is happening to him, an underlying issue inherent in his way of life, such as incorporation into excessive consumerism, relentless pursuit of efficiency, and one's critical thinking taken over by electronic media. The argument utilizes theories of Jean Baudrillard, Walter Benjamin, Sigmund Freud, Fredric Jameson, Jacques Lacan, Jean-François Lyotard and J. Hillis Miller. In relation to Chapter 6, the last chapter, "Televisual Appropriation and Fear in 'TV People' and *Ringu*," compares Murakami's short story with a pair of popular Japanese horror movies insomuch as both works, text and film, came out in the 1990's with a central image of a nonhuman form emerging out of a TV set, hinting at different kinds of fear intrinsic to the unconditional acceptance of pervasive electronic media.

Established critics tend to label Murakami's works as frivolous and irrelevant to grave, pressing problems of today's world, against which I believe I have made an effective argument, because his humanistic concern about how amiss society operates lies beneath the apparent lack of serious content. At the same time, in spite of its relatively simple style and the great popularity it enjoys in many parts of the world, his fiction often poses difficulty for readers to understand what might be meant. It is also my hope that this book presents possible ways to approach his literature.

Gitte Marianne Hansen & Joseph Thomas Milburn

Research on Murakami: past, present, and future

(Interview with Dr Gitte Marianne Hansen)

Joseph Thomas Milburn (JTM) *How did you first come across the work of Haruki Murakami?*

Gitte Marianne Hansen (GMH) *I first read The Wind-Up Bird Chronicle when it came out in Danish (Trækopfuglens Krønike). I think it was 2001. To be honest I didn't like it at all, and I even think I stopped halfway through. Then someone gave me the first English translation of Norwegian Wood, the one by Alfred Birnbaum.[108] It was an edition published by Kodansha International intended for Japanese learners of English. I was living in Ōita, Kyūshū at the time, and since my Japanese was still not that good, it was a true delight to be given something to read in English (the internet was not that advanced yet, and I didn't have a connection at my house). Seeing Murakami's name on the front cover made me a bit discouraged as I remembered my experience with The Wind-up Bird Chronicle, but I gave it a go. And that is when things really changed for me. I am not sure whether it was the circumstances I was in (living away from my family) or what, but I really connected with that book. Some years later, when I lived in Tokyo where I studied and worked at Waseda University as a teaching and research assistant to professor Katō Norihiro, I came to see a new value in Murakami, one that was more tied to research. Katō-sensei's weekly lectures were so fascinating and inspiring, and I came to read Murakami in way much more connected to the history of contemporary Japan. I am very grateful for the time I had with Katō-sensei (he sadly passed away in 2019) and I can say for sure that he is the direct reason that I, in one way or another, have worked on Murakami's works ever since. Looking back now, it is of course interesting to note that Waseda is the university Murakami himself attended as a student in the sixties, and that today it is the home to the new 'Waseda International House of Literature' or as it is also called, 'The Haruki Murakami Library.'*
I suppose I should end my answer to your question by saying that since my first encounter with The Wind-Up Bird Chronicle, I have read it many times, and while perhaps not my favourite, I see it as a very important work.

(JTM) *So, your meeting Professor Katō Norihiro partly explains why you started researching Murakami. But how does your work differ in scope?*

---

108   **Editorial note:** *Norwegian Wood* (1987) was first translated into English by Alfred Birnbaum in 1989; it has since been re-translated by Jay Rubin in 2000, and the Birnbaum translation is no longer in print.

(GMH) *I am particularly interested in Murakami's female characters and gender representation, a point Katō-sensei didn't really work on. By the time I came to Waseda, I was already interested in gender studies, specifically representations and character construction, but as someone who worked in this field, it perplexed me why I didn't seem to agree much with the general statement that Murakami's women figures are merely objects for male subjectivities. Yes, we do of course find images of women that are rather problematic, but it seemed too simplistic to me to read them only in this way, and yet I wasn't sure exactly why I felt like this—still now I am trying to look more carefully into this point. Then, when I came across the short story 'The little green monster'[109] and realised that this story was one of very few with a female narrator, it was clear to me that I wanted to do a full-scale project on his female characters.*

(JTM) *Could you explain your current research on gender and the representation of female characters a bit further?*

(GMH) *For a while I have been working on a book-length study of women in the world of Murakami. The task I have set for myself could at a first glance seem like a classic feminist project—an examination of women in writings by a male author. We do indeed find female characters who seem to fit right in with the typical criticisms of his works which suggests that his fiction mirrors Japanese patriarchy with female characters written as objects for male subjectivities and sexualities. To realise this, we only need to think of the most typical narrator strategy Murakami employs in his stories—the male first-person narrator who, through his very position as narrator, exclusively holds the power to construct the world we read and the women in it. However, as I just mentioned, my idea for this project came when I realised that we also find works with a female narrator as in the short story 'The little green monster.' Having read all his works—which are not few—I found that there are three other works in which the narrator is female, namely 'Asleep,' 'The ice-man' and the untranslated work, 'Kanō Kureta.' Reading these works made me realise how female character construction changes significantly depending on whether 'she' is constructed by him or by herself. Let me give you an example, we meet the character Kanō Kureta—or as Rubin translated her, Creta Kano—twice in Murakami's works. First in 1991 in the short story 'Kanō Kureta' and then again, a few years later in The Wind-up Bird Chronicle. In the short story, the character Kanō Kureta occupies not only positions of voice and focaliser, she also acts as narrator and her construction is therefore different from Kanō Kureta's story in The Wind-up Bird Chronicle, where the male narrator boku is the overall grammatical narrator despite the passive listening position he assumes during Kanō Kureta's tale about the violence she has encountered. As is typical to Murakami's stories with a male narrator, in The Wind-up Bird Chronicle, Kanō Kureta is then a plot device that drives boku's tale forward, while in 'Kanō Kureta,' she is herself the narrator in search of a device that can drive her plot, which here is the numerous violent men whom she encounters. In both stories Kanō Kureta is a voice for victims of men's violence against women, but it is*

---

109   **Editorial note:** Available in *The Elephant Vanishes* (1993). Translated by Alfred Birnbaum and Jay Rubin. New York: Knopf. Interestingly, the Japanese edition of the short story collection was published in 2005.

due to the difference in her narratological position that we can read her in the short story as an empowered subject, whereas in the novel she becomes a mysterious object.

Overall, I am not saying that Murakami's works with a female narrator portray successful feminist empowered female characters, yet they do seem to give voice to a different perspective of female. Stories with female narrators have largely been left out of the discussion about Murakami's representation of gender, but I find that if we bring them into our readings of his works more generally, we come to see new possible readings. The short story 'Kanō Kureta' ends strangely with the narrator explaining how her own neck is being slit by a big man, and if we decide to read the two Kanō Kureta characters as connected, that then means something for how we can understand The Wind-up Bird Chronicle because what does it mean if Kanō Kureta is already dead when the male narrator tells her story? It is dilemmas like these that really sparks my interest.

(JTM) *Could you provide an overview of the "Eyes on Murakami" research project that you led at Newcastle University?*

(GMH) *Eyes on Murakami is the webpage (https://research.ncl.ac.uk/murakami/) and event series for the UK Arts and Humanities Research Council (AHRC) funded project with the rather longish title 'Gendering Murakami Haruki: Characters, Transmedial Productions and Contemporary Japan.' While the official project has ended, many aspects of it are still ongoing. The project aimed to examine the worlds of Murakami, the processes of translation, transmedial production and the gendering of his characters. I did this through individual research as well as through an event series which included an art exhibition and catalogue; a translation symposium and translation workshop; a film event, and an academic conference. I was very grateful to have the support of leading scholars in Japanese literature and Murakami studies (full list can be found here: https://research.ncl.ac.uk/murakami/people/). While I knew events related to Murakami would probably attract a large audience, I was truly surprised when we were able to welcome scholars and students from all over the world, including various European countries as well as places as far away from the UK as Taiwan, Japan, Hawai'i, Australia, the USA, and even Puerto Rico. This resulted in a highly international atmosphere where thoughts and ideas could be exchanged and developed. Some of the presented work has now been published through two outputs, a special issue of Japan Forum (Vol 32, (3), 2020) and in Murakami Haruki and Our Years of Pilgrimage (Routledge, 2022), both of which I edited with the then project Research Associate, Michael Tsang, who is now a lecturer at Birkbeck College, University of London.*

(JTM) *You said "Eyes on Murakami" had a huge international interest, but why do you think Murakami's works have become so popular around the world?*

(GMH) *This is a question I get asked a lot. I don't think we can find just one single answer; marketing obviously has a lot to do with the success of any author who reaches a global audience, and as you can read from Murakami's first English editor Elmer Luke's recollection of the early days (included in Murakami Haruki and Our Years of Pilgrimage), Murakami's success is certainly also owed to his translators, editors, and* *publishers. However, it is of course too brutal to simply use that explanation. I also believe that Murakami has become so popular globally due to his ability to write to the inner worlds of humans, the inner feelings we may hold as humans in this world rather than as citizens of nation states. Due to his style, these feelings can probably be 'translated' in the mind of readers to fit their own specific cultural realities.*

(JTM) *The Art event, "Beyond Words: Transmediating Murakami Haruki"[110] refers to transmediality; what is the relevance of this term for Murakami researchers?*

(GMH) *Transmediality is a useful term when seeking to explore the movement of stories (in the broad sense) between mediums. Murakami's works are now translated into more than 50 languages and his stories and characters have increasingly inspired global producers of cultural products such as film and theatre makers, artists, travelogue writers, computer game programmers and dance choreographers. We see both official adaptation products and those that are probably not. By examining Murakami beyond his Japanese written word, we gain insight into how his stories and characters are understood, interpreted, and imagined. Through the events held in Newcastle, the project facilitated dialogues with both translators and transmedial producers of Murakami's worlds. The art exhibition was an experiment where I asked Japanese and European artists to respond to Murakami in their own medium. It was fascinating to see their work and hear their process of reading Murakami and creating their own Murakami world through their respective art. In 'Politics in/of transmediality in Murakami Haruki's bakery attack stories' (Hansen and Tsang in Japan Forum Vol 32, (3), 2020), we also discussed the transmediality of Murakami's 'Panya shūgeki,' 'Panya saishūgeki,' and the movement of these 'bakery attack stories' from literary text to other mediums (films, comics, translations). Focusing on the themes—ideology, race, and gender—and their representations across the different genres and media, our aim was to explore what sort of politics is involved in the transmediation of these stories to new platforms. As transmediations of Murakami's works are increasingly reaching large audiences—the international success of the film Drive my Car (2021) by director Ryusuke Hamaguchi is obviously a clear example of this—I think more research is needed in this field.*

(JTM) *Another key concern of your project was translating Murakami and the English-reading marketplace. Do you think there is anything essential lost (or altered?) when Murakami is translated?*

(GMH) *Of course, there will be elements lost when we translate any text—I am, for instance, very interested in Murakami's use of first-person pronouns (boku and watashi, for example) and such an interest will not make much sense to pursue in English translations of his works since English (as with most European languages) does not have several options when referring to oneself. In English, 'I' is 'I'—you could say there is 'me' of course, but that is a grammatically specific way of referring to 'I,' not an alternative. However, rather than focus on what is lost in translation, I think we should think of*

---

110   Catalogue available online: https://research.ncl.ac.uk/murakami/publications/

translated works as works of their own. Translators create new texts, and these should be appreciated in their own right—this also means that in the academic context we must choose whether to base our analysis on the Japanese, the English, or the Polish (and so forth) version. We cannot necessarily say that one analysis fits all. I try to make my students aware of this. Although my field is Japanese studies, I am happy to take students who work from the English version of Murakami's works, for example. It just needs to be a conscious decision because the two texts and their contexts are not the same. Murakami is himself a translator. Akashi Motoko has worked on this (included in Murakami Haruki and Our Years of Pilgrimage) and although Murakami the translator may be less known outside Japan, within Japan, his translations and retranslations of literary works written in English rapidly increases the sales of that author. It is really quite fascinating. But not only that, with the success of Murakami's own works, we are also starting to see a new trend where his translators often become recognized, even famous. The documentary Dreaming Murakami *(2018) about the Danish translator Mette Holm is an example of this kind of interest. In the past, such interest has not been typical for literary translators whose names often are just hidden away in the copyright page. Translation is an art and a huge responsibility. I think it is great to see that more emphasis is now paid to translators.*

(JTM) *What are your thoughts on the future of Murakami research?*

(GMH) *When Murakami first began writing in the late 1970s and early 1980s, his works saw much criticism from established literary circles in Japan. This may be hard to imagine today when his novels and stories have become so popular globally, but that is how it was. Through the past forty years plus, we have gone from strong criticism of his works within a discourse that even claimed he was not writing 'pure literature' (whatever that is), and which therefore also dismissed research on his works as unimportant, to now when his popularity sometimes prevents us from saying anything critically about him at all. As one of the very few who saw the significance of Murakami in the early days, this shift was of great concern to Katō-sensei at the end of his life.*

When Michael and I decided to go with Murakami Haruki and Our Years of Pilgrimage *as the title for our edited volume, it was, on the one hand, intended as a fun and obvious reference to Murakami's novel* Colorless Tsukuru Tazaki and His Years of Pilgrimage *from 2014. As we like to point out, 'pilgrimage' is used here not in the religious sense— by no means are we suggesting that Murakami is some sort of 'holy figure' in Japanese literature—but instead as a long, usually taxing journey in search of new meanings to one's belief, thought, and philosophy. Just like how Tsukuru is trying to make sense of his past in the novel, so have 'we'—and here we mean all readers, including those who read for entertainment as well as students and scholars who may read for other reasons—spent 'years' trying to think about his works, and so just like with the conference and 'Eyes on Murakami' event series in Newcastle, we wanted to create a space where we could exchange 'our' thoughts about Murakami beyond these two restrictive poles—that is, 'not significant enough' on the one hand and 'too popular' on the other. We are very happy to have been able to gather and edit truly fascinating works that discuss Murakami's literature from various angles, but at the same time, I feel this is just a beginning. Considering that Murakami has been writing for more than forty years and literary critics and academics have worked on him almost just as long, this perhaps sounds a bit strange, and yet there seems to be so much more to say because his worlds are in constant development. For example, as I already mentioned, his stories are increasingly moving beyond the boundaries of (Japanese) literary texts and into other mediums, and this is just one area I think we will come to think more about.*

Further Reading:

Hansen, Gitte Marianne, and Michael Tsang. 2020. "40 years with Murakami Haruki." *Japan Forum*, 32:3, 311–315.

Hansen, Gitte Marianne, and Michael Tsang (eds.). 2022. *Murakami Haruki and our years of pilgrimage*. London: Routledge.

Interviewee:

GITTE MARIANNE HANSEN is Reader in Japanese Studies at Newcastle University. As AHRC Leadership Fellow (Feb 2017–July 2018), she led the research project *Eyes on Murakami* and is currently working on a monograph about women in Murakami's works. She is the author of *Femininity, Self-harm and Eating Disorders in Japan: Navigating contradiction in narrative and visual culture* (Routledge, 2016) and *Murakami and Our Years of Pilgrimage* (Edited with Michael Tsang, Routledge, 2022).

Website: https://www.ncl.ac.uk/sml/our-people/profile/gittehansen.html;
https://research.ncl.ac.uk/murakami/
E-mail: gitte.hansen@ncl.ac.uk

Interviewer:

JOSEPH THOMAS MILBURN is a Ph.D. candidate in Philosophy at the University of Sofia. He holds an MA in Jungian and Post-Jungian Studies from the Centre for Psychoanalytic Studies, University of Essex, and a BA (Hons) in English Literature and Philosophy from Newcastle University.

Website: https://orcid.org/0000-0003-4792-2785
E-mail: joseph.t.milburn@gmail.com

Midori Tanaka Atkins

Killing Commendatore Book Review: From *Boku* to *Watashi*, Healing on Canvas and in the Darkness of the Pit

Transnational author Haruki Murakami's novels have been recognised and awarded prizes for their chronotopes, their treatment of language and their organization of space and time, as defined by Bakhtin (see Bakhtin 1981). They suggest the possibility of other types of chronotopes of immeasurable physicality which serve as the locus of Murakami's protagonists' searches for identity. His 14th novel *Killing Commendatore* (2017) features many of his familiar motifs and themes in depicting its protagonists' self-explorations. The novel's sixty-four chapters are populated by solitary individuals who display an omnipresent sense of vacuity, loss, violence, and repressed memories—unfolding over two volumes: 1 "The Idea Made Visible" and 2 "The Shifting Metaphor" in the Japanese. As these titles imply, the main protagonist's introspection combines involvement in inexplicable and emblematic events with immersion in a dark, deep space of the subconscious that collapses the notion of realist chronotope.

With the thirty-nine-year-old portrait painter *watashi* ("I") recalling events that had taken place during a nine month period three years earlier, *Killing Commendatore* picks up where Murakami's first novel, *Hear the Wind Sing* (1979), leaves off. Underscoring the influence of his (fictional) writer hero Derek Hartfield's personal history and novels, the cynical protagonist *boku* ("I") of *Hear the Wind Sing* nonchalantly dismisses the therapeutic benefit of writing—despite his sense of vacuity and loss. *Boku* is skeptical that writing can adequately capture perception. His unfounded optimism for his future self and for his future writing is limited only in that in "a few years or many decades," he might be able to write about a "salvaged self" in beautiful prose (Murakami 2016, 4). For Murakami, who has opined about creative writing, inasmuch as *Hear the Wind Sing* pivots on the discourse about writing, *Killing Commendatore* is about both the broader creative process and about pictorial representation. This framework is a departure from the many Murakami novels that vest their main character in the world of letters as writer, copywriter, translator, librarian, or publisher. However, *Killing Commendatore*'s use of visual art can somewhat resemble the ways in which the main protagonist of *Kafka on the Shore* (2002) is immersed in the world of letters—a world of literature and the private library—in his maturation process. *Killing*

Commendatore successfully deploys the immersive, colourful, and textured creative process of creating visual art as a device to propel *watashi's* progress in self-examination, thereby helping *watashi* move forward in life with clarity.

Watashi's eventful nine months begin after his wife Yuzu unexpectedly dissolves their marriage. Having wandered through northern Japan, the indignant *watashi* becomes a house-sitter for the famous painter Amada. The house atop an Odawara mountain is permeated by Amada's fierce spirit even as the painter is elsewhere—in a bed in an Izu Peninsula sanitarium. We see *watashi* house-sitting and taking up a quiet life as an art teacher, interspersed with assignations with married women who, like the other female characters in the novel, are narrowly portrayed as bodies. Things take a turn, and the narrative becomes filled with inexplicable events after *watashi's* discovery of and absorption in Amada's secret painting 'Killing Commendatore,' hidden in an attic. This breathtakingly violent painting's depiction of a scene from Mozart's opera *Don Giovanni* contrasts heavily with Amada's other known works that depict historical events in a utopian setting of the Asuka period (592–710). A repressed memory lies behind the painting's metaphorical composition—the bloody killing of Donna Anna's father, Il Commendatore, observed by a long-faced man situated in a hole in the ground, and drawn as traditional *nihonga* (Japanese painting), with figures in Asuka period dress. A bold blank space on the canvas (a *nihonga* technique) speaks to *watashi* of the underlying, unspoken narrative: The solitary and reticent Amada has suppressed memories of torture and imprisonment that he had received at the hands of Nazis and of their killing of his Austrian fiancée—in reprisal for Amada's and the fiancée's failed assassination attempt on a Nazi shortly before the 1938 Anschluss. We also learn of the Amada's brother's suicide, stemming from his experiences as a victim of bullying and as a (forced) perpetrator of atrocities committed during the 1937 Nanjing Massacre.

The painting's historicity connects the trauma of these past events to the subconscious, violent impulses of the present. Three otherwise isolated individuals are linked over their losses: *Watashi's* new patron, the reclusive, mid-fifties, Gatsby-esque Menshiki; thirteen-year-old Mariye from *watashi's* art class; and *watashi* himself. Murakami thereby underscores two aspects of violence: one that is systematically executed by a nation or an institution and another that is deeply suppressed within the individual. Menshiki has lost his raison d'être, having suffered brutality and injustice when the Japanese judicial system kept him imprisoned for a crime that he had not committed. Menshiki also aches for a deceased former girlfriend and now lives to find a way to form a relationship with Mariye, whom he suspects is his daughter by that girlfriend. Mariye herself is also not immune to loss, with vanished memories of her mother, who suddenly, violently died when she was a child. *Watashi's* life is in turn overshadowed by the childhood trauma of his twelve-year-old sister Komi's chronic illness and ensuing death. *Watashi* also has a suppressed, violent impulse which manifests in his raping his wife Yuzu in an inexplicable episode. This transgression of social boundaries and the suppressed urge to kill are also felt in a brief sexual encounter that *watashi* has with a stranger.

The novel shows *watashi* going through three phases of self-exploration, with Menshiki and Mariye following similar paths in parts. In the first two phases, art coerces progression. Murakami demonstrates what John Berger describes as a three-way relationship between perception, image, and other (see Berger 1972). First, *watashi's* chance discovery of 'Killing Commendatore,' "a requiem to the dead's memories" (Murakami 2017, 621), prompts introspection and *watashi's* undertaking of a commission from Menshiki for a portrait of Menshiki. They make a discovery of an old, hidden pit by Amada's house which becomes an integral place for further introspection. This is followed by *watashi's* undertaking of another commission from Menshiki for a portrait of Mariye, by *watashi's* painting of a stranger who drives a Subaru Forester (thereinafter "Subaru Forester Man"), and by *watashi's* drawing of the pit. *Watashi* depicts Menshiki in a bold, three-dimensional image, heavily layered with paint atop an outlined, realist painting. Conversely, *watashi* cannot fully decipher his portrait of Subaru Forester Man, done in the same style as the Menshiki portrait—dissolving the boundary between abstract and figuration, while speaking to the viewer of anger and violence. The other two paintings reveal some shift within *watashi*. In his rough sketch of Mariye, *watashi* discovers her image to be intertwined with that of his sister Komi. And the superrealist, meditative drawing of the pit becomes intensely alluring for *watashi*. Although Murakami's descriptions of these fictional paintings are flat and simplistic, the suggested images culminate in tension between realism and abstraction, surface and depth, and reality and illusion, all caught in colors and lines on the canvas, representing the fabric of *watashi's* exploration. *Watashi* experiences his craft as a therapeutic agency for self-healing through a dialectic introspection with his creations, their subjects, and with 'Killing Commendatore.' Thus, *watashi* is a vessel and catalyst for his sitters Menshiki and Mariye's introspection and for Amada's release from painful and violent memories and attainment of salvation.

Watashi's last phase of self-exploration shifts from the canvas as he visits Amada in Izu, the day after Mariye goes missing. Seeing Komi in Mariye, *watashi* embarks on a search for Mariye by plunging into a hole, like the one in Amada's painting, which mysteriously appears on the floor of Amada's sanitarium room. Murakami uses the search as a metaphor, with *watashi's* descent into the darkness of the pit resulting in self-discovery and coming to terms with Komi's death. He also gains better awareness of his violent impulses and subsequently decides to return to Tokyo and to welcome a child with Yuzu. The pit's construct and function share some characteristics with the well in *The Wind-up Bird Chronicle* (1994), as well as with other dark spaces that take various forms in Murakami's other novels—operating as the "root of collective unconsciousness" on "the sub-basement level" within an assembly of the self (Kawakami 2017, 108). In *The Wind-up Bird Chronicle*, the protagonist Tōru descends to the well's bottom to simulate the near-death experience that his acquaintance Lieutenant Mamiya had in a well near the China-Russia border during World War II. Loaded with a sense of historicity and violence, the well becomes Tōru's place for self-exploration that metamorphoses to another place of non-lineal spatio-temporality. In *Killing Commendatore*, the deep stone chamber-like pit becomes an expansive realm of *watashi's* trauma and unconscious. Murakami renders the enormity of the strains on *watashi* via forcing his claustrophobic protagonist through the "darkest and narrowest tunnel" and "the most desolate plain" where time does not exist (Murakami 2017, 681).

Depicting self-search in the inherent collective unconsciousness in a contemporary Japanese setting, Murakami juxtaposes the real and non-real with various sources beyond the pit. The story's universal themes, historicity and detailed descriptions of a particularised world are reminiscent of European realist technique. Murakami also draws upon the treatment of the real and non-real in Japanese narrative traditions to formulate the nature of self-search by destabilizing the narrative form through the deployment of traditional Japanese poetics. His postmodern treatment of time and space as fragmented, multiple, and destabilizing is found in his protagonists' self-exploration in his other work, most prominently in *Kafka on the Shore*. For Kafka's collapse of the realist chronotope and associated transcendence to the fantastic, Murakami borrows motifs of out-of-body experiences and living spirits found in Japanese classics such as the vengeful spirit of the Lady at Rokujō of *The Tales of Genji* (eleventh century), or the loyal samurai of Ueda Akinari's (1734–1809) *Tale of Moonlight and Rain* (1776). In *Killing Commendatore*, Murakami incorporates out-of-body living-spirits from such classical reality in three scenes. One is set after *watashi's* discovery of 'Killing Commendatore' and before his unearthing of the pit, when he hears a bell tolling from the bottom of the pit in the dead of night. Here, Murakami connects a narrative from Ueda's classic, "Fate over Two Generations" (1808) to the present, describing a similar phenomenon as an example of the separation of body-spirit. In another scene, *watashi* has the out-of-body experience of raping Yuzu in Tokyo, while his body remains in the North. In the third scene, *watashi* witnesses Amada's living spirit traverse time and space, visiting his studio to have a last look at 'Killing Commendatore' while his body remains in Izu. This type of 'reality' is further mixed with Murakami's use of characters called Idea, a guide for *watashi's* (and to a lesser extent Mariye's) exploration, and Metaphor, embodied as the Commendatore and the long-faced man respectively, thereby defying linear spatio-temporality. Murakami demonstrates the strain of inexplicability that is found in the bell sounds, in the enigmatic pit, and in these out-of-body episodes, as integral both to an individualised realm that is immersed in the expanse of historicity and to an alternate plane of reality.

Killing Commendatore's storytelling about the excavation of the unconscious unfolds within the familiar spectrum of Murakami's particular configuration of time and space. However, unusually and potentially foreshadowing a new authorial direction, fuller depiction of male characters and their dialogical relationship is helped, particularly in the Japanese text, by Murakami's unprecedented use of the first-person singular pronoun *watashi* for the narrator—a more formal word when used for the male voice—instead of his usual *boku*, which connotes intimacy and a youthful casualness. A survey of Murakami novels from early to recent periods reveals that he continues to craft a distinctive narrative style and to carefully choose language, style and sound in accordance with his themes and characters. The choice of *watashi* as the voice of *Killing Commendatore*'s portrait painter narrator, a man who is equipped with the social skill to quickly build trusting client relationships while painting images of those clients as he perceives and interprets, is a conscious shift from the past *boku* pronouns for Murakami who also refers to himself as *boku* in his interviews and essays, including *What I Talk About When I Talk About Running* (2007), the book which he calls his memoir.

While *Killing Commendatore*'s *watashi* seems a pertinent choice for the character, a short-story "First Person Singular" (2020) in the collection of the same title suggests that the *watashi* designation for a Murakami male narrator is one of many components to portray his 'I.' The eight short pieces in *First Person Singular*, written between 2018 and 2020, have the appearance of an 'I-novel'[111] in which the protagonists narrate with details from Murakami's

---

111   Japanese literary genre 'I-novel' took its shape during the development of Japanese modern literature in the first decade of the 1900s. I-novel adopts a confessional mode and

personal realm. The *bokus* in seven of these stories profess their inner thoughts through their recollections of impactful and sometimes bewildering encounters in periods ranging from high-school years to more recent adult-hood. "First Person Singular" stands out because it keeps its focus on *watashi's here* and *now*; its message is more ambiguous and symbolic than others in the collection. In this story, the narrator *watashi* is a "respectful adult of many years" and an intellectual (Murakami 2020. 222). On a warm, spring full-moon night, when he sees the reflection of himself in the mirror of an unfamiliar bar, dressed in his rarely worn British designer suit and Italian tie, he ponders whether there exists another 'I' besides *watashi* in as many multiple worlds as his life's unpursued paths. Such wondering manifests in the subsequent twists of the night: He has unpleasant exchanges with a stranger who claims to have met him and accuses him of committing an awful deed in the past. His voice no longer sounds like himself. When *watashi* exits the bar, he steps into a cold moonless street, with snakes on tree trunks and faceless people walking on an ash-covered ground. This experimental story questions the legitimacy of the first-person singular *watashi's* voice, the possibility of the untapped selves within *watashi*, and the boundaries of *here* and *now*. Mature and older *watashi* in *First-Person Singular* may or may not be a separate being from those characters' "I" that are synonymous with the *boku*s. In comparison, *Killing Commendatore's* fully-developed "I," the mature voice in the pronoun *watashi*, synchronises with and sets the tone for the narrative theme, development, and character settings, even though this may not be conveyed in translation.

Killing Commendatore tells the story of an unwavering sense of personal loss and torment, stemming from the heavy burdens of individual and collective memory. Highlighting this narrative's difficulty, Murakami instills verisimilitude by drawing from Japanese narrative tradition and by expanding on his theme that "[w]hat we see isn't the only reality" (Murakami 2017, 205–6). Echoing earlier works, Murakami blurs the border between the real and non-real, creating a time and space continuum that exists outside the realist chronotope. For the subconscious to emerge, he constructs two spaces for *watashi's* self-discovery: one familiar to a Murakami reader, experienced in the enclosed, dark pit, and the other innovative and unfamiliar, created on the canvas. With *watashi's* mature and introspective resonance, his scrutinizing gaze, and a considered and subtle emotional distance from others, *Killing*

---

focuses on a protagonist's inner psyche while observing his or her "particularised, personal, narrowly defined world" through personal experiences (Fowler 1988, 290).

Commendatore may become "the new beginning of (the author's) first person world" that Murakami anticipates (Kawakami 2017, 285). It remains to be seen in what ways Murakami may or may not incorporate the new language of *watashi,* this shift from *boku* to *watashi,* in his narrative world.

References

Bakhtin, Mikhail. 1981. "Forms of Time and of the Chronotope in the Novel: Notes toward a Historical Poetics." In *The Dialogic Imagination: Four Essays,* edited by Michael Holquist, 84–258. Austin: University of Texas Press.

Berger, John. 1972. *Ways of Seeing.* London: Penguin Books.

Fowler, Edward. 1988. *The Rhetoric of Confession.* Berkeley and Los Angeles: University of California Press.

Kawakami, Mideko and Muraami, Haruki. 2017. *みみずくは黄昏に飛びたつ 川上未映子 訊く/村上春樹 語る (Haruki Murakami, A Long Long Interview by Mieko Kawakami).* Tokyo: Shinchōsha.

Murakami, Haruki, Trans. Ted Goossen. 2016. *Hear the Wind Sing.* New York: Vintage International.

Murakami, Haruki, Trans. Philip Gabriel and Ted Goossen. 2017. *Killing Commendatore.* London: Harvill Secker.

Murakami, Haruki.

— 1979. *風の歌を聴け(Hear the Wind Sing).* Tokyo: Kōdansha-bunko.

— 1994. *ねじまき鳥クロニクル (The Wind-up Bird Chronicle).* Tokyo: Shinchōsha.

— 2002. *海辺のカフカ(Kafka on the Shore).* Tokyo: Shinchōsha.

— 2007. *走ることについて語るときに僕の語ること(What I Talk About When I Talk About Running).*   Tokyo: Bungei-Shunjū.

— 2017. *騎士団長殺し(Killing Commandetore).* 2 vols. Tokyo: Shinchōsha.

— 2021. "一人称単数" *(First Person Singular)* In *First Person Singular.* Tokyo: Bungei-Shunjū.

— 2021. *First Person Singular.* Tokyo: Bungei-Shunjū.

Ueda, Akinari, Trans. Yasushi Inoue. 2010. "二世の縁 (Fate of Two Generation)." In *春雨物語 (Tales of Spring Rain).* Tokyo: Kadokawa Bunko.

Ken Lawrence

Murakami Pilgrimage Reflections:
How Murakami's Fiction Makes the Mundane Magical

I'd been living in Japan for nearly a decade when I decided that it was finally time to move on. But before leaving, I couldn't shake the feeling that there was something I needed to accomplish—an idea that I'd been toying with in my head since fairly early on in my stay.

The plan was to make one last trip around the country, but with a twist. I was going to view Japan through the lens of the fictional characters of my favorite Japanese author, Haruki Murakami. Little did I know at the time what I'd be in for.

The project would be a fitting farewell to the country I'd long called home, as my initial encounter with Murakami's fiction happened during my very first visit. I was in my late teens then and was in the country as a foreign exchange student. In the small rural town I'd been sent to, reading books was one of the few ways to pass the time.

The problem was, however, that I was hours away from the nearest English bookstore, and this was in the days before e-books. The sleepy little town was home to no more than a handful of foreign residents, all of whom were dealing with the same conundrum. And so we'd occasionally meet up and trade English novels as if they were rare collectibles.

During one of these exchanges, someone handed me an English translation of a book called *A Wild Sheep Chase* by a Japanese author I'd never heard of before. Opening it up, I quickly devoured it in a single weekend. I'd never read anything quite like it but I knew I wanted more.

The following Monday, I was already asking around if anyone had something similar. I was in luck, as before long, I got my hands on Murakami's latest novel that had just been translated to English: *Kafka on the Shore*.

To my complete shock, I soon discovered that the story takes place in the same rural prefecture I'd been living in: Kagawa, the smallest of four prefectures of Shikoku, itself the smallest of Japan's four main islands.

To put it mildly, Kagawa wasn't the most thrilling place for a young adult to be. But after reading *Kafka on the Shore*, I could no longer perceive my immediate surroundings in the same way. Visiting the prefectural capital of Takamatsu, the ordinary shrines and shopping arcades I'd grown used to took on a whole new air of magic and mystery.

It was my first time visiting—let alone living in—a place from one of my favorite novels. And the more I began to observe Kagawa from the perspective of Murakami's characters, the thinner the line between my everyday reality and Murakami's fantasy world became. This early experience planted the first seed of what was to become *The Murakami Pilgrimage.*

Fast forward to roughly a decade later and I was living in Japan again, now in Tokyo. By this point, I'd already read through most of Murakami's bibliography. But for whatever reason, I put off picking up his latest novel at the time, *1Q84,* until a few years after its release. When I finally did, I experienced yet another eerie coincidence.

While most of Murakami's characters live somewhere in Tokyo, I wasn't quite expecting Tengo, one of the book's protagonists, to be residing in the neighborhood of Koenji, just the next station over from my flat.

And so whenever I could, I'd take my book over to Koenji to read in a public park or coffee shop. Immediately after putting the book down, I merely had to look around and I was right there in Tengo's world. Walking through the same streets as the characters from such a surreal novel was in itself a surreal experience.

With dedicated Murakami fans all over the world and with Japan's tourism industry on the rise at the time, I surely couldn't be the only one intrigued by such an experience, I figured. And so, feeling that my days in the country were numbered, I decided to finally get started on a travel guidebook to Murakami's complete body of fiction.

I couldn't begin my journey right then and there, of course. To be as thorough as possible, I first had to go through the long process of re-reading every single Murakami novel and taking copious amounts of notes. Only then could my adventure officially commence.

Sure enough, my travels took me to a lot of unique and interesting places. Following in the footsteps of Murakami's protagonists, I traveled to sheep pens in the remote corners of Hokkaido, smokey jazz bars in bustling Kobe, and of course, back to Kagawa, a place I hadn't visited in years. Getting to see Kagawa again with fresh eyes, I gained a much deeper appreciation for what's one of Japan's most historically significant prefectures.

It was also there that, when visiting an ancient yet largely overlooked shrine, I came face to face with the real-life "entrance stone" that likely inspired the fictional version in *Kafka on the Shore.* Without giving away too much, the stone in the novel functions as a portal between worlds—a motif that comes up again and again in Murakami's fiction.

Yet another symbolic portal between worlds is that of the emergency stairway from the opening scene of *1Q84*. Back in Tokyo, as I wandered alongside a busy highway in the trendy Sangenjaya district with my DSLR in hand, drivers were giving me strange looks, surely wondering what a foreigner was doing taking photos.

But to me, it was no longer just a stairway, but a potential portal to an alternate reality. In the novel, this alternate reality looks and feels mostly like the "real" world, and even the characters have a hard time telling the difference. By the end of my project, I could definitely relate.

In addition to far-off exotic places and tours through some of Tokyo's most lively districts, the project also led me to neighborhoods in the capital that I never would've visited otherwise.

One such neighborhood was Nakano Ward's Nogata, yet another setting from *Kafka on the Shore*. Walking past the police box outside the train station, an otherwise completely ordinary place, I couldn't help but picture mackerel falling from the sky. And just nearby, I found a vacant lot that could've been the place where Nakata sits and talks to cats.

While Murakami names plenty of real-life locations in his novels, others are only vaguely described and some are left as complete mysteries. As such, a fair amount of research and detective work was called for. But sometimes I could do nothing more than walk around and see what I could find.

One of my trickier hunts was seeking out the place where Toru, the protagonist of *The Wind-Up Bird Chronicle*, might've lived. The book only tells us that he lived in the 2-*chome* area of an unnamed district in Setagaya Ward. We also know that nearby his house was a library and a pool.

It's entirely possible that Murakami had no particular block in mind and was purely using his imagination. But for whatever reason, I felt compelled to find the closest possible match.

Interestingly enough, in the 2-*chome* area of Gotokuji, Setagaya, I encountered Gotokuji Temple. It's the supposed birthplace of the "beckoning cat" figurine that's now a common fixture at Japanese restaurants throughout the world. Fittingly, *The Wind-Up Bird Chronicle* begins with a search for a missing cat.

While that was a lucky find, I didn't come across anything particularly noteworthy during some of my other excursions to places like Kunitachi or Ichikawa, Chiba. But simply exploring them with Murakami's fiction in mind was enough to make these otherwise mundane neighborhoods somehow exciting.

The fact that visiting these ordinary places could become such unique experiences speaks a lot to Murakami's talent as a writer. He often starts his novels by introducing us to an everyday character with a typical job. He tells us what music they listen to, what food they like to cook and what cigarettes they smoke. From the onset, we're drawn into a very believable universe.

But in many cases, things are not quite how they first seem. Strange occurrences start to happen. And even if the protagonist can make it back to their original reality, they're never completely the same person they once were.

Putting myself in these characters' shoes, I often got the sense that something magical could happen at any moment, even while walking through the residential backstreets or sterile business districts of Tokyo I'd long grown used to. And for a first-time visitor to Japan, this sense of wonder is only bound to increase.

While, thus far, I've described the strange sensation of being drawn into Murakami's dreamlike settings, what if the reverse could also occur? What if something from Murakami's fiction suddenly appeared one day in our world? As farfetched as it may sound, I learned during my travels that such an event just may have really happened.

At one point in *A Wild Sheep Chase*, the protagonist comes to stay in a large house surrounded by birch trees that also faces a sheep pasture. In the book, it's located on the outskirts of a small town called Junitaki-cho. While Junitaki-cho is a fictional name, it was likely based on the town of Bifuka in northern Hokkaido.

When *A Wild Sheep Chase* was first published in the early 1980s, no such house existed—at least as far as residents of Bifuka, a town of just several thousand people, are aware. But a structure eerily similar to that of the novel did indeed appear sometime in 1995.

The owners had never read a Murakami novel when the house was built. And ordinarily, such a house wouldn't attract much attention. It wasn't long, however, before passersby began pointing out the similarities to the house of the book. Seeing its potential as a tourist attraction, the owners have since familiarized themselves with Murakami's fiction and the inn now attracts his fans from around the world.

But the question remains: Was it merely a series of coincidences that led a family, completely unaware of the novel, to build a strikingly similar house in the same town and set amongst identical surroundings? Or was it perhaps the mysterious Sheep Man who somehow willed it to take form in our world? And if so, what might be coming next?

Several years have now passed since the publication of *The Murakami Pilgrimage* and my departure from Japan. My pilgrimage, however, is not yet complete. When given the opportunity, I'm looking forward to revisiting the country and creating new chapters for more recent novels like *Killing Commendatore* and whatever else the author may have up his sleeve.

Whether someone's a first-time visitor to Japan or a long-time resident, I hope that the guidebook can help deepen Murakami enthusiasts' appreciation for his novels, while also enriching one's travels through the Land of the Rising Sun.

Eric Siercks

Just Like Breathing: Celebrating the Opening of the Haruki Murakami Library

> … Learning is really no different from breathing. Whether you're in a class-room or not, you are constantly taking in the world around you. I hope that this library will become a place of learning where you can breathe easy, a place that will allow you to pass through walls of all kinds—whether those erected within academic institutions or along national borders.
>
> **Haruki Murakami**

These words welcome visitors to the Waseda International House of Literature, also known as the Haruki Murakami Library or WIHL, located in Waseda University's main Waseda Campus in Tokyo. This newly renovated facility opened on October 1, 2021 in the midst of both the COVID-19 pandemic and a typhoon. Planning for WIHL began in 2018 following a public announcement that Haruki Murakami would be donating and loaning valuable items from his personal collection to Waseda University, the author's alma mater. These plans began with a comprehensive renovation of Waseda's Building 4—a building, Murakami noted in WIHL's opening press conference, that played center stage to dramatic aspects of the student protests in the 1960s.

To execute a full renovation in line with Murakami's literature, Waseda University and Murakami turned to visionary architect Kengo Kuma. Through a long series of proposals and revisions, Kuma devised a building that would house a distinctive hidden world. The Library's external appearance hints at the transformed space within, embodying WIHL's architectural concepts: tunnels and hollows. Kuma sees this kind of spatial transformation in Murakami's novel *The Wind-Up Bird Chronicle*, writing, "I designed the structure of the Haruki Murakami Library based on the spatial concept of a tunnel. One of the fundamental structures within Murakami's literature is a hole suddenly opening in the ground of our everyday lives, whereupon we suddenly wander off into—or perhaps find refuge in—an alternative underground world."[112]

---

112 Cited from Kuma's recommendation for *The Wind-Up Bird Chronicle* in WIHL's opening exhibition, *Literature in Architecture, Architecture in Literature*.

Kuma's aim to create a new, alternative world in the middle of the Waseda University campus informed WIHL's layout and design. Rather than crafting a "memorial hall" to Murakami's literature, the Library's form invites public utilization of space. The first floor's tunnel entrance opens into a multistory stairwell lined with bookshelves. Rotating selections of books are organized into broad literary themes: The Depths of the Spirit, Crossing Boundaries, The Ordinary and the Extraordinary, Expanding Language, etc. Other books are directly connected to Murakami's oeuvre. A section covers published materials cited in WIHL essays or exhibitions. While another portion of the stairwell is dedicated to recommended readings in world literature by authors such as Bryan Washington, Mieko Kawakami, Hideo Furukawa, and others. The stairwell is flanked on one side by a gallery, chronologically displaying all of Murakami's published works as well as translations of those books into more than forty languages. Visitors are welcome to read books from the stair bookshelves and gallery at their pleasure. Opposite the gallery is an audio room, where visitors can listen to records donated by Murakami (including a large selection of records from his jazz café, Peter Cat).

Descending the stairs to the basement floor, visitors find themselves before two large stage props from the dramatization of *Kafka on the Shore*, as well as the original grand piano from Peter Cat. Around the corner is the Library's student-run café, Orange Cat, which takes menu inspirations from Murakami's work. Adjacent to Orange Cat is a reproduction of Murakami's home study, allowing visitors to envision the space where Murakami spends his days writing. The second floor features a large exhibition space with new exhibits rotating twice a year. The Library opened with the exhibition *Literature and Architecture, Architecture in Literature*, an exploration of WIHL's renovation and the interwoven processes of spatial design and cultural production. The second floor also houses a recording studio and a multi-purpose "lab" space where live audiences can listen in to studio recordings, or organize presentations, research activities, and reading groups.

WIHL's upper floors are dedicated to research space. In addition to researcher's offices and seminar rooms, this section of WIHL holds the Library's research stacks. Open research stacks include a substantial collection of loaned books from Murakami's personal collections, with a particular focus on translations—including both his works in translation and his own translations of novels by authors like Raymond Chandler, Raymond Carver, F. Scott Fitzgerald, Truman Capote, and many others. The Library also collects secondary research volumes in a variety of languages that address Murakami's works. Closed research stacks are accessible with consent of WIHL staff. These stacks include a large collection of scrapbook files organized by Murakami and his office staff that cover reviews, articles, advertisements, and commentary on his body of work from the late-1970s to the present. WIHL looks forward to future donations of valuable research materials, including original manuscripts and ephemera.

Research activities stretch beyond the stacks, with WIHL regularly hosting major literary events and symposiums. In just a few short months, the Library has already played host to "Authors Alive!"—a series of public readings co-hosted by Tokyo FM that have included Murakami, Yōko Ogawa, Hiromi Kawakami, Hiromi Itō, Sayaka Murata, Ryō Asai, and guitarist Kaori Muraji. An international research symposium based on the Library's motto, "Explore Your Story, Speak Your Heart," featured discussions between Yōko Ogawa and Robert Campbell (Advisor, WIHL), as well as Waseda professors Richi Sakakibara (Assistant Director, WIHL) and Hitomi Yoshio with the recent Akutagawa-prize winning author Li Kotomi.

Moving forward, WIHL intends to maintain a busy schedule of open and international research reading groups (most recently hosting Rebecca Suter to discuss the book *Two-World Literature*), panel discussions on contemporary research trends (such as the panel "An Invitation to Digital Humanities"), public readings by contemporary authors, and boundary-pushing collaborations between the worlds of literature, music, art, design, research, and public outreach. Many of these events will be held free and online and we look forward to welcoming audiences from around the globe. And of course, we also look forward to welcoming all Murakami researchers to the library in person next time you are in Tokyo.

Biographical Notes

KAREN CONNIE M. ABALOS-ORENDAIN finished her graduate and doctoral studies in Kobe University under the *Monbukagakusho* (Japanese Government Scholarship). In 2018, she returned to the University of the Philippines, Diliman where she teaches Socio-Political Philosophy, Contemporary Philosophy, as well as Comparative/Japanese Philosophy. Her research focuses on Cosmopolitanism and Migration as well as Feminist Thought.

Website: https://pages.upd.edu.ph/kcabalosorendain
E-mail: kmabalosorendain@up.edu.ph

MIDORI TANAKA ATKINS is an independent researcher of Japanese literature, and was Senior Teaching Fellow (2014–2015) at the School of Oriental and African Studies, University of London (UK). Her principal research areas are post-WWII Japanese fiction; time, space, memory in literature; literature from suburbia; transnational literature; and Haruki Murakami. Her publications include "In-between spaces in Haruki Murakami's *Kafka on the Shore:* Time and space in Japanese realism" in *Landscapes of Realism: Rethinking Literary Realism in Comparative Perspectives. Vol 1: Mapping Realism* (John Benjamins Publishing Company, 2021).

E-mail: mail@midoriatkins.com

YPE DE BOER is a Dutch philosopher and translator, who has recently submitted his PhD on ethics in the work of contemporary Italian philosopher Giorgio Agamben at the Radboud University Nijmegen, where he teaches at the department of Metaphysics and Philosophical Anthropology. In 2017, he published a book on the philosophical value of the fiction of Murakami Haruki, *Murakami en het gespleten leven* (Murakami and the Split Life). His second book, *Het erotisch experiment* (The Erotic Experiment), came out in 2019 and consists of a philosophical exploration of the role, nature, and possibilities of the erotic in modern western culture. His translations include two works by Agamben, *Profanaties* (*Profanazioni*, 2015) and *Epedimie als politiek* (*A che punto siamo? L'epidemia come politica*, 2021) and one by French philosopher Alain Badiou *Ode aan de liefde* (*Éloge de l'amour*).

Website: http://ypedeboer.nl/
E-mail: ype.deboer@ru.nl

JONATHAN DIL is an Associate Professor of Foreign Languages and Liberal Arts in the Faculty of Science and Technology at Keio University. He is the author of numerous articles and book chapters on Murakami Haruki as well as the book *Murakami Haruki and the Search for Self-therapy: Stories from the Second Basement* (Bloomsbury, 2022).

Website: https://keio.academia.edu/JonathanDil
E-mail: dil@keio.jp

GITTE MARIANNE HANSEN is Reader in Japanese Studies at Newcastle University. As AHRC Leadership Fellow (Feb 2017–July 2018), she led the research project *Eyes on Murakami* and is currently working on a monograph about women in Murakami's works. She is the author of *Femininity, Self-harm and Eating Disorders in Japan: Navigating contradiction in narrative and visual culture* (Routledge, 2016) and *Murakami and Our Years of Pilgrimage* (Edited with Michael Tsang, Routledge, 2022).

Website: https://www.ncl.ac.uk/sml/our-people/profile/gittehansen.html;
https://research.ncl.ac.uk/murakami/
E-mail: gitte.hansen@ncl.ac.uk

KEN LAWRENCE is a writer, photographer, and designer with a passion for world cultures and literature. He is the author of the travel guide books *The Murakami Pilgrimage: A Guide to the Real-Life Places of Haruki Murakami's Fiction* and *Chasing the Emerald Buddha: An Alternative Journey Through Thailand, Laos & Angkor*.

Website: https://murakamipilgrimage.com
E-mail: ken@murakamipilgrimage.com

AMBER A. LOGAN obtained her PhD in Creative Writing from Anglia Ruskin University in Cambridge, UK, defending the thesis "Men Who Lose Their Shadows—From Hans Christian Andersen to Haruki Murakami: A Slipstream Novel and Conceptualizing Commentary." She holds an M.A. in International Relations from Webster University, a M.L.A. from Baker University, and a B.A. in Psychology from the University of Missouri at Kansas City. Dr. Logan has been an adjunct instructor with Baker University in Kansas since 2009.

Website: www.AmberALogan.com
E-mail: amberlogan@fac.bakeru.edu

JOSEPH THOMAS MILBURN is a Ph.D. candidate in Philosophy at the University of Sofia. He holds an MA in Jungian and Post-Jungian Studies from the Centre for Psychoanalytic Studies, University of Essex, and a BA (Hons) in English Literature and Philosophy from Newcastle University.

Website: https://orcid.org/0000-0003-4792-2785
E-mail: joseph.t.milburn@gmail.com

MASAKI MORI is a Professor of Comparative Literature and Intercultural Studies at the University of Georgia. He has publications on the epic tradition, Asian-American literature, and Kawabata Yasunari. His recent book is *Haruki Murakami and His Early Work: The Loneliness of the Long-Distance Running Artist* (Lexington, 2021).

Website: https://www.cmlt.uga.edu/directory/people/masaki-mori
E-mail: mamo@uga.edu

CHIKAKO NIHEI is a lecturer in Faculty of Global and Science Studies at Yamaguchi University. Her recent publication includes *Haruki Murakami: Storytelling and Productive Distance* (Routledge, 2019) and "Food culture, consumerism and Murakami Haruki: The kitchen in 'Zō no shōmetsu'" in *Murakami and Our Years of Pilgrimage* (Routledge, 2022).
E-mail: cnihei@yamaguchi-u.ac.jp

GEMMA SCAMMELL is a PhD candidate at Cardiff Metropolitan University. Her thesis *The Use of Heterotopic Space in the Fiction of Haruki Murakami* examines the use of space throughout Murakami's oeuvre. In 2018, Gemma was funded by the AHRC to present her research *Murakami's use of Magical Realism in the Creation of Heterotopic Space in the novels Dance Dance Dance (1988) and Kafka on the Shore (2002)* at Liverpool John Moores University. Gemma is also an Associate Lecturer at Cardiff University.
Website: https://orcid.org/0000-0002-0544-8408
E-mail: scammellg@cardiff.ac.uk

OLAF SCHIEDGES is an Associate Professor at Tokushima University, Graduate School of Technology, Industrial and Social Sciences. He is the author of numerous articles on Murakami Haruki. He also published the book *Die Raumordnung in ausgewählten Romanen des japanischen Schriftstellers Murakami Haruki* (Ergon, 2016).
Website: http://pub2.db.tokushima-u.ac.jp/ERD/person/292991/profile-en.html
E-mail: olaf@tokushima-u.ac.jp

ERIC SIERCKS is a Research Associate at the Waseda International House of Literature (The Haruki Murakami Library). His research addresses local literature, archival practices, and censorship. He has published on Occupation censorship and has forthcoming chapters detailing archival holdings in northern Japan and US libraries and archives.
Website: https://w-rdb.waseda.jp/html/100002989_en.html
E-mail: siercks@aoni.waseda.jp

MATTHEW C. STRECHER is Professor of Japanese literature at Sophia University in Tokyo. He is the author of *Dances With Sheep: The Quest for Identity in the Fiction of Murakami Haruki* (2002; University of Michigan Press), *The Forbidden Worlds of Haruki Murakami* (2014; University of Minnesota Press), and many scholarly articles dealing with Murakami Haruki, contemporary Japanese literature, literary history, and genre studies.
E-mail: mstrecher@sophia.ac.jp

TOMOKI WAKATSUKI is an independent researcher. She is the author of *The Haruki Phenomenon: Haruki Murakami as Cosmopolitan Writer* (Springer, 2020), as well as a book chapter in *Haruki Murakami: Challenging Authors* (Sense Publishers, 2016) and an article in the journal *Celebrity Studies* (Taylor & Francis, 2018).

Website: https://unsw.academia.edu/TomokiWakatsuki

E-mail: tomokigato@gmail.com

MEGUMI YAMA is a Professor of Clinical Psychology and Depth Psychology at Kyoto University of Advanced Science. She was a visiting researcher at Harvard University in 2015 and Essex University 2008–2009. She is also engaged in clinical work as a psychotherapist based on Jungian principles. She was educated in Clinical Psychology at Kyoto University under Prof. Hayao Kawai, where she received her PhD. Her interest is in images and words; what is taking place in the invisible silence, seemingly 'nothingness.' She deals with the theme by exploring clinical materials, formative art, myth, literature, and Japanese culture. Her publications include *To the Depth of Words* (Seishinshobo, 2003), *Yasuo Kazuko: his work and creative activity* (Tomishobo, 2016), and *Haruki Murakami: novel as method, a descent into the depths of memory* (Shinyosha, 2019).

Website: https://orcid.org/0000-0002-1893-0869

E-mail: memeyam2008@gmail.com

Call for Papers

In Statu Nascendi—Journal of Political Philosophy and International Relations is now inviting new submissions. Authors are welcome to submit *articles, book reviews, and polemics* for our next volumes that will be published in 2022. Manuscripts should relate to the mission of the journal, which may include, but are not confined to:

- International Relations theory, Political Theory & political, economic, cultural, and geopolitical dimensions of the contemporary decision-making process,
- Issues related to rising powers, new types of global cooperation, the global pursuit of power, especially matters related to foreign policies of the leading political powers in the modern architecture of power,
- Various aspects of political radicalization; contemporary conflicts and conflict resolution strategies; cross-border development, inter-regional migration,
- Matters related to globalization, regionalization, localization, multiculturalism, various new demographic trends, as well as emerging global challenges related to climate change and environmental degradation,

Papers will be accepted for publication only if they meet high scholarly standards of originality, significance, and rigor in advancing an understanding of area development and policy. Authors of accepted papers will be notified by e-mail after their paper has been reviewed.

Subscription

Please contact
ibidem Press
Leuschnerstr. 40
30457 Hannover
GERMANY

Tel.: 0049 511/2622200
Fax: 0049 511/2622201
info@ibidem-verlag.de

Inquiries

For any other inquiry please e-mail us at
irinstatunascendi@yahoo.com

or visit our website at
https://irinstatunascendi.wixsite.com/journal

Previous Editions of the Journal

<u>Issue 2021:2</u> comprises, amongst others, the following interviews & articles:

- United Nations Peacekeeping Missions in Haiti (1993–2019),
- Immanuel Kant and Niccolò Machiavelli's Traditions and the Limits of Approaching Contemporary Conflicts—the Case Study of the Syrian Conflict (2011–Present),
- The Mental Health of UCAV Drone Operators and Deployed Soldiers: a Comparative Study of PTSD and Moral Injury Using an Example of US Soldiers,
- The Economic Partnership Agreement in the Context of Globalization and Africa's Development the Opportunities and the Threats,
- Spillover-effects in International Railway Cooperation: The Case of V4 Countries,
- Aristotle's Phronesis and Socratic Skepticism: A Starting Point for the Development of Applied Ethics,
- Literature as a Modern Art (Letërsia si art modern),
- Culture as Understood in the Thought of Emmanuel Levinas and Hans-Georg Gadamer,
- Hegel's Notion of Recollection in Comparison to Agnes Heller's Notion of Imagination,

<u>Issue 2021:1</u> comprises, amongst others, the following interviews & articles:

- Constructivism in the Study of Sustainable Development,
- "Why should Russia not be gifting Kaliningrad Oblast to Ukraine?" (Interview with Dr Krzysztof Żęgota),
- 'Democracy to come': Derrida's 'undecidability' and Laclau's 'Ethical' as Investment Everydayness,
- Every-no-where: A brief comparison of Paul Ricoeur's "Imagination in discourse and in action" (1994) with Hegel's philosophy of imagination as expressed in Donald Phillip Verene's Hegel's Recollection: A Study of Images in the Phenomenology of Spirit (1985),
- A Hidden Tenderness for the World: Reconstructing Marx's Ethics,

Issue 2020:2 comprises, amongst others, the following interviews & articles:

- "Clarity is what I seek first": An interview with Professor Tamara Albertini,
- Reinventing Politics: An Epistemic Conversion of Information Technologies,
- Information Society and a New Form of Embodiment,
- The Analysis of the Economic and Political Determinants of the Venezuelan Presidential Crisis since 2019,
- Balance of Power and the 21st Century Iron Law of International Relations or an Outdated Idea,
- North-South Railway Construction Projects in the Visegrád Four Countries (V4),

Issue 2020:1 comprises, amongst others, the following interviews & articles:

- Interview with Dr. Zoran Kojcic on his unique form of philosophical counselling,
- Paul Tillich's Critical and Political Theology and his Critique of Modernity,
- The Phenomenology of Women. On Female Discourse in Julia Kristeva's and Simone de Beauvoir's work,
- The Implications of Relativity in Translation and vice versa,
- The Republic of Korea—United States of America's "Strategic Patience": A counter measurement of the Alliance in Responding to Democratic People's Republic of Korea' Nuclear Development Program (2013–2017),
- Dueling with Disinformation: Disinformation and Information and Communication Technologies in the Middle East,
- How would Realists Interpret People Republic of China's wish to "cultivate the image of a responsible great power"?

Issue 2019:2 comprises, amongst others, the following interviews & articles:

- Donald J. Trump's policy toward North Korea and the Islamic Republic of Iran—a Comparative Study,
- Contrariwise and inconsistent positions on Turkey´s EU membership—Do party politics matter in German foreign policy?
- Charity Begins at Home: Resolving the Tensions of Liberalism(s), "White Privilege" and African Corruption via Rawls and Transnational Digital-Communitarianism,

- Lukács, Kojève and Verene's interpretations of Hegel's recollection in his "Phenomenology of Spirit",
- Madonnas and whores or blood and gore? Roles for women in the so-called Islamic State,

Issue 2019:1 comprises, amongst others, the following articles:

- Interview with Prof. Marcin Grabowski on the Political Situation in Asia in general and North Korea in particular,
- Cecin'est pas Artemis Papachristou,
- The EU and The Migration Crisis 'The EU-Turkey Deal': policy effectiveness and challenges of implementation
- The Syrian Conflict (2011–2017): How a Perfectly Winnable Uprising has been transformed into a Civil War, Only to End up as a Ferocious Proxy War,
- Under what circumstances Ukraine can get the Crimean Peninsula back from the Russian Federation?
- Interview with Prof. Maria Dimitrova on continental philosophy in general, and Emmanuel Levinas' Philosophy in particular,
- Patristic Tradition, Criterialism and Levinasian Quasi-Theological Conditions of the Self,
- Reconsidering the Notion of Creative Genius in Postmodern Philosophy and Art,

Issue 2018:1 comprises, amongst others, the following articles:

Corporate Instrumentalization of Deliberative Democracy in Global Governance,

- A Comparative Study between Levinas and Kierkegaard on Subjectivity and the Self,
- The Kremlin's Reaction to the St. Petersburg Metro Attacks seen through the Prism of Russian Intervention in Syria,
- Donald Trump's visit to Saudi Arabia, Saudi Iranian Relations, and the Future of the Iranian Nuclear Deal,
- The United Kingdom on the Verge of a "Constitutional Crisis": Between the Possibility of a Second Referendum on the Membership in the European Union and a Potential Second Vote on Scottish Independence,
- Was it Greece last decade (2007–2017) or just a culmination of the process that has led Athens to the brink of the economic collapse?

What We Stand for
in Nineteen Different Languages

"To learn a language is to have one more window from which to look at the world"
Mandarin proverb

1. Albanian

"**Në Statu Nascendi** (ISN) është një ditar i rishikuar nga bashkëmoshatarët që aspirojnë të jenë në një platformë studimore të klasit botëror që përfshin hulumtime origjinale akademike kushtuar rrethit të Filozofisë Politike, Studimeve Kulturore, Teorisë së Marrëdhënieve Ndërkombëtare, Politikës së Jashtme dhe vendimit politik-proceseve të krijimit. Revista heton çështje specifike përmes një qasje socio-kulturore, filozofike dhe antropologjike për të ngritur një lloj të ri të vetëdijes qytetare në lidhje me kompleksitetin e krizës bashkëkohore, paqëndrueshmërinë dhe situata të luftës, ku "faza-e-bërjes" luan një rol jetësor."

2. Arabic

In Statu Nascendi يوجد مجلة جديدة لاستعراض الأقران تطمح إلى أن تكون منصة علمية من الطراز العالمي تشمل البحوث الأكاديمية الأصلية المخصصة لدائرة الفلسفة السياسية ، الدراسات الثقافية ، نظرية العلاقات الدولية ، السياسة الخارجية ، وعملية صنع القرار السياسي وتحقق المجلة في قضايا محددة من خلال نهج اجتماعي ثقافي وفلسفي وأنثروبولوجي لرفع نوع جديد من الوعي المدني حول تعقيد الأزمات المعاصرة وعدم الاستقرار والحرب ، حيث تلعب "مرحلة الانطلاق" دوراً حيوياً.

3. Bulgarian

In Statu Nascendi (Ин Стату Насенди)—е нов академичен журнал, който се стреми да бъде научна платформа от световна класа, включваща оригинални академични изследвания, посветени на политическата философия, културните изследвания, теорията на международните отношения, външната политика и политическия процес на вземане на решения.Журналът изследва конкретни проблеми чрез социално-културен, философски и антропологичен подход за издигане на нов тип гражданска осведоменост относно сложността на съвременните кризи, нестабилност и военни ситуации, където "състоянието на зараждане" (in statu nascendi) играе жизненоважна роля.

4. *Croatian*

In Statu Nascendi (ISN) je časopis s dvostruko slijepom recenzijom koji teži postati platformom visoke kvalitete u originalnom akademskom istraživanju posvećenom krugovima političke filozofije, kulturnih studija, teorije međunarodnih odnosa, vanjske politike te političkih procesa donošenja odluka. Časopis istražuje specifične probleme kroz socio-kulturalni, filozofski i antropološki pristup kako bi podigao građansku svijest o kompleksnosti trenutnih kriza, nestabilnosti, ratova u kojima "početne faze" igraju vitalnu ulogu.

5. *Belarusian*

In Statu Nascendi—гэта новы часопіс, які рэцэнзуюць эксперты. Мэта часопіса-стаць навуковай пляцоўкай сусветнага ўзроўню. In Statu Nascendi публікуе акадэмічныя даследаванні, прысвечаныя палітычнай філасофіі, культурным пытанням, тэорыі міжнародных адносінаў, замежнай палітыцы і палітычнаму працэсу прыняцця рашэнняў.Задача публікуемых даследаванняў—спрыяць фарміраванню новага тыпу грамадзянскай свядомасці ва ўмовах сучаснага крызісу, нестабільнасці і ваенных сітуацый.

6. *Dutch*

In Statu Nascendi is een nieuw wetenschappelijk getoetst tijdschrift dat ernaar streeft een academisch platform van wereldklasse te zijn en te vormen. Het omvat origineel academisch onderzoek met een focus naar politieke filosofie, culturele studies, theorie van internationale betrekkingen, buitenlands beleid en het politieke besluitvormingsproces. Het tijdschrift onderzoekt specifieke kwesties door middel van een sociaal-culturele, filosofische en antropologische benadering om een nieuw type van burgerbewustzijn op te wekken. Aangaande de complexiteit van de hedendaagse crisis, instabiliteit en oorlogssituaties, waarbij het 'stadium van wording' een vitale rol speelt.

7. *English*

In Statu Nascendi (ISN) is a peer-reviewed journal that aspires to be a world-class scholarly platform encompassing original academic research dedicated to the circle of Political Philosophy, Cultural Studies, Theory of International Relations, Foreign Policy, and the political decision-making process. The journal investigates specific issues through a socio-cultural, philosophical, and anthropological approach to raise a new type of civic awareness about the complexity of contemporary crisis, instability, and warfare situations, where the "stage-of-becoming" plays a vital role.

8. *French*

In Statu Nascendi est un nouveau journal des revues par les pairs qui aspire à devenir une plate-forme scolaire globale. Il englobe des recherches académiques dédiées aux: Philosophie politique, études culturels, théories des relations internationales, politiques étrangères et les procédés des décisions politiques. Le journal étudie des questions particulières, par une approche socio-culturelle, philosophique et anthropologique, afin d'accroître un nouveau type de sensibilisation civique concernant la crise contemporaine ; sa complexité, instabilité et situations de guerre, dont la phase de lancement joue un rôle vital.

9. German

In Statu Nascendi ist eine neue, wissenschaftliche Zeitschrift, die Beiträge der politischen Philosophie, Kulturwissenschaften, Theorie internationaler Beziehungen, Außenpolitik und politischer Entscheidungsprozesse veröffentlicht. Die Artikel werden im Peer-Review-Verfahren geprüft und untersuchen konkrete Themen mithilfe einer soziokulturellen, philosophischen und anthropologischen Herangehensweise. Ziel ist es, zu einem neuen Bürgerbewusstsein über die Komplexität von gegenwärtigen Krisen, Instabilität und Kriegssituationen, bei denen die Phase der Entstehung eine wesentliche Rolle spielt, beizutragen.

10. Greek

Το επιστημονικό περιοδικό **In Statu Nascendi** δημοσιεύει μετά από κρίση πρωτότυπες μελέτες πάνω σε θέματα Πολιτικής Φιλοσοφίας, Κοινωνικών και Πολιτισμικών Σπουδών, Θεωρίες Διεθνών Σχέσεων, Εξωτερικής Πολιτικής, Πολιτικής Διπλωματίας και Ανθρωπολογίας. Το περιοδικό πραγματεύεται κυρίως εξειδικευμένα άρθρα που προσεγγίζουν πτυχές της κοινωνικο-πολιτισμικής, φιλοσοφικής και ανθρωπολογικής επιστήμης και έρευνας με σκοπό την διαμόρφωση ορθής πολιτικής και κοινωνικής συνείδησης σχετικά με την πολυπλοκότητα της σύγχρονης 'κρίσης,' την αστάθεια και τις εμπόλεμες καταστάσεις που αναδύονται στην σύγχρονη πραγματικότητα, όπου το πλαίσιο του κοινωνικο-πολιτικού γίγνεσθαι χρίζει ιδιαίτερης αναφοράς.

11. Hungarian

Az **In Statu Nascendi** (ISN) egy lektorált folyóirat, amely a politikafilozófia, a kulturális tanulmányok, a nemzetközi kapcsolatok elmélete, a külpolitika, valamint a döntéshozatali folyamatok témájában íródott egyedi tudományos kutatások világszínvonalú akadémiai műhelye kíván lenni. A világban zajló válságjelenségekről, instabil helyzetekről és háborús eseményekről kialakítandó új típusú társadalmi véleménynyilvánítás elterjedése érdekében a folyóirat társadalmi–kulturális, filozófiai és antropológiai megközelítéssel, azok teljes összetettségében vizsgálja a konkrét történéseket, különös tekintettel a kialakulás állapotában lévő jelenségekre.

12. Indonesian

In Statu Nascendi (ISN) adalah jurnal yang diulas oleh para sejawat yang bercita-cita untuk menjadi media ilmiah kelas dunia yang mencakup penelitian akademis orisinal yang didedikasikan untuk bidang Filsafat Politik, Studi Budaya, Teori Hubungan Internasional, Kebijakan Luar Negeri, dan proses pembuatan keputusan politik. Jurnal ini mengkaji berbagai isu-isu spesifik dengan menggunakan pendekatan sosial-budaya, filosofis, dan antropologis untuk meningkatkan jenis baru kesadaran kewarganegaraan tentang kompleksitas krisis kontemporer, instabilitas, dan situasi peperangan, di mana "tahap menjadi" memainkan peran yang sangat penting.

13. Italian

In Statu Nascendi—è una nuova rivista accademica che aspira a essere una internazionale piattaforma di ricerca dedicata allo studio di tematiche legate alla Filosofia Politica, gli Affari Internazionali, gli Studi Culturali e le diverse Teorie delle Relazioni Internazionali. La rivista analizza tali specificità tematiche attraverso un approccio socio-culturale, filosofico e antropologico per costruir una nuova consapevolezza civile sulle tante complessità della società odierna, della sua instabilità e conflittualità, all'interno della quale nuovi "processi-in-divenire" interagiscono tra loro in modo rilevante

14. Polish

In Statu Nascendi jest nowym recenzowanym czasopismem akademickim, które aspiruje do światowej klasy platformy naukowej obejmującej oryginalne badania naukowe poświęcone kręgowi zagadnień zwiazanych z filozofią polityczną, kulturoznawstwem, teorią stosunków międzynarodowych, polityką zagraniczną i złożonością współczesnego procesu decyzyjnego. To czasopismo analizuje konkretne zagadnienia za pomocą podejścia społeczno kulturowego, filozoficznego i antropologicznego, w celu podniesienia poziom świadomości obywatelskiej na temat złożoności współczesnych sytuacji kryzysowych, niestabilnosci miedzynarodowej, i wojen w których kluczową rolę odgrywa "etap stawania się."

15. Russian

In Statu Nascendi—это новый журнал, рецензируемый экспертами, цель которого—стать научной платформой мирового уровня. In Statu Nascendi публикует академические исследования, посвященные политической философии, культурным вопросам, теории международных отношений, зарубежной политике и политическому процессу принятия решений. Задача публикуемых исследований— способствовать формированию нового типа гражданской осознанности в условиях современного кризиса, нестабильности и военных ситуаций.

16. Serbian

In Statu Nascendi (ISN) je časopis s dvostruko slepom recenzijom koji teži postati platformom visokog kvaliteta u originalnom akademskom istraživanju posvećenom krugovima političke filozofije, kulturnih studija, teorije međunarodnih odnosa, spoljne politike te političkih procesa donošenja odluka. Časopis istražuje specifične probleme kroz socio-kulturalni, filozofski i antropološki pristup kako bi podigao građansku svest o kompleksnosti trenutnih kriza, nestabilnosti, ratova u kojima "početne faze" igraju vitalnu ulogu.

17. Spanish

In Statu Nascendi es una nueva revista con revisión paritaria que aspira a convertirse en una plataforma de investigación académica mundial dedicada al campo de la Filosofía Política, Estudios Culturales, teorías de las Relaciones Internacionales, Política Exterior, y procesos de toma de decisión política. Esta revista analiza asuntos de relevancia internacional a través de un enfoque socio-cultural, filosófico y antropológico. Nuestro objetivo es crear un nuevo tipo de conciencia cívica que tenga en cuenta la complejidad de las crisis coetáneas y la problemática de la inestabilidad y la guerra en las que el 'stage-of-becoming' juega un rol crucial.

18. Turkish

In Statu Nascendi—Siyaset Felsefesi, Kültürel Çalışmalar, Uluslararası İlişkiler Teorisi, Dış Politika ve siyasi Karar verme sürecine adanmış özgün akademik araştırmaları kapsayan dünya çapında bir akademik platform olmayı amaçlayan yeni bir hakemli dergidir. Dergi, "kriz aşamasının" hayati bir rol oynadığı çağdaş kriz, istikrarsızlık ve savaş durumlarının karmaşıklığı hakkında yeni bir sivil farkındalık yaratmak için sosyo-kültürel, felsefi ve antropolojik bir yaklaşımla belirli konuları araştırıyor.

19. Ukrainian

In Statu Nascendi—це новий рецензований науковий журнал метою якого стати науковою платформою на світовому рівні. Опубліковані академічні вивчення присвячені політичній філософії, культурології, міжнародним відносинам та зарубіжній політиці, і також політичному процесу прийняття питань. Вивчатимуться дослідження соціально-куль-турними, філософськими та антропологічними підходами та направ-лені на створення нового виду громадської свідомості в умовах сучас-ного кризисну в світі, нестабільності та військових ситуацій.

Coming up next on In Statu Nascendi

Our Next Special Edition (Volume 5. Number 2.) on Gender Equality in Politics and International Relations; comprises, amongst others, the following articles & book reviews:

- Interview with the Revolutionary Association for Women of Afghanistan (RAWA) on 'Feminist Resilience in Afghanistan'
- The Feminist Other
- On the State's Being-with and Being-toward as a "Personality of Higher Order"
- Kierkegaardian Religious Dialectics: God and death as a scandalous paradox
- Book Review: Negarestani, Reza, and Kristen Alvanson. 2008. *Cyclonopedia: complicity with anonymous materials*. Melbourne: Re. Press.

In Statu Nascendi—Journal of Political Philosophy and International Relations is a peer-reviewed journal that aspires to be a world-class scholarly platform encompassing original academic research dedicated to the circle of Political Philosophy, Cultural Studies, Theory of International Relations, Foreign Policy, and the political Decision-making process. The journal investigates specific issues through a socio-cultural, philosophical, and anthropological approach to raise a new type of civic awareness about the complexity of contemporary crisis, instability, and warfare situations, where the "stage-of-becoming" plays a vital role.

We welcome all types of partnership and collaboration for fostering a knowledge-based society, organizing events, and framing new projects. If you are an academic institution, research institute and investigation team, group, a non-profit organization, research center, or research think tank, and you are willing to become a long-term partner for *In Statu Nascendi's* activities, please email us. We will get back to you as soon as we can.

***ibidem*.eu**